Now You're One of Us
The Incredible Story Of Redd Kross

Now You're One Of Us
The Incredible Story Of Redd Kross

Jeff and Steven McDonald with Dan Epstein

Typeset by Evolution Design & Digital Ltd (Kent)
Printed in Poland

www.omnibuspress.com

CONTENTS

Contents

COME ON LOSE YOUR MIND: A NOTE FROM THE AUTHOR

Long-haired friends of Jesus
In a chartreuse microbus
Come on lose your mind
Now you're one of us

The first time I ever heard the above verse, it was September 1987, and I was listening to *Neurotica*, the new album by a band called Redd Kross, while reading along with the hand-written lyrics reproduced on the record's inner sleeve.

'Neurotica', the album's opening track, was the first song I'd ever heard by the band. I knew nothing about them, beyond the fact that they'd completely blown the mind of a college buddy and bandmate of mine when he'd caught them in Cleveland that summer.

Bob had returned to school that fall as a raving Redd Kross evangelist, and as his friend and musical partner in crime, he immediately targeted me for conversion. But before he would even deign to spin *Neurotica* for me, I first had to listen to his blow-by-blow account of their live show, which had apparently included KISS songs, Zeppelin-esque hard rock grooves, wild bass solos, wilder clothes, hilarious between-song banter and such sublimely over-the-top, arena-show-in-a-nightclub moments, with the band's two brothers suddenly locking eyes and whipping their impressively long manes around together in perfect unison. These guys were flying their freak flags high, and Bob was way, way into it.

The *Neurotica* album cover, with its four freaky-looking dudes surrounded by even freakier-looking Papier-mâché heads, looked promising enough in itself – but then I also noticed that the record had been released by Big Time, the same Australia-based indie label that had launched the Hoodoo Gurus, one of my and Bob's favourite bands. To paraphrase the Magic 8 Ball, all signs pointed to 'Yes.'

But it was the aforementioned lyrics, declaimed over a martial, Beatle-esque psychedelic throb, that really sealed the deal. Who the hell would quote 'Convoy', C. W. McCall's 1976 CB-sploitation hit, in the opening track of their album? A band that was clearly custom-made for a seventies-damaged weirdo like me, that's who.

Ask any Redd Kross fan, and they'll tell you a similar story. The specific details will differ, of course, and the record that lured them into the cult of Redd Kross could come from anywhere in the band's lengthy and varied discography. But that moment of epiphany – that flash of connection where certain clues, cues and musical elements combined to make them understand with every fibre of their being that this was *their* band – will be pretty much the same. Because Redd Kross's music has always been a clarion call to outsiders, freaks and musical obsessives like themselves, offering the alluring invitation to ignore the trends of the moment and join in celebrating the timeless joys of hook-filled songs and knowing references to the trashier end of the pop culture spectrum. Like the films of Russ Meyer or John Waters (two major influences on the band's vision), the music of Redd Kross has never been for everyone, but those who 'get it' inevitably become fans for life.

Redd Kross have never had a Top 40 hit, and their only Gold record (so far) was the 1998 soundtrack to the film *Varsity Blues*, which (thanks to some savvy and friendly music supervisor) included the band's 1997 album track 'Teen Competition.' But nearly half a century since brothers Jeff and Steven McDonald first began plotting world domination through rock'n'roll, their ardent cult of fans continues to grow, and their flamboyant and ferociously tuneful music remains as potent as ever.

The story of Redd Kross is fascinating, compelling, uproariously funny, and at times maddeningly frustrating. Check the scrapes and dings on their chartreuse microbus, and you'll find evidence of collisions with everything from the original LA punk scene of the 1970s and the Sunset Strip hair-metal ridiculousness of the 1980s to the massive alternative rock and Britpop explosions of the 1990s. Redd Kross are the direct link between Black Flag and The Bangles, between The Seeds and Shonen Knife, between The Partridge Family (both the group *and* the TV show) and L7. Their influence has impacted everyone from alt-rock legends Sonic Youth and Mudhoney to filmmakers Quentin Tarantino and Allison Anders. They are the rare male-driven rock band of their era who looked as much or more to female heroes as male ones for inspiration, and who made no bones about letting the world know it.

Now You're One Of Us isn't just a 'rise and fall and rise of a rock band' tale. It's also a story of figuring out your identity and searching for your tribe, gleaning inspiration and enlightenment from pop cultural detritus, and struggling to persevere through soul-crushing personal adversity. It's the story of whip-smart, free-range, overstimulated Gen-X kids bursting with creativity, but too often tripping themselves up with their irrepressible sense of mischief or their neurotic tendency to overthink. It's the story of two brothers who decide to form a band – a fateful decision which, as anyone who knows anything about such sibling-based musical concerns as The Everly Brothers, The Kinks, Creedence Clearwater Revival or Oasis can tell you, almost never leads to the smoothest of sailing.

Now You're One of Us is, to the best of my knowledge, the first rock autobiography where two brothers have teamed up to tell the story of their band. By now, you've hopefully already seen *Born Innocent*, Andrew Reich's excellent Redd Kross documentary. From the moment my agent Lee Sobel brought me together with Jeff and Steven for this project (thanks, Lee!), I knew I wanted *Now You're One Of Us* to serve as a companion piece to Andrew's doc, as opposed to a printed version of it. That's why there are only three voices in this book: Jeff's, Steven's and mine. The brothers do most of the talking here; I just occasionally pop up as the narrator to set the stage, offer additional context or move the story along. The McDonalds are both so articulate, thoughtful, engaging and hilarious that I wanted as few distractions from their versions of events as possible. (If you're one of the many folks who generously reached out to me and offered yourself as an interview subject, I hereby apologise for not taking you up on it. This was never going to be that kind of book).

As for said versions of events: As I learned from working with them on this project, Jeff and Steven are profoundly different people with profoundly different ways of viewing and interacting with the world around them. Though they share so much – not least their enduring passion for Redd Kross – their memories, opinions and emotions don't always sync up. Where these things diverge, I've tried to include both of their perspectives. Maybe Jeff is right, maybe Steven is right, or maybe the truth lies somewhere in between. It's up to you, the reader, to decide for yourself.

If you're a longtime Redd Kross fan, I sincerely hope that this book will give you new insight into the band, the brothers and their music, while also entertaining the hell out of you. And if you're new to the band, I hope this book will inspire you to search out their music, whether online or in the bins of your local record store, and discover that one Redd Kross song or album that makes you wonder where they've been all your life. And once that magical moment occurs, well, now you're one of us.

Dan Epstein
New York, March 2024

PREFACE: AN APOLOGY FROM REDD KROSS

Dear Poison,

Long time. Hope you dudes are well.

It's been, what, nearly forty years since we played with you guys and Leatherwolf at the Country Club in Reseda? Crazy. That prom limo you rented for the show sure was classy. How's CoCo Smith doing these days?

Anyway, we're really sorry for repeatedly calling Enigma Records, pretending to be you guys, and telling them how pissed off we were because Stryper's new album was in all the record stores but copies of Look What The Cat Dragged In were nowhere to be found.

Bret, we're also really sorry for leaving messages on your voice coach's answering machine, and telling her that you were going to sue her for blowing your voice out with her vocal exercises. We know you're a consummate professional with dynamite pipes, and it was totally wrong for us to jeopardise your business relationships with our immature prank calls.

This apology is long overdue, but we hope you'll accept this tortilla as a token of our sincerity.

Eat It,

Jeff and Steven McDonald
Redd Kross

FOREWORD BY CHARLOTTE CAFFEY

Let's just say I was a little late to the party. Redd Kross had already been creating music and mayhem for over a decade while I was busy being a Go-Go along with all the breakups and makeups that came with it. Our worlds collided in 1990 when Redd Kross joined us on our 'reunion' tour.

Fast forward to backstage at the Riviera Theater in Chicago, November 29, 1990. The first person I met was Steve McDonald. He was tall, thin, with waist-length hair parted down the middle, wearing a long-sleeve shirt and bell bottoms. Then Jeff came into my view – he was a Vision of Nowness. Just as skinny and standing even taller than Steve, he was wearing striped pants, a patterned shirt, long, straight Cher-'65 hair (bangs included) and platform shoes which made him close to 7 feet tall. I shyly said 'hello' and then went to the side of the stage to watch their show.

I found myself transfixed the second they started to play. I could only see Jeff and Steve. The way they moved on stage was mesmerizing, with their hair flying; Steve doing his Davy Jones dance as he played his bad-ass bass, Jeff shredding with rad guitar sounds, and both singing classic sibling harmonies to their perfect songs. I was an instant fan. They were hands down one of the best bands I had ever seen. My mind was blown, and my first thought was 'How can we go on AFTER them?'

The next stop was the legendary First Avenue in Minneapolis. At soundcheck, I saw Jeff bending down and Jane Wiedlin whispering something in his ear. She had let it slip that I thought he was cute. Of course I was mortified, wondering what could have possessed her to spill my secret, but that one moment changed the trajectory of my life. We had a day off in St. Louis where Jeff and I had the opportunity to hang out and ended up talking all night. The rest is history.

Jeff and Steve have always been people magnets – attracting only eccentric, artistic, hilarious, one-of-a-kind personalities who are all big, brilliant freaks. I had been living like a hermit for so long but my house on the hill quickly became a revolving door for what I called the '30 best friends.' We would watch bizarre Public Access shows and have roundtable discussions about all things pop culture, rock music, art, KISS and, as Jeff puts it, 'the non-ironic appreciation of Jimmy Osmond.'

Jeff and I got married in 1993, and our daughter Astrid was born a couple of years later. Steve married genius singer-songwriter/composer Anna Waronker, and their addition to the group was Alfie in 2009. All of us play music and have collaborated with each other on various projects. Personally, I am waiting to finally record the follow-up Ze Malibu Kids family band album.

There was an unintentional but beautiful reunion of the '30 best friends' at the first screening of the upcoming documentary *Born Innocent: The Redd Kross Story*. Although some of them are no longer with us (Bill Bartell, Howie Pyro, Kim Shattuck) they live on in infamy within our group and beyond.

Over four decades and many albums later, Jeff and Steve remain unwavering and relentless. They have just finished their self-titled double album. What could be more rock'n'roll than that?

Janet and her boys, moments before Jeff and Steven dragged their parents kicking and screaming out of the square 1950s and into the groovy 1970s. (Photo by Pat McDonald)

Chapter 1

A CONSTANT BATH OF MUSIC AND POP CULTURE

Surf music was enjoying the final weeks of its last big summer on August 10, 1963 when Jeffrey McDonald was born in Southern California. The Surfaris' 'Wipe Out' could be regularly heard hammering away on KRLA, one of the biggest radio stations in the region, where the song was just beginning to slip from its peak position of number two on the station's 'Tune-Dex' chart. Holding off the twangy 12-bar instrumental from the chart's top spot was 'Surfer Girl', a sublime Brian Wilson-penned ballad from The Beach Boys, local heroes who hailed from Hawthorne, a small city just a few minutes south from where Jeff's parents Terry and Janet lived in Inglewood.

Lurking in the lower reaches of the KRLA Tune-Dex was a band that would soon outpace The Beach Boys and everyone else on the chart, though absolutely no one could have predicted it at the time. 'From Me To You', a snappy mid-tempo rocker by a British quartet called The Beatles, had stalled out at number 32, though this was still better than it had done anywhere else in the country; the single, released by Chicago independent label

Vee-Jay, had managed to squeak to number 116 on *Billboard's* 'Bubbling Under' charts almost entirely by virtue of KRLA's support. Six months later, The Beatles would become the biggest band in the world, just in time to take up a formative and permanent residence in young Jeff McDonald's consciousness.

JEFF: I loved The Beatles from the very first; they're part of all my earliest memories. I think it was because I had teenage aunts and uncles that were very into rock'n'roll. There has always been the influence of the older, sibling-type people in our lives – whether they were aunts and uncles, or teenagers on the block.

My dad's family is very large, and everyone lived in Southern California, so we would have Sunday dinners together no matter what. I'd always hang with my young uncles and aunts; my dad's the oldest of nine, so the ones that were way down at the bottom were more like siblings to me. My aunts would try to teach me Beatles lingo; they were basically brainwashing me, because I was still a toddler.

I saw The Beatles in 1965 with my Aunt Colleen who was still a teenager, my grandma and my mom. I was two years old, and all I remember was just, like, horror and screeching. I remember my aunt saying, 'Oh, there they are! There they are!' It was in a baseball stadium in San Diego, and I remember sitting on a wooden bench, very far away. But I fell asleep during the show, and I remember nothing else about it – just the screaming, and being stuck in traffic. I get certain flashes of what it looked and sounded like when I'm floating through YouTube and watching people's Super 8 films of The Beatles taken from the nosebleeds. And then it's like, 'Oh yeah, that's the way it looked!' – all tiny and blurry.

I do remember a few years later, when The Beatles were supposed to be on Ed Sullivan. I couldn't wait to see them, but it turned out to be scenes from the rooftop concert of them doing 'Get Back', which was the new single. They weren't actually there on the TV show, which was really disappointing.

I used to bring records to kindergarten; if you had records from home that you wanted to play, you could bring them. One time I brought *Magical Mystery Tour*, and the teacher refused to play it. She was this horrible witch with 'cat's eye' glasses; this was 1968, but it seemed like she was from the 1940s. My only memories of her are in black and white. And she was like, 'I will *not* be playing this!'

I remember that feeling. She was shaming me – 'I will not play this record!' – and I didn't know why. I didn't know about rock'n'roll as being a rebellious form of music. I was too young and innocent to know why anyone would have such an adverse reaction to The Beatles.

Jeff's little brother Steven arrived on the scene on May 24, 1967, by which time pop music had already undergone several more upheavals. KRLA Beat, the radio station's weekly magazine, had just run a cover story on LA's groovy 'It Couple' Sonny and Cher, along with a feature article on Beach Boy Carl Wilson's refusal to report for induction into the US Army, rumours of a Rolling Stones breakup, and a full-page ad for *Surrealistic Pillow* from Jefferson Airplane, one of several psychedelic San Francisco bands slated to play the upcoming Monterey Pop Festival. And of course The Beatles were serving up some psychedelic whimsy of their own with 'Penny Lane', which was currently lodged at number five on the KRLA Tune-Dex.

STEVEN: I was incubated in a constant bath of music and pop culture, if you will. The earliest record I remember as a constant was *Sgt. Pepper's*. We had a copy on clear red vinyl that our Uncle Kevin had brought back for us from Japan in like 1969. There was never a time that that record didn't exist in my life.

JEFF: I still have that original *Sgt. Pepper's* from Uncle Kevin. The label was Paramount Records, which was very strange; it was in a soft cover, like all the records from Japan had in those days, and at some point it got cracked down the middle. But if you put it back together, if you just kind of jimmied it a bit, it would still play.

STEVEN: I remember *Meet The Beatles* being a constant, as well. We had a Mickey Mouse record player, which had a big Mickey hand that held the stylus. You'd put Mickey's glove down on the record to play it.

JEFF: I still have all the records that I had when I was a kid, but they're all in terrible condition, because I actually played them, and those plastic record players would just chew them up. Today, people have this nostalgia for vinyl, but I didn't really care what format the music came on. It was just such an important part of my life. It was always in the foreground.

Jeff and Steven grew up sharing a bedroom in the small Hawthorne tract home where Terry and Janet had moved shortly before Steven's birth. A landlocked working-class town then populated largely by employees of the local aerospace industry – Los Angeles International Airport lies just a few miles to the north – Hawthorne had already lost much of its Beach Boys-era suburban shine by the time the McDonalds moved in, and both the McDonalds' home at 5259 W. 115th Street and the Wilson family's home at 3701 W. 119th Street would be among the many residences demolished in the mid-1980s to make room for the 105 Freeway. But until the city finally tore it down, Jeff and Steven's shared bedroom would serve as a playroom, listening booth, fantasy stage, practice space and a launching pad for countless schemes and pranks, not to mention a place for the brothers to sleep.

JEFF: Steven and I were roommates until I was around 18. At first, our parents were always trying to control what we did with the room, like, 'You can't put posters up!' But we turned it into our den pretty quickly. It was close quarters, but that was good for sharing toys or records, or musical instruments later on.

STEVEN: Jeff always had pretty sophisticated taste, and he always wanted to share his music with me; he wasn't the kind of older brother who didn't want his younger brother hanging around. We shared a small bedroom in a 1000-square foot house, so we were always at each other's throats; we definitely didn't avoid that brotherly cliché. We argued constantly, but music was always something that we agreed on, something that we liked to do together. Jeff really liked me being a part of whatever he was into. I guess nowadays the terminology is 'inclusive', but I don't know if it was necessarily a case of inclusivity. It was more like strength in numbers.

Our families were free-flowing Coca-Cola drinkers, and you would get a five-cent return on each little green bottle. Jeff and I collected and returned a hundred of them and cobbled together enough nickels between us to buy the Beatles' *White Album*. This would have been 1970 or something, so the record was a couple of years old, but it was already mythological to us, like the *ultimate record*. And I remember when I was 5 years old, I had *two* double records – one was a Dr. Seuss double record set with 'The Star-Belly Sneetches', and one was the *White Album*. I had those two double record sets and held them in equal esteem, which gives you a pretty good idea of my early musical experience. I also had a cheap off-label *Sesame Street* record, Bert and Ernie's 'Rubber Duckie'; Jeff thought it was cool that I liked 'Rubber Duckie' and I also liked, you know, 'Don't Bother Me' by The Beatles. I just never *didn't* have this music that was odd for my age group.

JEFF: Non-musical interests? I guess I liked those 'Creepy Crawler' Mattel toys, anything like that. And I liked Saturday morning cartoons, and *I Love Lucy* re-runs every day after

5

school – and in the seventies, you had *The Brady Bunch, The Partridge Family*; all that stuff spoke to me as a child.

The Partridge Family first came out in 1970, when I was 7. Those first hits like 'I Think I Love You', the kids at school liked them, and I liked them too; I thought those were great songs. But even more fascinating to me was seeing on the show that they had instruments in their garage and played them together in a band. I was always into electric guitars and amplifiers and all that kind of stuff; those were *my* hot rod cars. So seeing little kids playing them, it was like, 'Oh my god, I wanna be in a band!' Just thinking that you could actually put a band together with your friends and play in your garage – that was like the first little spark of, 'Oh, we could do this too.'

STEVEN: Records were like serious currency for us. And Jeff's thinking back then was that you have to be careful because you only have a very limited budget with which to procure these different songs – and sometimes you get tricked, because one song might appear on several records, and if you double up on a song then you're somehow getting killed. But at this point, I wasn't so savvy to this…

JEFF: Records were really expensive, so I'd always ask for albums for the holidays. I did have a small collection of singles back then, but I was kind of discouraged to buy them. My dad told me, 'Why buy singles? It's a rip-off!' It cost you a dollar for a single and you only get two songs. So, you save up a couple of extra dollars so you can get a whole album. I remember I traded two Creedence singles with my former babysitter for *The Supremes A' Go-Go* album. .

STEVEN: When I was about five, my mom took me to get my booster shots or whatever, and as a reward she took me to the Muntz Stereo; they had a big store in West Hollywood, but there was a smaller one in Hawthorne which had records as well as stereo equipment. She told me I could pick out any two records, and we went home with Alice Cooper's *Killer* and The Rolling Stones' *Get Yer Ya-Ya's Out!*

These were the first two records I'd ever bought on my own, and I remember playing them in our little bedroom while waiting for Jeff to get home from school, being really excited about them and just being really excited for Jeff to see and hear these records that I chose. Obviously I really wanted his approval, and I really thought I was gonna impress the fuck out of him. But when Jeff got home, he was bummed about the Stones record; he said that we already had a bunch of those songs that were on it.

JEFF: See, there you go – that's my dad's influence. I mean, Alice Cooper was cool, because we'd discovered Alice from the teenagers next door. But yeah, every purchase we made was so planned out ahead of time, and that he went off the beaten path for *Get Yer Ya-Ya's Out!* was just unacceptable. I mean, obviously he was right, but he has never forgotten. It was like I punched him or something horrible.

STEVEN: He was probably just lightly critical, but I took it really hard; I remember freaking out, just being so devastated and crying, but also not quite knowing why I was so upset. Life is an emotional rollercoaster when you're 5. I wanted my older brother's approval, and I really thought that I was gonna wear the crown for a day; unfortunately, it came with caveats, and I wanted it unconditionally. Jeff has since apologised, not that he necessarily even remembered his critique. And he has since revised his earlier criticisms of my *Get Yer Ya-Ya's Out* choice.

JEFF: I was always just different than other kids, in the sense I was already buying records when I was, you know, 10, 11 years old. All my other friends were playing baseball and didn't really care much about music. I don't even know why I didn't just grow *out* of liking music. I was just obsessed, always digging for cool things and trying to read as much as I could about what was happening. And I became *really* obsessed with the next phase after the sixties phase – I loved Elton John, Cat Stevens, David Bowie.

STEVEN: Our Uncle Shane, who was like 16 in 1972, got an 8-track tape of *Ziggy Stardust* as a Christmas present that year. But he was more of a Cream and Doors enthusiast, and it wasn't really in his wheelhouse, so Jeff and I asked him if we could borrow it. He thought it was kind of funny that we were interested in it, so he lent it to us; we took that copy home and never gave it back.

JEFF: My friend Annette lived down the street, and her parents had one of those big consoles with a record player and an 8-track. After school, we would put *Ziggy Stardust* in their family console and just listen to it in a tape loop until her mom got home and made us turn it off. On 8-tracks, some songs would have to be split into two parts. I always remember 'Soul Love' would fade out, then there was a big click, and then it would fade back in the middle of it.

I always had loved The Rolling Stones, and I kind of thought David Bowie was the next step from Mick Jagger, and it seemed like a natural fit with the British pop stuff like Elton John and Cat Stevens. But I think my parents were concerned with his gender-bending, androgynous thing, like, 'What is this?' My dad's a macho guy, so I think the image scared him more than anything else.

Elton, being more mainstream, kind of softened that blow after a while. But there was a year or two where Bowie was really shocking even to the older siblings of my friends. They were all into Cream and early Led Zeppelin, and we were 11 and 12 years old and listening to Bowie, Lou Reed and Mott The Hoople records – people think that stuff was part of the mainstream in the seventies, but all these older kids were like, 'Oh, this is '*fag*' music.' That's how they judged it, and they didn't see it any other way.

I remember buying *Hunky Dory* at a record store, and this hippie girl who was working behind the counter looked at the cover with utter disgust and said, 'Have you actually *heard* this?' She was looking at me with such harsh judgement, like I was purchasing pornography or something.

STEVEN: And then the funny thing was, a couple of years later, Uncle Shane gave me Lou Reed's *Rock 'n' Roll Animal* for Christmas. I was 7 years old, and he gave that to me specifically. I don't know what that was about. 'Hey, Steven should like this – it's got a nine-minute version of 'Heroin' on it!'

Get in the van: Jeff and Steven with a foreshadowing of their rock'n'roll future, 1970. (Courtesy of McDonald Family Archives)

Chapter 2

THIS IS OUR GARBAGE

Often unfairly derided as a cultural wasteland, 1970s America was actually a tremendously vibrant and imaginative place, especially in comparison to the conservative conformity of the 1980s that would follow. The social and political upheavals of the 1960s spilled over into the new decade, colliding with mainstream pop culture to produce new movements in music, art, film and fashion, the ripples of which continue to be felt today.

The sense of excitement and creative possibility was apparent even to a couple of pre-adolescent brothers living on the landlocked edge of SoCal's South Bay. The LAX-adjacent suburbs may not have offered as much in the way of freedom or intense stimuli as, say, New York City below 14th Street did, but thanks to increasingly fine-tuned cultural antennae and a lot of luck, Jeff and Steven were able to discover, explore and cherry-pick from the disparate influences – mainstream, underground and completely off-the-wall – that would eventually gel into a singular vision of their own.

JEFF: All of the music that we found when we were kids was accidental, essentially. I mean, we were lucky; there were a few positive influences within our lives to point us in the right

11

direction, but there were also times where we just somehow managed to find things we needed. Like Black Sabbath's *Paranoid* and Deep Purple's *Machine Head*, two favourites from my childhood – I was walking home from school one day, and there was this trash can in front of someone's house with mint-condition copies of both albums sitting on top. It was like someone found Jesus or someone's religious fanatic parents threw them out, but they were neatly placed on the top of the trash. It was the strangest thing.

We lived on a long block; on our side were mostly boys, and we were all kind of the same ages. And then my friend Annette and her sister and brother lived at the other end of the block. At first Annette and I hated each other; we had mud fights and wars and myths and stories of how, you know, *disgusting* the 'other side' was. And then our parents were going to go on a date or something, and our new babysitter turned out to be Annette's older sister Joanie. She was wearing go-go boots and she looked like Katharine Ross; I instantly had a crush on her, and she turned out to be extremely cool. So I dropped my other friend group and started hanging out with Annette, since we were the same age.

We were both really into music, and both really into reading rock magazines, which were hard to find where we lived. There was a liquor store down at the corner of our block, and they had a small magazine rack next to the porno mags that would occasionally have an issue of *CREEM* or *Rock Scene*; they would just sort of pop up randomly, and we were the only people that bought them. But whenever they'd come in, we'd get to read about all these people that we had been following, and that information was more precious because it was so hard to come by. It's how we started discovering groups like the New York Dolls, and other stuff that you couldn't find anything about in *Rolling Stone*.

Annette's mom gave her a subscription to *Circus* magazine, so we were always waiting for the next issue to arrive. The magazine went downhill when it started covering television shows, but it was really great for a while. That was where I heard about the Ramones for the very first time, because someone had written in complaining about a *good* review that this group the Ramones had gotten from the magazine, when their songs are so fast and 'they don't even have any guitar solos in their songs.' And that was like the first thing that really stuck in my head about the Ramones, because everything the guy was complaining about was everything I was looking for.

STEVEN: I didn't really discover music from the radio; that was more Jeff's thing, and he kind of delivered the good stuff to me on a silver platter. I remember him putting me up to calling the AM stations and requesting songs – I remember calling KHJ a lot and requesting '48 Crash' by Suzi Quatro over and over again. I think we already had the album, but we just wanted to hear them play it. I remember that the DJ or whoever answered the phone finally asked me who the hell was making me call up and request it; I think they probably assumed it was some flunky from Bell Records.

I don't know where Jeff discovered Suzi, but I guess it was same place where he discovered the New York Dolls and Mott The Hoople or whatever. But it wasn't necessarily all that mainstream. I mean, I think LA teenagers would have been hip to '48 Crash' and maybe would've seen her at the Santa Monica Civic or somewhere. But you've got to remember that Jeff is only 10 years old at the time.

JEFF: Being a very young, very precocious rock'n'roll person, I wanted to go to concerts, but it was tough talking my parents into it. 'You're not going to a concert – you're 10 years old!' But I convinced them that it was really no different than dropping me and Annette off at the movies and picking us up afterwards. I finally sold them on Elton John in 1974 on the *Caribou* tour; that was my 11th birthday present, my first post-Beatles concert that I'd ever gone to, and it was the greatest thing. But it took months to talk them into letting me go, because in those days you actually had to go to the venue and camp out for tickets.

13

My mom let me and my friend skip school and dropped us off at the Forum at like 6 a.m. the day the tickets went on sale. And that was another thing I realised – if the concert was at the Forum, we'd have a better chance of being able to go, because it was only like 4 miles from our house.

STEVEN: Elton John was a mind-blowing discovery for us. I remember being in kindergarten or first grade; they were playing some kids' music, and I remember just feeling way too cool for it, literally rolling my eyes and thinking, 'This is so lame – I wish they were playing Elton John!'

We had *Don't Shoot Me I'm Only The Piano Player*, and we bought *Goodbye Yellow Brick Road* right when it came out. I especially loved that one, because the album's booklet had a drawing for each song. I was particularly fascinated with the one for 'All The Girls Love Alice.' I remember thinking that these women were not necessarily 'goody two-shoes'; they were up to no good, and there was some trouble going on there. And then there's that name again, Alice, which seemed like it was everywhere in my childhood.

You had Alice Cooper, a *guy* named Alice. 'She asked me why the singer's name is Alice/I said listen baby, you really wouldn't understand' – that's a lyric in the second song of the first album I ever bought for myself. And then here's this Elton John song about lesbianism, so you've got that gender-bending, sexual ambiguity association with it. You had the psychedelic element to it, with *Alice in Wonderland* and *Go Ask Alice*, which was a seventies novel about a teenage girl who takes acid and runs away from home. And then you had *Alice Doesn't Live Here Anymore*, the Scorsese film; we really loved that film when we were growing up, especially the Tommy character who's into Mott The Hoople and is like the coolest kid ever.

It was a big thing for us, this seventies Hollywood archetype of the kid who was wise beyond their years and didn't take any shit. Like Bess from *The Mary Tyler Moore Show*, who called her

14

mother by her first name, or Tommy in *Alice Doesn't Live Here Anymore*, or the iconic Tatum O'Neal character in *Paper Moon*, these precocious kids that smoked and cussed and had snappy comebacks and great taste in music. I can't profess to have had an ounce of the cool that Tatum possessed in 1973; I don't know who did. But these kids, these characters, they were up there alongside all these rock stars that we loved. These were our idols; these were the people that we aspired to be.

Danny from *The Partridge Family* was another one. I loved the dynamic between Danny and Keith – Keith was a sexy teen idol, but he was also often the comedic foil and the stooge. I'm sure there was something that appealed to me about this idea of the precocious younger brother outwitting the dominant older brother.

JEFF: I was influenced by a lot of stuff at school, just not the reading, writing or arithmetic. But any time they would show a film, they had my attention. They would show us these 1940s industrial films about agriculture whenever it was too rainy for us to go outside, and oh my god I just loved those films. We'd just sit there watching oranges on conveyor belts going through heavy machinery and all this just insane weirdness. I think it must have influenced my love for noise music later.

They would also have these drug education programmes where police officers would come to our classrooms, with these display cases where it was like, 'This is a joint, this is a tab of acid…' and all this stuff. I don't know if they were confiscated real items or if they were just fake, but you could walk over and look at them. They would always be like, 'People take LSD and they see a million colours and believe they can fly.' And you're thinking, 'Oh my god, that sounds awesome!'

I remember this one film they showed us where a girl's rolling around on the floor going, 'I'm a cookie, watch me crumble! I'm a cookie, watch me crumble!' Or this film strip where these girls are having a sleepover and they're all wearing curlers and sniffing spray paint; one of the girls ODs, and she gets taken

15

away in an ambulance. It was always kids who looked like the older sisters of your friends, so the idea of them ODing on spray paint at a sleepover was just very relatable and hilarious.

These films and film strips were like our introduction to camp entertainment, even though it would be years before I was able to identify them as the art they were on a certain level. But watching really bad police-produced anti-drug films at school, and evangelical preachers on TV, that was a big influence – along with Elvis movies and *Beach Party* movies. It was all stuff that I was clued into before punk rock. Some people, like Henry Rollins at the time, they thought it was garbage and wouldn't have understood the value of that stuff. But we were like, 'No, this is *our* garbage.'

I'd always say back then that I was never gonna smoke pot or drink, because we'd go to all these concerts at the Forum where all these older people were smoking weed and stumbling around. It was part of the show, just watching it. It was the height of stoner rock back then, but I was like, 'These idiots!' I wanted to be present at the show fully, and I didn't want to forget anything about it.

We saw so many great shows at the Forum over the course of like four years. Some of the best were Rod Stewart and the Faces with Foghat opening, Aerosmith opening for ZZ Top on the *Fandango!* tour, and Led Zeppelin. And the first KISS *Alive!* tour, that was like the Holy Grail show for us – and then we saw them again with Cheap Trick opening for them when they were recording *Alive II*, and that's how we got into Cheap Trick.

STEVEN: KISS with Montrose opening at the LA Forum, that was my first-ever concert – February 1976. I was 8 years old, and the average age there was probably 18 or something. We were sitting very close to the back row of the Forum, but I can still remember the wave of heat hitting us when the pyrotechnics went off. I knew that KISS *Alive!* record so well even by then, just four months or so after it had come out. They played almost the same exact setlist, in the same order, and Paul Stanley was pretty much saying the same things between each song as he did on the record.

JEFF: I had never seen or heard KISS before *Alive!* came out, but once we discovered them we got really obsessed with them. We got tickets to see them on that tour, but it was like the second leg of it – the record had broken, so it was like their victory lap. It was fantastic, it was so great; when I look back at films of that tour on YouTube, they really were much better on that tour. That was like the sweet spot for KISS. I mean, they were always great, but that was *the* moment. And we were into KISS before kids our age really knew who they were yet.

STEVEN: We were already doing a lot of posing in the bedroom mirror with tennis rackets and cheap microphones while listening to our records, and KISS was a big part of that. You know, most bands are a press photo before they're anything else, and we were no exception to that; even if you couldn't play an instrument yet, you could mock-perform in your own room. And this was the era when kids were dressing up as KISS at high school talent shows across the country. I remember hearing about a group of girls who did a KISS lip sync performance at Hawthorne High in 1976, maybe for Halloween, and they were basically rock stars in our minds.

I think we went as KISS that Halloween, too, with our best friends Annette and Linda, who had gone to the concert with us. We dressed up like they did on the cover of *Alive!* I was Ace, and I had the Saturn rings around my shoulder blades that were achieved with paper plates wrapped in tinfoil. And it's funny that I ended up the bass player in our band, the Danny Partridge, because Jeff was Gene that year. I think Gene was the immediately attractive figure to young boys, because he was this dominant, evil monster – a demon. And that meant Annette and Linda would've been Peter and Paul.

It was just sort of this first taste of the effect of being part of that tribe; you got to put on the costume and traipse around in public with other people that had these identifying markers that they were part of the same gang as you. It was exciting and inspiring, and kind of a shaping experience. It was in the same vein of when Jeff and I started plotting to get guitars; it hadn't happened yet, but it gave us that same feeling.

17

Jeff and Steven at their grandparents' house in Palos Verdes with their uncle Kevin McDonald, friend Mike Tanaguchi, and parents Terry and Janet McDonald, mid-1970s. (Courtesy of McDonald Family Archives)

Chapter 3

THE SECOND COMING
OF THE BEATLES

If Jeff and Steven were a few months ahead of the curve within their own age demographic when it came to KISS fandom, they were light years ahead of their schoolmates in their embrace of another artist, one whose music – along with that of The Runaways and the Ramones – would nudge the brothers not just towards making their own music, but in the direction of the then-burgeoning LA punk scene.

JEFF: Everything seemed to be happening at the same time. I mean, we were already Patti Smith fans by the time we first saw KISS.

STEVEN: There were a couple of places in Hawthorne where we would buy records – Muntz Stereo was the big one, but there was also a drug store at the corner of La Cienega and Imperial Highway that had a small bin of records. There was a headshop at the Hawthorne Mall, which opened around 1977. And then there was The Eardrum, which was like this high-end audiophile stereo shop. It was like something from a Paul Thomas Anderson movie, with these guys that looked like they were in Three Dog Night having their minds blown by listening to *Dark Side Of The Moon* between two speaker towers. They also had a small selection of records, but it was not a big part of their business. I'm sure the guys who worked there hated us, because we'd always come in barefoot and dirty and just start thumbing through their records. That's all we cared about.

The Eardrum was where we bought *Frampton Comes Alive*, just because it was *the* record to have that summer. Jeff and I brought it home, and we were dropping the needle on each song. 'No. Next song. No. Next song. No.' We flipped the record over, and it was the same thing – 'No. No. No.' We got to the end of Side Four, and we were like, 'Oh, man – fuck this record!'

JEFF: I liked heavy guitar rock, and that record was very misleading. He's playing this iconic triple pickup black Les Paul on the cover, and it looks like the record really rocks out, but it's just so light. It was just a horror.

STEVEN: We finally got up the nerve to go back to Eardrum and say, 'This record skips. It's broken.' They were so pissed off; they were like, 'You're not getting your money back. Grab something else and get outta here.' So after much deliberation, we picked *We Sold Our Soul For Rock 'n' Roll*, which was kind of like Black Sabbath's greatest hits at the time. But before that, Eardrum was where we discovered Patti Smith.

JEFF: I remember seeing this record by this woman. It had just come out, and I didn't know anything about her, but I really liked the way she looked. I immediately thought, 'This is like The Rolling Stones,' because she looked like Mick Jagger *and* Keith Richards. I wanted to buy it and find out what 'The Rolling Stones girl' sounded like, but I didn't have the money.

Shortly after that, Steven and I were forced into going on a family trip to Big Bear, where we were snowed in in this big mountain cabin. I was bored shitless; there was no TV, there was nothing. I turned on the radio, and I managed to get a signal from a college radio station in Riverside. And the one song I noticed that they played was this song 'Free Money.'

STEVEN: As soon as we heard it, Jeff was like, 'What is this? *Who* is this? I bet it's that weird Mick Jagger chick that they've got at The Eardrum.' He totally intuited it. And then when we got home, he got that record – *Horses* – and he was right.

JEFF: She was on *SNL* shortly after that, and we were instant fans. We played *Horses* all the time in the house, and her next records when they came out. We finally saw her at the Santa Monica Civic, which is like my all-time favourite venue in Los Angeles, in 1978 on the *Easter* tour, and it was great. We begged our parents to let us go get tickets; they knew we were big fans because we were always playing her records in the house. And our parents actually didn't mind Patti Smith, for some bizarre reason.

STEVEN: Our parents weren't music obsessives like we were. My dad listened to the radio a bit, but he was more into country stuff like Waylon Jennings. But for all their sort of conservativeness, they never discouraged us; they were very supportive of us being so passionate about something. I think they figured that even though they might not understand what we were into, the fact that we were so into it was a good thing, or at least harmless.

JEFF: If we were getting ready for school, we'd blast a record and listen to it, but anything that would get us up and going out the door was okay with my mom. They might be like, 'Turn it down!' if we were playing it loud in the evening and my dad was being a grouch after getting home from work, but they never said, 'Oh, that's horrible' about anything we ever played. It was never an attack on what we were listening to, even with punk rock. The Ramones were the first punk rock music we ever played, and my dad was like, 'Oh, this sounds like Jan and Dean.' Which was very true – it did!

Before Ramones records ever blasted through the McDonald household, however, Jeff and Steven had become completely obsessed with another seminal band – The Runaways. Assembled by Hollywood producer/impresario/sleazemeister Kim Fowley, the all-female quintet was widely panned by male rock critics of the day, who either dismissed The Runaways' self-titled 1976 debut as yet another cheap Fowley gimmick, or simply couldn't wrap their heads around the idea of teenage girls playing electric guitars. But for the McDonald brothers, The Runaways were a total revelation.

JEFF: We worshipped The Runaways. I've always considered The Runaways the very first band in the LA punk scene, because they were the one band that everyone, every single group, was influenced by whether they liked it or not. For some women it might have been like, 'I hate The Runaways because of Kim Fowley – but if they could do it, I can do it too.' And then there were bands like the Germs who were totally unapologetic about how much they loved them. The Runaways were the first teenage band of our era to have a record out and play shows at these Hollywood venues where, at that time, you couldn't do live shows unless you were a cover band… or unless you had a record deal.

My friend Annette bought the first Runaways album, and I had never heard of it. I remember hearing it for the first time at her house and looking at the record cover, which had their pictures on the back and their ages. They were only a few years older than us, and they were *girls*. At the time, you never saw girls playing electric instruments; even when Heart came on the scene, you never saw Nancy Wilson playing an electric guitar – she was always playing her Ovation acoustic. When Suzi Quatro came out, it was part of the intrigue, like, 'This girl plays electric guitar!' Even though she actually played bass, and we didn't know the difference between guitar and bass at the time.

STEVEN: It's crazy to think about that first Runaways record. It comes out in 1976, and Joan Jett is 16 – I think they're all 16 except for Lita Ford, who's 17. Granted, I'm only 8 or 9 years old at the time, but they still seemed young to me, like they were still kids. We were definitely not above being affected by that stigma of, like, 'Chicks can't play'; I mean, we respected them immediately, but we were absolutely mesmerised by the idea that they knew how to play.

JEFF: The Runaways looked like the older sisters of our friends, and the music was raw and very different and not slick. Everything about the whole package was so great. It was obviously aimed at 12-year-old boys, but it was so great, and it made me want to be in a band. I tried to get my friend Annette to start a band with me, but she wasn't into it, and I didn't know how to play a guitar yet. But The Runaways really pushed me into making sure I learned how to play guitar as quickly as possible. I didn't have an electric guitar, and I didn't know how I was gonna get one. But I just had this urgency; I just *had* to learn how to play.

STEVEN: It really felt like if *they* can do it, then we've got to try. So that Christmas of '76, we mounted an unsuccessful campaign to get an electric guitar from the Sears catalogue for Christmas. My parents wound up getting Jeff an acoustic guitar, a cheap student model of an Ovation called an Applause. It had like a steel fretboard, and it was really hard to play. I mean, even now I would struggle to hold down the strings. It was that typical thing of, 'We'll try acoustic guitar first, and if you like that, then maybe you can move on to an electric.' But it's such a backwards way of thinking because electric guitars are so much easier to play than acoustic guitars.

JEFF: My aunt had a good acoustic guitar, so when I'd go to my grandma's house on Sundays, I would just go into my aunt's room and play her guitar. She had a Cat Stevens guitar book for the *Tea For The Tillerman* album. And it had the chord diagrams, which showed you where to put your fingers.

I'd tried a few years earlier with a Beatles guitar book, but the original Beatles sheet music was notoriously wrong; they would always have the wrong voicings for chords that were like these insane jazz voicings that The Beatles never used, and that you can't play as a beginner. So that was a discouragement. But with the Cat Stevens guitar book, the chords were a lot simpler; and because I knew the tunes so well, I knew where to change the chords – all I had to do was be able to hold the chords down. And once I got through learning that, then I learned how to play bar chords. And then I instantly started writing songs.

And then Steven joined the school orchestra because they allowed electric basses. He started with a standup bass, but that was part of the whole thing – like, if he could get an electric bass, and I could get an electric guitar…

STEVEN: We had a standard public school orchestra ensemble with flutes and clarinets and all that stuff, but electric bass was the one electric instrument they always allowed. The kid who played electric bass in the orchestra played a late-sixties Vox three-quarter scale bass, like a student model, and he was going to be graduating soon. So it seemed to that if I played my cards right, I could fill that position in the orchestra – but I would first have to learn to play the standup bass. So I joined the orchestra, and they gave me your typical public school standup bass to learn on. Which in reality was probably worth thousands of dollars, but it wasn't well maintained.

I practised, practised, practised; I learned to play the riff to the Roger Miller song 'King Of The Road', and this funky kind of blues riff from a song called 'Little Rock', and I really impressed my parents with it. So after a year of playing standup bass in the school orchestra, my parents bought me a Fender Musicmaster bass for Christmas. And then, after I blew the speakers out of my first amp – a Sears Silvertone that I'd bought from a girl in the neighbourhood – my parents bought me a little Peavey 115 combo, and that was it. I was 10, going on 11.

JEFF: Steven was a very good student, and my parents were encouraging him with his bass playing, but I realised that I was really gonna have to work for the electric guitar. I think my dad just thought I wanted to make noise – 'Oh, you're just gonna make a racket.' Which was totally wrong, but it was probably good because I had to actually get a job in order to pay for my guitar. That first guitar I found was a used Fender Stratocaster copy at a guitar store in Hawthorne. It was $40, so you can imagine how great it was, but it was better than anything I had. So I got a job at the local fish and chips place and got $40, which was probably like a week's salary at the time. And then I got the guitar, and I quit almost immediately after.

STEVEN: Which was probably the last normal job Jeff McDonald ever had; he got that cream Strat copy, and that was it. And then he got an amp from our next-door neighbour, Jimmy. Jimmy was in between my age and Jeff's age, and he was always keeping up with us; but he was an only child, so he would get things quicker than we would. I remember he got a Les Paul copy off the back of the Sears catalogue, and a Peavey Backstage 30 amplifier. Within a year's time, Jeff ended up with that Backstage 30, and the first thing we did was start playing along to Ramones and Runaways records.

JEFF: The Ramones were the second coming of The Beatles to me, because a lot of the music I loved from the early seventies had kind of fallen off. Like, Elton was terrible at that time, you know? Cat Stevens was awful. And David Bowie was making music I couldn't relate to at the time. It was just like anything coming from England was just kind of bloated. And then, hearing the Ramones for the first time, it was just like hearing The Beatles again – their songs were so good, and the music was so exciting. I felt they were mine, and I was convinced that they were gonna be gigantic.

STEVEN: Discovering punk rock didn't mean we stopped appreciating the old stuff. But when Bowie or Elton John increasingly got into American soul music, we felt like it got too soft – too *not* rock. And it would just kind of turn us off, you know?

Punk rock would've been sort of like this natural destination because it reduced the music to its hardest components, kind of like how Mick Ronson played the guitar riffs on the *Ziggy Stardust* album. The Ramones would have been the ultimate example of that – just great riffs and loud, aggressive guitars. It was like, 'This is exactly what we've been looking for!'

Jeff bought the second Ramones album, *Leave Home*, first; he bought it right when it came out in early 1977, and then we went back and got the first one, and then we bought *Rocket To Russia* when it came out later that year. So by the end of 1977, we had all three Ramones albums.

That first Ramones record, the way it's mixed is, there's no guitar overdubs. It's just guitar on one side, bass on the other side; the bass isn't in the centre, and there's no guitar doubling left and right. So if you just take the balance knob on your stereo, and you turn it all the way to one side, the mix becomes drums, bass and vocals; you turn the knob the other way and it's drums, guitar, and vocals. We would use that as a tool – we would take turns replacing the missing instrument.

JEFF: After seeing Johnny Ramone on *Don Kirshner's Rock Concert*, I realised you could play a whole song with bar chords; you don't have to switch shapes from D to G to A, you can keep your hand still in one shape and just slide it around…

Today, people think of the Ramones as part of American culture, as if they suddenly burst out and became famous. But back then, they really were not famous at all – and if you were a Ramones fan in LA, you were among maybe a thousand people in the county of Los Angeles who even knew who they were. I was barely a teenager at the time, and now some of the friends I was hanging out with at school were starting to get into music because it was cool. And I thought, 'I'm gonna rule this; I've made this great discovery, and it's gonna be the next big thing!' But people had the same reaction to the Ramones as the hippies that would scowl at us for buying Bowie records in the early seventies.

The surfers at school were really into music because it was part of their whole pot/surf culture. But it was always Led Zeppelin and/or Black Sabbath, and I was always kind of like, 'Yeah, I was already into them years ago, and they're past their prime.' I was *that* kind of snob; I would just have disgust for people who had just discovered Black Sabbath on *Never Say Die!*

The Ramones actually toured with Black Sabbath in 1978, and they did some West Coast dates together. In Los Angeles, they played the Long Beach Arena; I could not get our parents to drive us, and I didn't know anyone who could give us a ride, so I was devastated. But I knew people who were going to the show just to see Black Sabbath, and I was like, 'Just you wait! You're gonna hate Black Sabbath. Ramones rule – Black Sabbath is over with!' But the next day, boom – everyone who had gone to the show was like, 'Punk sucks! Ramones, they're goofy! Blah, blah, blah.' And it was just like pure hatred for them. So that whole movement that would later become surf punk rockers, those people initially were the most adamant punk haters.

And then there was a horrible NBC television special on punk rock in England; I remember seeing it, and it was really embarrassing. It was shot at the 100 Club in London, and all these safety pin punk kids were mugging for the cameras, doing the fake strangulation thing. And the news reports were talking about how 'punk rockers like to vomit on each other,' all that kind of stuff. I was already into punk rock, and I was sitting there watching it and going, 'Oh my god.' It was just so humiliating.

Many years later, I heard either Joey or Johnny Ramone talking about how they knew they were cooked the minute that thing aired, that that's what basically killed their career. The way punk rock was portrayed as just this moronic, stupid, goofy crap – dumb people vomiting on themselves – kept the people away who would have and should have transitioned into Ramones fans, and fans of the new music of the late seventies didn't embrace it. Even if it was only on some stupid news special, there was only three networks and a couple of other channels at the time, so everyone saw everything that was on TV. It was so powerful then. The FM radio stations wouldn't play them because they were too goofy. They weren't serious. And what was serious? The Eagles?

So, it was a struggle. Having musical taste and being kind of ahead of the curve, even as a child, always came with a sense of frustration and irritation.

Surfer dudes, 1977. (Photo by Janet McDonald)

Chapter 4

ANNETTE'S GOT THE HITS

Finding cool new music could be a serious challenge in the late 1970s, even for an inquisitive lad like Jeff McDonald. Mainstream newspapers and magazines rarely covered anything edgier than major label-approved new wavers, while FM rock stations – once a bastion of creative free-form programming – had become increasingly corporate and set in their ways.

Fortunately for Jeff, Steven and a whole lot of other open-minded LA listeners, there was KROQ. Launched in late 1972 (and then shuttered for two years due to cash-flow issues), the station re-emerged in 1975 as a champion of cutting-edge music, making 106.7 the preeminent destination for listeners who wanted to hear something more challenging than the album-oriented rock that was in constant rotation further down the FM dial.

One of the station's most popular programmes was Rodney on the ROQ, a weekly Sunday night show hosted by Hollywood scenester and club promoter Rodney Bingenheimer, which debuted in the summer of 1976 and regularly played current punk records from both sides of the Atlantic, along with their 1960s antecedents. The show would have an incalculable influence not just upon the McDonalds' musical education, but also their future musical endeavours.

JEFF: I was in seventh or eighth grade, and some other kid I knew who was open to cool music said, 'Have you heard Rodney? He plays all this great stuff. He plays Ramones.' I tuned in, and I was immediately hooked.

Rodney is one of *the* most important figures in LA music. His show was like rock'n'roll university for me because it taught me about Brian Wilson's importance in music, and the connection between Phil Spector and punk rock. Rodney loved the same sixties beach movies that we did, and he'd play a set with, like, the Avengers, Annette Funicello and the Ramones. This was all stuff that I'd already discovered on my own, but he tied it all together for me; he also got me going back and thinking about other things I used to listen to, like The Partridge Family. That education gave us *such* a leg up.

STEVEN: I was always proud of Hawthorne's connection to The Beach Boys, but back when we were into KISS and hard rock, their stuff seemed really corny to me. We were so obsessed with KISS *Alive!* and the whole world KISS had created, that The Beach Boys just seemed like squares to us. The Ramones were the ones who really sold me on The Beach Boys – it was like we found our way back to our local heroes via these weird punk rockers from Queens. And it was Rodney who helped us draw that connection, as well as the connection between those bands and The Ronettes and Blondie and Annette Funicello and beach movies. We realised that we could embrace all that stuff while simultaneously learning about punk rock, like all the local stuff that was coming out on Dangerhouse Records. And all of this would go into that first batch of songs that Jeff and I were writing together.

It felt like we were owning our heritage a bit, while also giving a bit of a 'fuck you' to our peer group who had feathered hair and maybe a feathered roach clip hanging from one ear, and who still thought that Robert Plant was God and Stevie Nicks was the ultimate babe. Compared to that stuff, an Annette Funicello song like 'The Monkey's Uncle' – which she sang with The Beach Boys, who grew up just a mile down the street from us – felt a lot more in keeping with this new music that we were getting turned on to.

JEFF: When I was 14, I somehow convinced my parents to buy me a used moped, and I started riding it up Sepulveda all the way from Hawthorne to Westwood. It was pretty scary – you couldn't go fast enough to keep up with traffic, but you went fast enough to kill yourself – but it was exciting to be able to escape to a completely different land for the first time. I'd meet my friend Chris, who lived in Brentwood, and we'd go to Rhino Records, which usually carried the punk singles that Rodney was playing on his show.

There was a woman named Connie Clarksville, who was in the original LA punk rock scene, and she was the one who cut everyone's hair. We found out where her salon was, so Chris and I rode our mopeds over there to get our first punk rock haircuts. She cut my hair extremely short for the time – nothing close to skinhead or anything like that, but just that kind of mod, spiky kind of look you see on bands from the pre-hardcore era. But people at school looked at me like I was absolutely insane.

I'd started growing my hair really long when I was about 9 or 10, down to shoulder length. I'd fight my parents about it, because they wanted me to get it cut, and I remember one time my friend Annette's grandmother asked her to ask me to leave their house; I asked Annette why, and she said, 'She hates you because you have long hair. She says you have lice.'

So, I'm old enough to have been hassled for having long hair when I was a kid, and then later get hassled for having short hair by surfers who thought I was a freak because they didn't know what punk rock was yet. People our ages in the suburbs didn't know what it was that we were trying to be or look like. Just having short hair in California was enough to send people through the rafters; they didn't know what was wrong with you.

STEVEN: We'd spend all summer at the beach when we were kids, from the second we got out of school in early June until September when we had to go back to school. Someone would drop us off in the morning at Manhattan Beach or El Porto Beach – which has a big refinery behind it but is actually quite a popular surf spot – and we'd hang out there all day. The highest status you could have on the beach was to be a surfer, but we rode boogie boards, and the surfers were really rude to boogie boarders and little kids. Jeff once got ran over by a surfboard while he was on his boogie board, and he came back to the sand looking like Carrie at the prom; he had a big gash in his head and had to get like twelve stitches.

But it was fun, and we went to the beach throughout the seventies, at least until we got into punk rock. In a very short time, we went from knowing about the Ramones and Blondie and the Sex Pistols to suddenly knowing about Darby Crash, and the Germs, and The Weirdos, and X, and the Bags, and all these other bands that were happening right in our hometown. At that point, the idea of being suburban surfer kids was like the lamest thing we could imagine. Not that we didn't desperately want to be cool among our ranks, but now we wanted to be part of this new culture, this punk rock scene. We no longer gave a shit about what some shirtless surfer dude would think of us. We cared more about what, you know, Alice Bag would think of us.

Having learned via Rodney on the ROQ that the Hollywood club scene was teeming with local punk bands, Jeff wanted to check out punk shows at venues like the Starwood and the Whisky a Go Go. But given that he and Steven lived a good 15 miles away from the Sunset Strip and were too young to drive, actually getting there was easier said than done.

JEFF: I was working on my parents to drive us to Hollywood, but there was also the issue that Steven was still a little intimidated by the idea of the punk rock scene. Our parents took us to the Ticketron at the Broadway department store at the Hawthorne Mall once, and they said we could go to one of the shows they had on sale. I wanted to see The Dickies and the Eyes, which was Charlotte Caffey's band before The Go-Go's, who were playing with The Jam at the Starwood. But Steven was like, 'I don't wanna go to the punk rock show! I don't wanna go to the punk rock show!' So our compromise was going to see Angel at the Long Beach Arena instead. Which was fine; I liked Angel, and I would have plenty of chances to see the other bands. Except for The Jam – I never saw The Jam.

STEVEN: The very first time we went to a nightclub to see a band was in July of '78 – we saw the Avengers at the Whisky, and X were supporting them. The Whisky would have two shows a night in those days, and the early shows would be all-ages. I'm very lucky that that practice existed at the time because it seemed reasonable to ask our parents to let us do something that was done by nine-thirty or ten; again, it was just like having them drop us off at the movies. But since they had to drive us however many miles to Hollywood, they were kind of stuck there; I guess they could have gone out to eat or something, but they weren't very adventurous. I just remember them sitting in their 1969 Toyota Corona in the Arco station parking lot across the street from the Whisky for the entire duration of the show.

JEFF: Joan Jett was like our local rock legend-slash-curiosity. She lived right around the corner from the Whisky, and if you got there for an early show you would always see her hanging out. We'd just kind of gawk at her because there was no difference in my mind between Joan Jett and, say, Rod Stewart. They both held the same mystique, they were both in the same magazines that I read, just like Mick Jagger and David Johansen and Joey

Ramone. So it was just insane to see her in person. We saw her play at the Whisky when our parents drove us there for a Runaways show – though it was *Waitin' For The Night* Runaways, after Cherie Currie had already left the band.

STEVEN: The Runaways were great that night. Looking back, they were kind of on the skids at that point, at the very end of their last lineup; Joan was in overalls, and Lita was in full rocker effect, but we loved them. And what was even more mind-blowing to me was the proximity effect; it hadn't even been three years since my first concert, and I was used to seeing all these idols that I held in such high esteem from hundreds of yards away, these little specks on the arena stage. And suddenly we're in these small spaces where you could not only be a fan and, you know, grab their foot at the front of the stage, but you could maybe hang out and have an exchange with them. That evolution was quite disorienting.

Seeing bands playing original music in such intimate venues lit a fire under Jeff and Steven to find other members for the as-yet-unnamed band of their own. Unfortunately, the pool of potential candidates seemed woefully limited, even without bringing punk rock into the equation. But in the fall of 1978, Jeff finally found a likely guitarist in a most unlikely setting: high school photo shop.

JEFF: I would audition anyone who had a guitar, whether they were into punk rock or not. I was in ninth grade, and almost no one had guitars at the time – they were like rare instruments, and it seemed like anyone who did have one was in bands like Seagull or Rage, these South Bay cover bands that could play Led Zeppelin note for note but never played any original material.

I remember this one kid came over and we showed him our songs, but that didn't go anywhere. And then another guy who

I met at Jack in the Box – he was a few years older than me, but he played guitar. But he was already living on his own, and he kind of drank a lot, so we were like, 'Not him.'

STEVEN: Jeff was taking a photo class in ninth grade at Hawthorne High. At the time, our bedroom walls were completely covered with the black and white photos he'd taken of punk bands, and Jeff was in class developing pictures he'd taken of X at the Whisky. Greg Hetson was there developing pictures he'd taken of The Dickies, and it was extremely uncommon for there to be two people in the same class who were into punk rock, so they started talking. And that's really where the band began.

JEFF: Greg was a senior, and he was like, 'Oh, you like punk rock? I love The Dickies. And I have a guitar.' Greg had grown up in Hawthorne, but his parents had divorced and he was living with his dad in Brentwood. He was worldly enough to have discovered punk rock, and he had a car so he could actually go to the shows. He was like the only other person I had met at school who had even heard of these bands, much less seen them; though I don't even know why he had a guitar, because he wasn't trying to be in a band. So I immediately had to talk him into coming over. I was like, 'Yeah, I have a band. We have an 11-year-old bass player, and we need a guitar player.' He was like, 'Oh, really? I don't know…'

STEVEN: Jeff was always playing up the '11-year-old bass player' angle. It was that Kim Fowley thing; he was always looking for a way to break into showbiz, and he saw his younger brother as a unique way of getting that attention. He's talked about how watching me watching Jimmy Osmond on TV was kind of a lightbulb moment; I just imagine me spacing out in front of the TV, and Jeff looking at the screen and seeing this cherubic Jimmy Osmond, then looking at me, cherubic Steven, and then looking back at the screen. It's like I'm a gigantic T-bone steak – potential fame, just right there for the taking!

JEFF: Groups that were made of family and where there were kids playing instruments – like The Osmonds or The Partridge Family – that was almost as strange at the time as girls playing instruments. It was another one of those things that you just weren't used to seeing. And I knew that you had to have some sort of image; you don't just have a band, you have to have a whole *mystique*. And Steven being a cherubic little kid with a high-pitched Osmond brother voice, I always said he was like the Jimmy Osmond of the band. I meant it as a compliment, but it was also very punk rock to say something like that, because saying 'We're very into The Osmonds' would be enough to make even people in the punk scene think we were completely insane.

STEVEN: In those days, I was extremely sensitive about being younger than everyone else we hung out with. Like, when we would go to Disneyland, I could get a discount with a child's ticket, and the teenagers would all be like, 'Go for it, dude!' They thought it was cool, but I would immediately feel humiliated by it. It's like getting the 'senior platter' offered to you long before you're ready for it.

JEFF: Greg wasn't too sure about playing in a band with an 11-year-old. But after having class together for a couple of months, I finally talked him into coming over with his amp and his guitar. We already had songs that were ready to play, because once I got my $40 guitar and I had some chords to work with, and Steven had learned a few licks on bass, the songs began to come out. I think 'Annette's Got The Hits' might have been one of the first songs we wrote.

STEVEN: We decided to call ourselves The Tourists, which was a reference to the beach culture. The whole thing was that if you didn't live on The Strand or, like, a stone's throw from the beach, then the surfers who ruled the beach would call you a tourist. And if you were a tourist, you didn't belong; you didn't own any real estate on the waves. So we were embracing our status with the name – like, 'Yeah, we're tourists. So what?'

If you listen to the lyrics of 'Annette's Got The Hits', we're making fun of beach culture – 'Ten foot boards/Strapped to our cars/We're just homely beach kids/We don't go to bars.' But at the same time, we're kind of celebrating Annette Funicello, and all those sixties beach movies we grew up watching.

JEFF: Steven had learned Henry Mancini's 'Peter Gunn' theme and Roger Miller's 'King Of The Road' in the school orchestra, and he repurposed those riffs for some of our early songs. 'Annette's Got The Hits' was kind of a sideways Mancini thing. People don't realise that Henry Mancini and Roger Miller were big influences on our early records, but there you go…

Greg had a couple of ideas, we wrote a few songs together, and everything fell together really fast. So then it was up to me to find a drummer – and the only person we knew with a drum set was a 13-year-old kid who was in the junior high school orchestra with Steven.

STEVEN: John Stielow was an eighth-grade kid that I kind of knew from playing with him in the school orchestra. He was kind of a star, because when the orchestra did 'Hawaii Five-O Theme', he did the drum solo at the beginning of it, and that was a big hit at our school.

John was just like a normal kid. He'd probably have been happier if we were doing Led Zeppelin covers, but he was pretty open-minded. Our first rehearsal as a four-piece was in his garage, and the cops came and shut us down. And then we tried to go rehearse in a little amphitheatre in a neighbouring park because John said there was an electrical socket we could plug in to. So we set everything up, and then they just came and stopped us again.

JEFF: I didn't play guitar in the band at first. I was able to write songs on guitar, but I wasn't confident enough to play guitar onstage; I was still kind of stuck in that whole thing of, it takes years to be good enough to play guitar in a band.

When I was in eighth grade, I had a friend who was a really good guitar player, but he was just into hard rock, not anything weird that I was into. But he was my friend, and he was putting a band together to do a song for the eighth-grade talent show, and he asked me if I wanted to sing. I said yeah, and I bought a cheap microphone, because I thought I had to have a microphone. But then he wanted to play 'Snakeskin Cowboys' by Ted Nugent, from the first Ted Nugent album, and once I started picking out the lyrics, I was like, 'This is so stupid.' I mean, the lick is great, but once you hear the lyrics, it's just rock'n'roll clichés strung together. And I remember singing along to the record and thinking, 'I'm not gonna be able to sell this.' So I bailed on them, and they just played it as an instrumental. I wanted to sing, but I knew I could write better lyrics than that…

Greg was a much better guitar player than me at the time, so I think it was just easier for me to wrap my head around coming up with the songs and singing them, because that was scary enough without also trying to play guitar at the same time. So I just used the Peavey Backstage amp as a PA system, and I plugged that cheap microphone into it. We learned some Beatles songs and some New York Dolls songs to go with our originals, so we had a whole set's worth of material pretty quickly. Now we just needed to get some shows.

The Tourists rock Polliwog Park, July 1979. (Photo by Spot)

Chapter 5

THE CHURCH

Despite the apparent scarcity of punks and punk gigs in the South Bay in the late 1970s, one of the most important punk bands to ever emerge from Southern California was actually taking shape just a few miles away from the McDonalds in nearby Hermosa Beach. Originally formed in 1976 as Panic, the band – led by guitarist Greg Ginn – changed its name to Black Flag in late 1978. They played their first gig under that name on January 27, 1979 at Moose Lodge 1873 in Redondo Beach, opening for LA punk bands The Alley Cats and Rhino 39. Jeff and Steven were in the audience, having forked over $2.50 apiece for admission to the show. That money – along with whatever they paid that night for a copy of *Nervous Breakdown*, Black Flag's debut 7-inch EP – would prove an unexpectedly fruitful investment.

JEFF: We found out about this very rare DIY punk gig in Redondo Beach; our parents were okay with us going, because it was kind of in our neighbourhood. I'd discovered The Alley Cats because there was an article in the *LA Times* about women getting into playing in bands because of punk; it included Diane Chai, who was the bass player of The Alley Cats, who were on

43

Dangerhouse Records and were one of the OG LA punk bands. My grandmother saw the article and was like, 'You know your cousin Carey? Diane is Carey's aunt!' Diane wasn't a blood relative of ours, but this was still an unexpected connection to someone in the scene – and the fact that her band was playing in our neighbourhood was so exciting.

STEVEN: We were big fans of Rhino 39 and The Alley Cats. But then there was this obnoxious band Black Flag opening for them at the Moose Lodge that were super loud, and to me they just sounded like a muddy mess. The singer was drunk, and I remember he tore down an American flag, which got some of the local Moose Lodge members really pissed off. It was just a bunch of shenanigans that I wasn't particularly impressed with. But they were selling that first EP, and we ended up getting it.

JEFF: We saw on the back of the record that their label SST Records was in Lawndale, which is the next town down from Hawthorne. I was like, 'Whoa, that band's actually from here!' So I got on the phone and called them the next day. I talked to Greg Ginn; I told him, 'Oh, we have this band, we have an 11-year-old bass player, and we really want to do some shows.' And he invited us to come over to their rehearsal space…

When we were starting our band, we had no idea how to get shows; we didn't know anyone, and we didn't get to enough shows to do any real kind of networking. I would always be on the lookout for potential venues in our area – like, 'Oh my god, this Mexican restaurant has a stage!' – and try and put a show together somehow, but I didn't have any luck. We called members of X and The Dickies to introduce ourselves and see if they wanted to play a show that we were gonna put together, but they both kind of laughed at us. But when I called the SST number and talked to Greg about our band, he was receptive because he was essentially trying to put together a scene of his own.

STEVEN: Yeah, of course Jeff pimped me out as the 11-year-old bass player. But whatever Jeff said to Greg Ginn on the phone, he was charmed by it and said, 'We're rehearsing tomorrow – you guys should just come down here.' Greg Hetson was the only person in our band with a car, a little yellow Toyota pickup truck, so he drove us down there with me sitting in the open bed.

The Tourists pulled up in front of 'The Church', a decrepit Spanish Mission-style building from the 1920s that had been home to a local Baptist congregation before being sold to developers in 1973. The building had changed hands several times since then, and was currently occupied by a disparate array of artists and musicians, including Greg Ginn and Black Flag.

STEVEN: The whole place was totally foreign and intimidating and bizarre to me. The church had been repurposed as an artisan space by these hippies who were renting out space for people to do macramé or make stained glass or sandals or whatever; but instead, Greg Ginn had shown up, and he was running his small electronics company and rehearsing his punk rock band there. There was a lot of hostility between Black Flag and the hippies.

Greg Ginn was also living there in one of the spaces, and I don't know if they necessarily had hot water. It was really gross, like probably five levels below your average college dorm. And he had an area where he was soldering his radio transmitters all the time, and they'd covered the walls of their rehearsal room with someone's 1950s carpeting that they'd dug out of a dumpster, so the odours of mildewy carpets, beer-soaked hardwood floors, dust and solder were all pretty overpowering.

JEFF: Yeah, that was really scary, because I'd never been in a place with actual bohemian types – like, people who lived in places without showers and ate potato chips for dinner and didn't have parents. So just going into their world was, like, insane. It was this stripped-bare church with no pews or altar left; and though they paid to rent it for rehearsal and for Greg Ginn's electronics company, they weren't supposed to be living there in this room, which was the size of a garage and had a big wall of really loud amplifiers.

STEVEN: We just sat down on the floor, Indian style, and they blasted us with their full-blown attack. Greg Ginn had his Sound City double cabinets with eight 12-inch speakers; and it was the classic lineup of Robo on drums, Keith Morris singing and Chuck Dukowski on bass, who was still called Gary at the time. Robo had his gigantic Ludwig Vistalite kit with the clear drums, and Keith was shouting through a Shure Vocal Master PA, and they just assaulted us with the same set that they had drunkenly done at the Moose Lodge. And then they were like, 'You guys are in a band? Come on, let's see it.'

Greg Hetson may have had his guitar with him. But I didn't have my bass, so Chuck Dukowski handed me his Ibanez Flying V, which was massive on me. And little John Stielow got behind Robo's gigantic Vistalites, which had like a John Bonham-sized kick drum. We played pretty much all the songs we had at the time, like 'Annette's Got The Hits', and two covers: 'Who Are The Mystery Girls?' by the New York Dolls, and 'I Want To Hold Your Hand' by The Beatles. I thought our arrangement of 'I Want To Hold Your Hand' was pretty clever – we'd do the first verse and chorus at Beatle tempo, and then we'd blast into, like, a Ramones-style super-fast tempo for the rest of it.

JEFF: It was scary because they'd also invited some of their friends, people from our area who were into punk rock but also turned out to be like-minded on just about every level. So we wanted to impress them, because they were in the know, and we honestly didn't know if we were any good. We had no way of knowing if what we were doing was like just a total joke and embarrassment, or if it had some kind of merit. But after the first couple songs, everyone got into it, and everyone was really cool; it was apparent that we were instantly accepted by Black Flag and their friends. So that was one of the great moments for us.

The Church would soon become a regular hangout for The Tourists, and ultimately a place to practise. Unfortunately, acceptance was harder to find outside of LA punk's small circles. As punk and new wave gained a higher profile in the media, the music, its fans and practitioners were viewed with mounting suspicion and disdain by everyone from South Bay surfers to the LA Police Department. While Jeff and Steven were increasingly harassed by their peers over their affinity for punk rock, it was nothing compared to the violence that the LAPD under the command of newly appointed Chief of Police Daryl Gates were inflicting upon audiences at local punk gigs. The infamous 'Elks Lodge Riot' of March 17, 1979 was but one grisly example, with an estimated hundred LAPD officers in full riot gear launching a brutal and unprovoked attack during a show that featured X, The Alley Cats, The Plugz, The Zeros, an early lineup of The Go-Go's, and a young band from Portland called Wipers. Jeff and Steven were among the estimated four to six hundred people in attendance that night in the ballroom of the Elks Lodge building, an ornate art deco skyscraper located across the street from MacArthur Park in downtown Los Angeles.

STEVEN: Only two or three bands got through their sets that night at the Elks Lodge before the LAPD riot squad came storming up the stairs, just indiscriminately bashing people in the head. The building has this grand staircase that leads up to the ballroom from four sets of double doors at the front entrance; Jeff and I were on the staircase talking to some people we'd met because it was between bands, and suddenly we saw the cops come flooding through the doors and up the stairs. People were trying to get out and get away from the cops, but there was a bottleneck because so many of them kept charging through the front doors, just swinging their clubs at anyone within their reach.

My parents were parked outside – they had driven us to the show – and they saw everything go down. They saw the riot squad assembling and then eventually charging through and bashing people. We were at one of the doorways trying to get out, and my dad saw us; he was like, 'Goddammit, Steven!' and he grabbed us, pulled us through, and saved us from getting unjustly beat up. I remember that he was so angry on the car ride home, but he didn't know who he was mad at – us for dragging them down to that situation and pressuring them to let us go into an environment that ended up being dangerous, or the LAPD for being so incorrectly aggressive. He was like, 'You're not doing that anymore!' But then we had a conversation with them soon after where I was like, 'Look, you know *we* weren't in the wrong,' and they relented.

These gatherings, these punk shows, were actually quite peaceful, and they weren't harming anyone. But just because the people going to them looked different, and the media was making a big deal out of it, they were being persecuted. The Elks Lodge thing was an early eye-opening experience for everyone, just seeing this oppressive use of power against people who really hadn't provoked it other than by looking different. And it was like, 'What's your problem with that?' So I think the whole thing kind of helped my parents open their working-class suburban mindset to what we had gotten ourselves involved in. I'm sure it probably added to the anxiety they had about us being in environments that may have been not the safest, but at the same time they were down for the cause.

JEFF: The summer of 1979, that first summer we spent in Hermosa Beach hanging out at The Church, that's when all the surfers were just getting hip to Devo. So they would see us and throw things and scream, 'Devo! Devo!' That was like a hardcore surfer putdown of the punkers. It would drive us insane. I mean, I loved Devo, but they were just starting to discover it; and you could tell that they were calling us 'Devo' because *they* were getting into Devo and they didn't know how to deal with these conflicting feelings around it. It's like the jocks all calling the one guy a 'faggot' – like, why are they so concerned, unless they have their own issues? It was *exactly* like that.

So, it took me a while to make my peace with Devo and get back on the Devo train, because it was really bad. And then of course, all of those people – all the surfers and skaters – became hardcore punk rockers. We'd started skateboarding in 1975, right when urethane wheels first came out, which was revolutionary; before that it was all clay and steel wheels. And it was really cool, until we got into punk and all these skaters were going, 'Devo! Devo! Devo!' at us. And then they transitioned into punk, which I guess in real time was about eight months, but at the time it seemed like an eternity. And oh my god, it was torture.

The Tourists inflicted some torture of their own in June 1979, when they made their official live debut at the eighth-grade graduation party of Lisa Stangle, one of John Stielow's classmates. Not only did the band accept her invitation to play the event, but they made the occasion extra memorable by inviting some other friends along.

JEFF: Lisa asked us to play at her parents' house. We said, 'We can get another band to play, too,' and we asked Black Flag. All these stoner idiots showed up at the party and booed us; all the older teens who weren't supposed to be there, they were like, 'Punk rock sucks! Play some Zep!' So I'd be like, 'Okay, this next song is an unreleased Led Zeppelin song.' And they'd all go 'Yeah!!!' And then we'd start playing and after thirty seconds they'd realise that we weren't playing a Zeppelin song, and they'd start booing us again. So then I'd say, 'Okay, this is an unreleased Black Sabbath song...' and they kept falling for it.

STEVEN: That was a bit of a trial by fire. We didn't back down, and I think we buffered each other's sense of confidence that night, but I still kind of felt like a failure – you know, I would have preferred standing ovations to being booed by older teenagers.

JEFF: It was our first time really performing in front of a live audience, and I think the adrenaline just kicked in and got us through the set. The experience gave us mad Bob Dylan 1966 playing-through-booing skills, which we'd have to use again later in life. And then Black Flag came in with their stacks of amplifiers and just blew their heads off. All the teens were horrified; it was so loud and so scary. We were kids that they could pick on, but these guys were like ten years older than us. They played until the cops came and shut it down. That was the weirdest, weirdest gig.

The Tourists opened for Black Flag again in July 1979, as part of an infamous outdoor concert at Manhattan Beach's Polliwog Park. This time, however, Jeff and Steven's band was tolerated by the crowd, while Black Flag were the ones who came in for abuse.

JEFF: At the time, Black Flag were always setting up weird shows. They were the original DIY people, and they'd play anywhere – I think they played an office break at the Richmond Oil Company, just weird shit like that. Polliwog Park was a big local park that had a little amphitheatre stage, and the Parks & Rec department was doing a summer concert series there.

STEVEN: The story I heard was that Black Flag misrepresented themselves to whoever it was at the city council who booked the entertainment; they gave them a tape of Steely Dan or some light jazz record and claimed it was their band. And these people took their word for it.

JEFF: They asked us to do the show with them, and we just jumped on it. It was a weekend, a Saturday afternoon, and we felt lucky to get on the bill. And it was a little scary because there were over three hundred people in the audience, including all these normal families who were having picnics. And this was at a time when your normal person didn't even know what punk rock was.

STEVEN: I was excited and really nervous and had no idea what to expect – except that it could probably go poorly as our first gig had gone. But we didn't choke, the audience was polite to us, and we finished all of our songs. We even *performed*; we had seen our favourite band the Avengers live onstage, and we were aiming to really stalk the stage like Penelope Houston – not necessarily be 'punk' or tough, but do our thing and move around a bit. And like the Ramones, we wanted to make a quick impression and then leave.

JEFF: I think we played, like, seventeen minutes; I don't see how it could have been any longer than that. And people were nice to us; we were really young, and I don't think these people had seen kids playing music before. And then the minute Black Flag started playing, everyone was totally shocked.

STEVEN: The audience were there to just, you know, maybe throw a Frisbee, fly a kite, have a picnic and enjoy some light jazz. And instead you had Black Flag unleashing this outrageous punk rock assault, and Keith was wasted and cussing a lot and saying offensive things just to bait the crowd. And the reaction was like the one we'd gotten a few weeks earlier at the graduation party, only more aggressive.

JEFF: I remember seeing watermelon wedges flying through the air. People were throwing whatever food was left in their picnic baskets at the stage. It would've been really sad for adults to attack us like that, because we were actual children; Black Flag were full grown adults, so I guess it was fair game. The local Redondo Beach newspaper reviewed the show, and all they said about us is that we seemed like the Vienna Boys' Choir compared to Black Flag. That was the first words we ever had in print about us – comparing us to the Vienna Boys' Choir!

Neither The Tourists' name nor their original lineup would survive the summer of 1979. In August, they rechristened themselves as Red Cross, and – in the first of many membership upheavals to come – replaced John Stielow with Church resident Ron Reyes. With Reyes on drums, the quartet recorded a four-song demo (featuring original songs 'Rich Brat', 'Cover Band', 'Clorox Girls' and 'Standing In Front Of Poseur') that was produced by Joe Nolte of The Last and engineered by future SST in-house producer Spot.

STEVEN: It was kind of becoming revealed to us that no one in Black Flag thought The Tourists was a cool name – it was kind of new wave instead of punk rock. And then we learned about this band from England called The Tourists who turned out to be an early incarnation of Eurythmics, and that sealed the deal.

JEFF: We had a complete block on what else to call ourselves; it wasn't like we had a million possibilities to choose from. I remember we were all in the basement room at The Church where Ron lived, and I just spit out 'Red Cross,' and everyone just said, 'Oh, that's fine.' It might have been a subliminal thing that Red Cross looked good on a flyer with Black Flag, but it wasn't intentional.

STEVEN: Black Flag had a gig at the Hong Kong Café in Chinatown where they were opening for U.X.A., and they asked us to open for them. But John Stielow couldn't do it because he was going to be visiting some relatives in the Midwest, so we just unceremoniously kicked him out of the band. And Black Flag suggested that Ron Reyes could learn how to play drums and do it. Ron was like an 18-year-old runaway; he and Joe Nolte lived in this little spray-painted room in the basement of The Church. And after he joined, that's where we practised. So we had a name change and a lineup change probably in the same week, and both encouraged by Black Flag, who were mentoring us.

JEFF: The LA punk scene was made up of a lot of bands that had singles, so we thought if we at least paid for a recording, we might be able to find someone to put it out. Because I had no idea how to do that. There was a recording studio just around the corner from The Church, and it cost like $30 an hour to record there; Joe Nolte had made records before, so he said he'd produce it for us. Steven made, like, probably $60 a month on his paper route, so that was enough to get us a couple of hours in the studio. And that's how we paid for it.

STEVEN: The studio was called Media Art. It's also where Black Flag recorded early on, and Spot was a house engineer there; that might even be where they met him. They had a 16-track 2-inch tape machine, and if you did the graveyard shift from midnight to eight in the morning, it'd be half price; and since I'm the 12-year-old bassist paying for it with my paper route money, that's what we opted for.

JEFF: 'Rich Brat' was the one song on the demo that never got re-recorded. It was just kind of a diss track about some older, overprivileged kids that we didn't like. In those days, we didn't know what you were supposed to write songs about. It wasn't like, 'Oh, I'm a teen poet. I have to express myself!' It was more like, 'We need words for these songs. What do we write about?' You knew you wanted to have your own songs, but then it required you to say something.

STEVEN: Recording for the first time was intimidating, but Jeff and I really kind of cheerleaded each other through it. All these new experiences were scary for us, but we were always just sort of thinking, 'This is the next step!'

JEFF: And the next step after that was to get Rodney to play it. Rodney on the ROQ was really big at the time, and he was always saying, 'I won't play cassettes – I only play acetates!' We only had the cassette, but Greg and I drove up to the KROQ studios to give it to him. I think he was probably into the teen vibe of it because he instantly started playing it.

Steven sings 'Standing in Front of Poseur' at King's Palace, December 1979. (Photo by Al Flipside)

Chapter 6

BAD VIBES

O n September 2, 1979, the new lineup of the newly rechristened Red Cross made its debut at the Hong Kong Café, opening for Black Flag and San Francisco punk transplants U.X.A. Black Flag's support gave Red Cross instant credibility and visibility in a Hollywood punk scene that had already gone through several upheavals and permutations since Jeff and Steven had begun to follow it. Between this date and Thanksgiving weekend, Red Cross would play ten more shows, mostly at the Hong Kong Café and King's Palace in Hollywood, appearing on bills with such already-established bands as the Germs, the Bags, The Mau-Mau's, the Descendents – and, of course, Black Flag.

The Hong Kong Café was a Chinese restaurant located in LA's Chinatown district, which had begun booking punk shows in July 1979 – a practice which put it in direct competition with Madame Wong's, a nearby restaurant and venue that had been booking shows since the previous fall. Wong's tended to book more mainstream-oriented new wave bands, while the Hong Kong Café generally featured more cutting-edge acts. It wasn't unusual to see celebrities and famous musicians hanging out at either club; none other than David Bowie was supposedly at the Hong Kong Café during Red Cross's debut appearance.

JEFF: I don't know if Bowie was at our first Hong Kong Café gig or the second one, because they were about three weeks apart, so let's say it was the first one – that's cooler. I remember hearing that Bowie was there, but I didn't see it. The thing about that place was that it had a really weird layout; you'd walk in the front door, turn right and walk up a flight of stairs into the venue, which was in a banquet room. And if you turned left from the front entrance, there was an old-timey 1950s-style lounge that served tropical drinks and had a lady who looked like Doris Day playing the organ and singing. It wasn't some sort of 'retro' thing – the lounge had actually been like that for decades, and we were just catching the tail end of that world. But we were too young to drink, so we weren't allowed in the lounge. And that's supposedly where Bowie was when people saw him; I have no idea if he actually saw our set.

There was a big rivalry at the time between the Hong Kong Café and Madame Wong's, which was kind of like the enemy at that time – only the 'skinny tie' people played there, and bands that had obvious commercial potential, or had been kicking around for a long time without any real success, so they were trying to ride the 'new wave' angle to success. But Wong's had a lot of really important early new wave shows there, like The Pretenders and The Police, and I'm sure The Knack played there. It's so weird to think that just across the street, all these really tragic, weirdo Hollywood art bands were playing.

As far as LA is concerned, I have to say that I saw some of the greatest shows by the greatest weird underground bands at their best moment at the Hong Kong Café; it was just a magical place. The Germs, for instance – the show where we opened up for them, it was just full-on chaos. Pat Smear was playing a borrowed Rickenbacker guitar, and all the guts, all the electronics just kept popping out of the guitar while he was playing, and he had to keep stuffing it back in.

And the Bags – we opened for the best version of the band, the one that did the 'Survive' single, and that was just so exciting. Alice Bag and Patricia Morrison, their friendship was breaking up at the time; at one point in the show, the audience was getting all rowdy, and Alice walked up to Patricia's bass amp, pulled out the plug and said, 'Call off the *dogs*, bitch!' Right there on stage, you know? And I was like, 'Whoa, bad vibes!'

STEVEN: The Germs were my absolute favourite band. They were the most dangerous, most extreme band on the scene, but they were also just a few years older than us, so they were kind of like relatable teenagers, too. Darby Crash was like the first rock star of the scene, the punkest person there was, and it was a revelation for me to see this guy up in close quarters in the prime *GI* era, stalking around onstage like a wild animal with his blue-black hair and gnarled teeth. To 12-year-old me, he was like Keith Richards meets Sid Vicious. And playing with the Germs at the Hong Kong Café kind of elevated me – like, not only am I a fan, but I'm also in a band, too!

The thing is, bands like X and The Go-Go's and the Bags, they were definitely image conscious and they were into fashion and doing their own thing. But in many ways, the original LA punk scene was all about ripping down the façade of the rock star, and getting rid of that distance between audience and band. Whereas I loved the fantasy; I bought into the fantasy. And Darby wanted to be a cult leader, you know? He had gone to Scientology school and learned certain mental control tactics that he was dying to try out on teenagers; he wanted to control people like me, and I was all about it.

The Hong Kong Café was also where Red Cross first encountered Robbie Fields, an American-born, London-raised former journalist who had recently begun releasing the music of local punk bands on his own Posh Boy label. Fields had heard the Red Cross demos on Rodney on the ROQ and approached the band about recording some songs for an upcoming Posh Boy compilation. The band entered Hollywood's Shelter Studios in October 1979 to record six tracks – 'Cover Band', 'Clorox Girls' and 'Standing In Front Of Poseur' from the demo, and 'Annette's Got The Hits', 'S&M Party' and 'I Hate My School'. Former Sparks bassist Jim Mankey engineered the session, which ably captured the young band in all its raw teenage (and in Steven's case, pre-teen) hyperactivity.

STEVEN: Shelter was a studio that Leon Russell built in one of those massive old farmhouses on Sunset Boulevard. I think Liberty Records may have been there before it – there used to be a whole row of indie labels on Sunset in the fifties and sixties, back when 'indie label' meant something much different than it does now. Tom Petty and Dwight Twilley had both recorded at Shelter only a few years before us.

JEFF: I don't know why we didn't record 'Annette...' for that first demo; maybe we didn't think it was strong enough, and it took Robbie to point out to us that it was a good song.

STEVEN: I really love that both 'Be True To Your School' by The Beach Boys and 'I Hate My School' were written about the same school: Hawthorne High.

JEFF: We were well-rehearsed, and we had only about twelve minutes' worth of original material, so we did everything very quickly. I did the vocals after the tracks were done, so it all took just a couple of hours including mixing. I only played guitar on one song, 'Standing In Front Of Poseur' – Steven sang on it and Greg played bass. We'd have this whole changeover onstage where I'd take Greg's guitar and Greg would take Steven's bass, and the song is only like forty-five seconds long.

STEVEN: Greg had a little 'My Generation'-style bass solo on there, which I thought was very cool.

JEFF: Poseur was a shop on Sunset in Hollywood. It was the only place that had, like, punk clothes from England. They sold Crazy Color for hair, and then a few really overpriced items, like T-shirts with safety pins in them that had been imported from London. That part of Sunset was also, like, a big prostitution area, with lots of street prostitutes. So that song was basically just an observation of prostitution on Sunset in the vicinity of a punk rock store.

The Ramones were really good at the observational-type song. People don't give them credit because of their cartoony image, but their songs are observations in the same way that you know what England's like just from hearing Ray Davies' songs, or you get a sense of New York from Velvet Underground records. They just wrote about their environment, and that was kind of what we were trying to do.

We actually grew up surrounded by prostitutes, because we lived just a block off Imperial Highway, which was one of the main thoroughfares to the airport, and all these guys would be picking up hookers on their way to or from the airport. There were all these vacant houses on our street because the city was buying them up to make way for the new freeway project, so a lot of the hookers would use the vacant houses as places to bring their johns or tricks or whatever they were called – that is, if they weren't doing it in cars, because we would see that a lot, too. I was in my early teens when we first really started noticing it.

STEVEN: They were usually African American women who looked like Foxy Brown or Sly Stone on the cover of *Fresh* – gigantic afros and platform heels. I remember this one girl wearing a Girl Scout uniform, but with platform shoes, a really high skirt, and a Girl Scout cap pinned to the side of her afro.

I would just look at these women and be so mesmerised by them on so many levels, because they looked like rock stars to me. And they were always really nice to me, never saying anything inappropriate; I'd be riding my bike down the street on my paper route, and they'd be like, 'Hey, Honey – how are you today?' They were brassy, outlandish, sparkly creatures, but always sweet to the little boy.

Jeff and I would break into those vacant houses sometimes, and there was one house where we found a bunch of burnt candles, hooker clothing everywhere and tubes of model glue. We were like, 'Whoa – devil-worshipping, glue-sniffing hookers!' So, flash-forward to the early eighties when we're dumpster diving for clothes at the Salvation Army drop-off bin, and the memory of seeing how those sex workers put themselves together really wasn't far at all from our minds, you know?

JEFF: Recording for Posh Boy was a big deal – just to be able to go into a studio and get something out, that wasn't a common thing at all back then. We didn't know how to put out a record, and there was no concept of, 'Oh, SST will put it out,' because at that point SST wasn't really a label; they were more Greg Ginn's electronics company. So here's Robbie Fields coming up to us after just a couple of shows and saying, 'I'll record you guys and put you on a compilation,' and it all just felt like everything was falling into place.

STEVEN: Robbie had just put out the *Beach Blvd.* compilation, which was great. It was like three pop punk bands from Southern California, and he'd had success with it, so now he was going to do another one, and we were going to be on that. That's how it was presented to us; it wasn't presented to us that we were recording an EP. But when the comp was finally done, it had two new wave bands on it that we didn't know – one was from San Francisco and the other was from Salt Lake City. We were like, 'Who are these guys?' The comp was called *The Siren*, and it was a weird record; we didn't think our music fit in with the other bands at all. But our songs turned out to be the ones that Rodney played all the time, and the ones that people got the record for. So eventually Robbie made an EP out of it.

The Siren – which also featured three songs each by 391 and Spittin' Teeth, as well as the six tracks Red Cross recorded at Shelter – was released in early 1980. By the time it hit the stores, Greg Hetson and Ron Reyes had already left Red Cross; Hetson formed the Circle Jerks with former Black Flag singer Keith Morris, while Reyes replaced Morris in Black Flag. Meanwhile, Jeff and Steven struggled to keep the band afloat. *Red Cross*, an EP containing only the six songs recorded at Shelter, would finally be released by Posh Boy in 1981.

STEVEN: We lost Greg Hetson and Ron Reyes within weeks of each other at the end of 1979.

JEFF: I don't know what eventually led to it. I mean, there were definitely some issues between me and Ron; he would mess with my head by saying that he'd been told by so many people we would be so much better if we had a better singer. But I was also going through this teenage identity crisis, where I felt like had to get drunk or wasted before a show. I did not know how to hold my alcohol in those days – not that I ever really learned, but I was extremely obnoxious then. I would almost get us into fights with people, and just be really horrible.

We had a show in November at King's Palace, which later became Raji's. I got really drunk beforehand, *teenage* drunk, and this girl I was hanging out with drew King Tut makeup on my face. And Ron was furious, yelling at me, 'We don't wear makeup!' So then I was really obnoxious during the show, and it just kind of disintegrated into a really sad display on my part, and both Greg and Ron just left the stage. I don't really remember it, but it all came to a head that night. We hadn't officially broken up, though; Ron left, but Greg hadn't quit yet. But that King's Palace show was definitely the last show of that lineup.

I don't know how long it was between Ron quitting our band and joining Black Flag, but it wasn't long. We tried out Lucky Lehrer as a drummer, but Steven and I were both kind of tripping on the fact that he had this gigantic kit and was so much older than us, so we weren't quick to pull the trigger on that. But Greg thought he was great, and he and Keith and Lucky decided to form a new group together. It all blends together in a weird sort of way.

STEVEN: A *lot* happened in that twelve to sixteen-month window, from Greg coming over to our house for the first time to the end of the first lineup of Red Cross; in between, we went from being The Tourists to becoming Red Cross, we played our first shows, and had our first two recording sessions. But instead of feeling like we'd accomplished so much, and that our dream was being realised, I was licking my wounds. I felt betrayed by Greg and Ron, and felt the frustrations of trying to keep a band together. And I was feeling all these things for the first time, at the same time, so it was intense.

The band was always extremely important to me. And Greg and Ron leaving, it was the first of several situations where I felt wronged – that people had misled us, led us on, used us as a stepping ladder or whatever. But it was also probably very difficult working with Jeff and I, in that we were very dysfunctional. And the way our dysfunction mostly manifests, and which is something we still struggle with, is that we argue, we bicker. And as much as I felt somewhat betrayed and used by Greg and Ron, I think our bickering was probably a difficult thing to cohabitate with, and it should be acknowledged that there was an annoyance factor there.

And you know, it was modelled by our parents. I love them, but they are both Olympic champion bickerers. I mean, it's insane – they *need* to be right, both of them. They also worked together at their own small business, Omni Welding; my mom did all the administration, and my dad did the welding, so they had a lot of shared responsibilities beyond parenting. They were stressed out, of course, but they didn't have great tools of communication, and they modelled a lot of crappy behaviour for us. I forgive them and all that stuff, but it's been a lifetime of trying to honestly take account of it, as well. I can't play the victim and pretend that everybody wronged us for no reason at all, because I think it really has been a lifetime project for us to learn how to collaborate in a more functional way.

JEFF: After that period with Greg and Ron kind of dissolved, we were out of commission for a while, and Chett Lehrer – Lucky's brother – started calling me and just chatting and trying to convince me to put the band back together. I had no designs on doing that, but he was very persistent. Then Dez Cadena joined on guitar for what was his first stint with the band; so we had a five-piece lineup with two guitarists, and I was just singing. I believe we played two shows at the Fleetwood in Redondo Beach with that lineup. One was opening for Black Flag, the night that Ron Reyes quit Black Flag. Another was opening for the Dead Kennedys. And then maybe a few more shows at other venues; I know that lineup supported the Plugz, on a bill with the Minutemen opening, which was one of the Minutemen's earliest shows.

There were a bunch of half-baked attempts to get it back together, but we were just being stupid and, like, total teenagers and really not functioning. It just seemed like such a hassle at that point; and being a kid, a lot of other things felt more important. I was just completely out of it, and not interested at all.

Now in seventh grade, Steven was also having to deal with the social stress that resulted from his extracurricular punk rock pursuits. Always a popular and well-liked kid in elementary school, he suddenly found himself bullied as an outsider upon entering junior high in the fall of '79.

STEVEN: When I was in sixth grade at Anza Elementary, we could bring records in to play at lunchtime; everybody was bringing in the *Saturday Night Fever* soundtrack, and I brought in a Dickies 10-inch. It was too weird for them, and the kids kind of acted like I'd overshared a little bit, but I was well known at the school and everyone liked me, so it wasn't really a big deal. It wasn't until the next year when I was trying to assimilate into this horrible, horrible world of junior high school that my taste in music really became a problem.

I went to Richard Henry Dana Junior High, which was comprised of three different elementary schools from Hawthorne; Anza parents had the lowest average income of the three schools, so I already had a bit of a leg down, status-wise. And then the summer between sixth and seventh grade is when The Tourists first started playing, so I was in full-blown early Red Cross mode by the time seventh grade started. I was immediately targeted by some eighth-grade bullies, and the Anza kids couldn't really help me out – they all kinda had to scatter. One bully eighth grader beat me up during PE, just because I had a little bleached patch in my hair. Like whoa, really *bold*, you know?

My hair wasn't even spiky. It was kind of like a Beatles '62, right when they started combing it down, but it was still really short. But I had a little bleached patch in the front, and so this kid could just smell that I was different and somehow alien. He decided I was an easy target; and as he's pummelling me, the whole class is circled around me chanting, 'Devo! Devo!'

A punk rocker is supposed to be truly authentic and not care what anybody thinks; this was the requirement to join that

66

club. But in my case, it meant there was gonna be this really nasty tradeoff: if I wanted my rank to rise among this older set that I really had no business being involved with, because I was way too young, I had to signal in certain ways; I had to make permanent changes to my appearance that were not hideable in normal daily occurrences. So even though it meant I was going to be beat up at school, I'm supposed to walk into that fearlessly and accept it; it would be proof that I was somehow authentic, that I was not a poseur. Because part of our outsider subculture is to be a nonconformist, yet we deeply needed to conform to the dictates of our supposed outsider subculture. And you're so cool, yet in the eyes of unsophisticated daytime peers, you're extremely uncool. It's a tough balance to strike; and if you live the duality of Clark Kent and Superman, ultimately you're a phony in both worlds.

So yeah, junior high was really when things kind of went south.

Steven, Jeff and Dee, 1980. (Courtesy of McDonald Family Archives)

Chapter 7

ON THE LAM

Red Cross played a handful of concerts in a variety of incarnations between March and September of 1980, but both Jeff and Steven's focus was largely elsewhere for much of the year. At 16 going on 17, Jeff was more interested in doing typical teenager stuff – skipping school, getting wasted, making prank calls, and going to concerts and shows with friends. On the other hand, 13-year-old-Steven found himself increasingly enmeshed in a twisted and inappropriately intense relationship with a much older woman from the LA punk scene. By the end of the year, he would be living with her in Las Vegas under an assumed name, while his family searched desperately for any sign of his whereabouts and well-being.

JEFF: High school was a drag. It's stressful to go – especially if you're like a weirdo punk rocker and you don't have your people there for support. I was more into just hanging out with my friends; we all kind of stopped going to school around the same time, at least the ones that were still in school.

I was pretty good at beating the system. My parents both worked, so they didn't know if I was going to school or not. I would be gone for like a month at a time and then go back, and if a teacher would say, 'You've been gone for twenty-eight days, we need a note from your parents,' I would just write a fake note, not even trying to imitate my parents' signatures. Because I figured, 'How are they gonna know?' But then I realised that it was just easier for me *not* to go back. I couldn't handle the stress of just dealing with the social aspect of being in school, and I also couldn't handle the stress of being behind from skipping school all the time.

The thing is, I'd never, ever ditched a day in school in my life, until I was in the middle of high school. But one day, I didn't go to school because I just didn't want to, and I didn't get caught – and then it immediately became an addiction. It was this very much like, 'Oh, I know this is really bad for me, but I can't stop doing this.' And then I just had to adjust my life to doing it, which also created an insane amount of stress. It was like a 'one day at a time' existence, just trying to not get caught. If I would've just went in the direction that I was supposed to, I would've been fine. But instead, I went into a lot of chaos. And of course, I'm the one who paid for it later in life.

I finally just told my parents that I wasn't going to school. At that point, they kind of knew, though I don't think they knew to what degree it was. There wasn't any pressure from them to go to college, or to get an education beyond just doing your duty as a kid by a finishing school. I never had that moment of being inspired enough to *want* to continue my education. Not until after I got out of school, not until I started reading and I started travelling; that's when I started wanting to learn about the world. But it didn't happen in school.

STEVEN: Junior high school was where I went from being a well-liked kid to a tortured, harassed kid. After I'd been humiliated that day in PE class, I picked myself up from the blacktop and marched into the principal's office. I was like, 'I'm gonna break the playground code and I'm gonna rat on these kids; I'm gonna advocate for myself and see if these adults can help me out.' And I remember sitting in the office waiting room, listening to these two secretaries talking about me while they were typing away on their IBM Selectric typewriters. They were saying, 'Well, look at him – he obviously wants the attention.' That's when I realised, 'Okay, so I'm getting blamed for this; this is *my* fault in their eyes, and there's not gonna be a lot of help here.'

Jeff was always about individuality; he was reading Lester Bangs when he was 9 years old, and he had just kind of internalised this romantic idea of the visionary, maverick artist who always does exactly what he wants. Whereas I was kind of like a normal kid who desperately wanted to fit in, and I felt a lot of peer pressure from my brother not to be a poseur – you know, 'If you're *really* punk rock, you have to go to school looking the same way you would go to a gig.' I had been seduced by rock'n'roll, too, but I wasn't simply some rebellious kid that didn't give a fuck; I gave *lots* of fucks, in all the different environments I was in, and being outcasted in junior high was such a miserable experience. And in some ways, it led to me being kidnapped.

JEFF: I don't really remember when Dee first popped into the scene. We might have met her at the Hong Kong Café, but all of a sudden she was hanging out in our little friend group at the time when we were getting into partying, drinking, smoking weed and experimenting with other drugs. All we knew was that she had original punk scene cred – and a car, which meant we now had transportation to all the shows that were happening. She was older, and my friend Janet Housden and I would be over at her place taking acid and staying up all night. I don't think she and Steven ever said, 'We are an item,' but all of a sudden it became, like, 'Oh – *this* is what it is.'

STEVEN: I suppose I first met her at The Church; Jeffrey Lee Pierce and other Hollywood punk scene types had started to talk about this band Black Flag and that things were going on down there, so she would have come down to check it out. She was kind of a lower-tier scenester of the original LA punk social scene – like, not someone that you'd see pictured in all those books documenting that era, but someone with purple hair whose self-esteem was based on their status as 'an original scene person,' someone who had been at The Masque in 1977 and had written gig reviews for various fanzines like *Flipside*. Someone who would have been very judgemental of poseurs, in other words. Connecting with her made me feel like I was being accepted by this world that I cared about and idolised so much.

I was experimenting a lot with drugs and alcohol at the time, and boundaries got blurred in ways that they wouldn't have without the inhibition-lowering that went on with that. We shared all these intimate moments – like, we'd be at a show, and everybody would be inside the Fleetwood or something, but her and I would be in the parking lot in her car, flying on some combination of like Southern Comfort and speed, just getting to know each other, but also just inappropriately oversharing.

I think a lot of the Dee story speaks to my dysfunctional relationship with my brother, and me trying to branch out and find my own identity. And sadly, I found a very unwell person that had a very large personality and a penchant for really young guys.

JEFF: We all kind of got used to the idea that she was his girlfriend – not my parents, but our friends. Like, 'Oh, maybe he's just more mature than his years.' By today's standards, people would label it as paedophilia, but we were just slowly kind of eased into it, and it just became normal to us. And we had a lot of fun hanging out with her at first, but then it got to the point where Steven was always missing out on everything, because he was always consoling her about something. Like, he missed The Cramps at the Whisky – the original lineup with

Bryan Gregory – because he was out in the car with her, talking her down. And he would always be bummed out because *she* was always bummed out.

STEVEN: She was a real drama queen. We sat in the Whisky parking lot that whole night while she had a breakdown about some mysterious other friend that was being really self-destructive; she was completely distraught about it. She had me thinking that she was somewhat polyamorous, and that she had this other relationship that was troubled, but she was always mysterious about who this other person was. And then, through various ridiculously dramatic scenarios, it was somewhat uncovered that her other troubled lover was Darby Crash.

JEFF: She was also the kind of person that would just go out and get into fights with people. She just had a massive chip on her shoulder, and she was always drunk or on speed or a combination of the two; I'm surprised we didn't get killed hanging out with her. But I didn't go too deeply into thinking about their relationship until our parents started becoming upset about it. And then the instinct was to cover for him, at least at first, because otherwise they were going to put the kibosh on us going out and doing stuff, because they didn't want him with her.

STEVEN: Every weekend she would come down to Hawthorne and pick me up, and we would hang out. And then, once our relationship became physical, I got cocky and wouldn't come home all weekend; I'd call my parents, and say, 'I'll be honest with you; we drank and it's not safe for Dee to drive me home.' My parents were in denial, for sure, but I also think they just didn't know what to do; I was a very intense, probably lawyer-grade negotiator, and I was very aware of how I could manipulate them through keeping certain lines of communication open, but then withholding other pieces of information. I gave them this story that Dee and I were just best friends, and that if they thought it was anything more than that they were being silly or dirty-minded. But it was also really nerve-wracking for me to keep up the whole ruse.

My parents eventually did the right thing, and started digging into my backpack and looking through my schoolwork to see what they could find out. They found my journals, which were filled with all this stream of consciousness stuff that was going through my mind about the whole experience, and they were like, 'You've been lying to us, this is not right, and this is ending now!' They threatened to take away my freedom to do my band, which was something I really cared about. I felt a lot of shame for lying to them, and painfully embarrassed that they knew I was having a sexual relationship. But at the same time, I once again felt trapped between two worlds, and the stakes were so high – I had a crying mom on one side, and a crying girlfriend on the other, and it's all my fault. I needed a way out, so I tried pulling the plug and telling her, 'My parents know, the jig is up, and I just can't do this anymore.'

But then she just got more and more erratic and unstable; I would try to put up boundaries, but I was so caught up in the drama of the relationship and the adrenaline; I thought I was in love, and that it was something that no one else understood. And every time I tried to get out of the relationship, she would find a way to pull me back in. She was filling my brain with all sorts of stuff, drawing a connection to the totalitarian fascist regime in George Orwell's *1984*, and how society – and my loving parents – wouldn't let us be together. Her idea was that the only way we could be together was to run away.

She, her mom and her mom's boyfriend actually hatched this whole plan where we would go on the lam together in Vegas; we would all change our names, and he was gonna make a fortune card-counting at the blackjack tables. For whatever reason, they thought that this was a reasonable thing to do, and that in due time my parents would probably give up, and we could just carry on in this new life as a family.

In my defence, I will say that I tried several times to avoid this plan. Like, her mom's boyfriend was supposed to pick me up on my way to school, and every day I walked a different way so I wouldn't see him. But then one night I ran into her at a show, and she was super-distraught and told me that she was pregnant, and that she was going to leave town and have my child – or the other option would be that she would get an abortion and I would leave town with her. And I was like, 'Ugh, I have to do this.'

I was so tortured and conflicted about what was happening, but it speaks volumes about the dysfunction in my family – particularly in my relationship with my brother – that as close as I am and have always been with them, I couldn't find the way to tell them the situation I was in. I was fixated on this idea that if I was only six years older, the age gap with Dee wouldn't really be all that weird, and then no one could say anything. I tried to argue that point to Jeff, and he just shut it down – 'Well, you're *not* 18.' So at that point, I determined that he was on my parents' side, and that I couldn't trust him, either. So now I had this problem that I couldn't talk to anyone about.

JEFF: I didn't really know what was going on. I didn't know about the mind games. Steven didn't talk about them. The whole thing was this major plot that I was completely oblivious to.

STEVEN: The other thing was that Darby Crash killed himself right before we left town. Looking back, Darby was really pretty sad – by the end, he was always really wasted or catatonic, or just on his way there, and he was a real mooch who was always trying to take advantage of his followers; instead of the puzzled panther prowling the stage, he had become just a wasted clown.

But at the time, he was my idol. Luckily, I wasn't directly in his circle, but I was still in the 'Cult of Darby' by proxy – and it *was* like a bona fide cult, with real power over people – and I was just 13 and really fucking impressionable. Put it this way: I was so preoccupied with Darby Crash that when John Lennon was killed, the day after Darby's suicide, I barely cared.

And then there was also the whole mystery surrounding Darby's alleged relationship with Dee. I have no idea how much of that was real or exaggerated; there were a lot of people in the scene who competed for his attention and affection, and Darby was very much a taker. And she was such a drama queen, she would have been up for all of his shenanigans. But at the time, I actually felt like I owed it to Darby to see this through, because I believed he might have killed himself because he was so distraught over our relationship. I mean, it's absurd and embarrassing for me to even think about that now; but I'd bought into this manipulation, and that possibility felt very real to me.

Steven left town with Dee's mother's boyfriend in December 1980, a week before Christmas. Their first stop was a trailer in Kingman, Arizona, where Steven stayed by himself until the whole family returned and picked him up on their way to Las Vegas. Once there, they stayed together at a downtown Travelodge Motel, until Dee's mother and her boyfriend found jobs and were able to move them all into an apartment. Back in Hawthorne, no one knew what had become of Steven, though his devastated parents certainly had their suspicions…

JEFF: It was right before Christmas vacation, and Steven just didn't come home one day. We were all in complete panic, trying to figure it out. My parents automatically thought that this woman had something to do with it, but I was like, 'She had *nothing* to do with it' – total Stockholm syndrome, protecting the captor. Our friend group was all in denial about it. But at the same time, I'm thinking, 'Was he murdered by someone? Was this a kidnapping?' I thought that something really horrible could have happened, because it was so out of the blue. It was horrifying for the first two weeks, because I thought the worst. But then it really did become apparent that Dee was behind his disappearance.

Dee's whole thing was to stay around at home and pretend that she didn't know what happened to him, either. In retrospect, her reaction was a little too calm, considering that she had feelings for this person. I would talk to her on the phone about it every night, and she would be like, 'I don't know what's going on.' I thought she was my friend, but I was being manipulated too. Eventually, I talked to her best friend, and I said, 'My parents think Dee has something to do with it. Do you know anything about that?' And she got quiet on me and was like, 'I can't talk about this.' So from that moment, even though she never admitted it and she wouldn't give me any details, I knew that Dee had something to do with it. And then shortly after that, Dee and her mom disappeared. So then it was like, 'Okay, he's probably all right – we just have to find them.'

STEVEN: The homesickness I felt was of just gigantic proportions, as was the guilt for causing pain and suffering to my family. It's still hard to think about that betrayal and the deep suffering that I was wilfully causing. But at the same time, I felt I owed it to Dee; I thought that she needed me, and that they just didn't understand. And that I needed to look out for myself, and not have to become a father at 13. It was such a big bag of fucked-up shit.

The first forty-eight hours were particularly intense. I was all by myself, staying down some rural road in this trailer. I had an AM radio, a couple of *Penthouse* magazines and the supplies her mom's boyfriend had bought me on the way out of town – Blue Diamond almonds, cans of Spaghettios' and a carton of Marlboro Lights, all the things that would sustain me until they came back to pick me up. Steely Dan had just released *Gaucho*, so 'Hey Nineteen' and 'Babylon Sisters' were on the radio a lot, and 'Love On The Rocks' by Neil Diamond. So I was listening to those songs over and over again, re-reading *1984*, looking at the *Penthouse* pictorials, eating Blue Diamond almonds and smoking. And crying – I spent the first night just apologising out loud to my mom, over and over and over. The whole thing was pretty traumatising; I eventually just became numb and gave into it.

Dee had an Instamatic camera that she would always take to gigs. And I remember at one point in Las Vegas, I stumbled on some snapshots of Red Cross that she'd taken at the Fleetwood. I remember looking at the pictures and talking to Jeff a little bit in my mind – making something like an apology, but also some kind of promise that this wasn't the end of the band. I thought, 'I don't know what's gonna happen, but somehow this is gonna work itself out.'

The police proved completely disinterested in handling this particular missing persons case – runaway punk rockers weren't a high priority for the LAPD – so Jeff and Steven's parents found a private detective who was able to track Dee and her family to Las Vegas and alert the local authorities. A SWAT team was dispatched to where they were living, and enacted a rescue that was nearly as traumatic for Steven as his kidnapping three months earlier.

STEVEN: It was like a drug bust kind of thing, like an episode of *Cops*. I heard them burst in through the doors downstairs, and all this screaming and yelling; Dee was like, 'Fuck you, you pigs! Get the fuck outta here!' I was lying in bed naked, so I just jumped into this closet with some foam padding from the bed, and hid behind it in the closet. I remember hyperventilating in this hot closet and feeling a mixed emotion of, like, wanting them to get me and take me home, but also thinking that I had *1984* ahead of me – that we were about to be captured and tortured like in the book. And I thought that even if they weren't tortured, Dee and her family were certainly going to prison together, and once again it was all my fault. It's like in Patty Hearst's memoir, where she talks about how the survival instinct kicks in, and you're protecting your captors and identifying with them – all that stuff definitely came into play. And then I felt this firm hand grabbing me…

I was completely undressed, which made me feel particularly vulnerable and horrible. The cops allowed me to put on some clothes, and then they handcuffed me and took me to this juvenile detention centre, where I spent the night in my own cell, with a stainless steel toilet, a stainless steel bench as a bed and a scratchy wool blanket. I remember at a certain hour they knocked on the doors and said, 'Butt wipes!' And you had to tell them whether or not you wanted toilet paper, and they gave you a few coarse squares.

I spent the night crying. That first night in the trailer, I would've been crying to my mom and to my dad and my brother, but I was crying this night because I didn't know what was going to happen, and was feeling responsible for everybody's pain and suffering. The next morning, I was ushered into the mess hall where I had breakfast among all these poor delinquent kids in the juvenile detention centre. Some of the kids asked me what I was in for – in my mind, I'm thinking of 'Dead End Justice' by The Runaways – and when I told them 'Running away,' they kind of nodded and identified with me, assuming that my parents had beat me and I was trying to get away.

I remember being completely grossed out by the soft scrambled eggs – I was still basically a finicky little kid, and these were nothing like my mom made for breakfast – but I had to eat them. And I was also completely stressed out because they were about to have PE in the gymnasium next to the mess hall. I'd had a rough run playing sports on the Dana Junior High playground, but the kids there were nothing compared to these kids. But then, right before I had to go do it, I was called out of the room and told that my parents were there to take me home. I was brought into some other area to get my clothes and my things, and then into the lobby where my parents were waiting.

I thought they would be mad at me, but they were just crying and happy and grateful and hugging me. I'd been missing for three months, but the story had a good ending; I didn't die and I came home. But I was very much *not* myself for a long time after coming home, and my mom's sleeping habits permanently changed; she no longer slept through the night, and she would catnap on the couch.

Once I came back, it was very clear that the narrative Dee had fed me was a lie; not only were they not being tortured or thrown in jail, but I actually had a say over what happened to them – I could choose whether or not to press charges. I chose not to, because after all the suffering it had caused my family, I just wanted the whole thing to go away.

'Charlie Saves': Red Cross at the Whisky, August 6, 1981. (Photo by Alison Braun)

Chapter 8

BORN INNOCENT

As traumatic as the events around Steven's kidnapping had been, the incident gave the McDonalds a chance to hit the reset button, both as siblings and bandmates. The year before, Red Cross had foundered in a sea of distractions, but now, in the spring of 1981, both brothers were determined to get the band going again.

JEFF: While Steven was gone, I started thinking, 'Okay, I wanna do something.' I was tired of being bummed out, so I started a band called Pig with some neighbourhood friends. They were people who weren't musicians; they weren't in the punk scene, and they didn't even go to shows. It was like early electronic punk, and it was just fun to kind of play around and do that stuff. So when Steven got back, I was like, 'Let's play music again.' And he was down.

STEVEN: It wasn't long before we got back into the swing of things. I mean, these were things that made me feel normal again. I liked the specialness of being in a band; I liked the identity of being a musician. And the more I played music, the more those three months in Vegas seemed unreal.

JEFF: Steven had only been away for a few months, but he'd hit his growth spurt during that time, and now he looked like a different person. To me, he was always like this short, chubby, Jimmy Osmond-looking kid, but now he was tall and thin. And my hair was starting to grow; the last kind of punk hairdo I had was before Steven went to Las Vegas, and I remember thinking like, 'I'll cut it when Steven returns.' But then I didn't cut it when he came back, so now we both looked a lot different than we had just a few months earlier.

STEVEN: I think Jeff stopped wanting to be a part of anything around 1981. I was more of a standard teenager who would've been *glad* to conform to whatever was popular in 1981, but I remember the day he told me he was no longer cutting his hair, and he suggested that I stop, too. I was like, 'Wow, I just *got* a cool punk haircut!' And he was like, 'Yeah, well, I don't know; I'm not doing it anymore.' And that was him rejecting the whole Orange County punk scene.

JEFF: When Steven got back, that's when we decided that I was gonna play guitar in the group. We found one kid to play drums with us for a while, but he was terrible and noncommittal. So we bit the bullet and called John Stielow to see if he'd come back.

STEVEN: John and I were both going to Hawthorne High at this point. John was really excited to be back in the band, and we went through a period where we rehearsed every day as a three-piece. We were really on top of it. We recorded the New York Dolls' 'Puss 'N' Boots' as a three-piece for the *Hell Comes To Your House* compilation, and if you listen to it, we're really tight. We recorded that at Kitchen Sync Studios, this old studio in East Hollywood where a lot of the Dangerhouse singles were recorded. We also did the demos for *Born Innocent* there.

JEFF: It was funny because Ron Gowdy, the guy who put that compilation together, he asked, 'Do you wanna be on this record? If you have something, we'll put it on.' So we went into the studio and recorded 'Puss 'N' Boots' and gave it to him. We didn't know we were supposed to say, 'Oh, this is a cover song!' But nobody in LA at the time except a few first-generation punk rockers even knew who the New York Dolls were at that point. They didn't realise it was a cover until the record came out.

STEVEN: They eventually took us off the record, because they didn't want to pay mechanical royalties to the New York Dolls. We didn't know anything about mechanicals when we recorded the song.

JEFF: I love that recording because it sounds so different to anything else on the record. And things were so rigid and small minded in the LA punk scene at the time that the fact that we used tambourine on the track was considered weird, and we got a lot of shit for it. The other thing I loved about that recording was that, right before we went into the studio, we spent the weekend on LSD at Lake Dolores, which was like this early waterpark out in the desert; it was the most unsafe, gnarly place you could ever imagine. We were sitting there in Janet Housden's parents' Winnebago, tripping all night, listening to the Ace Frehley solo album and *2112* by Rush, and laughing hysterically. Then we made it back to Hollywood by three o'clock in the afternoon, knocked out 'Puss 'N' Boots', and gave it to Ron Gowdy. That was about five minutes before Tracy Marshak – aka Tracy Lea – joined the band.

STEVEN: We were big fans of Castration Squad, this all-female proto-goth rock band featuring Alice Bag, and Tracy was this über-cool teenager who played guitar with them. She was Jeff's age, but she grew up in Hollywood and she had seen The

Runaways with Cherie Currie at the Whisky when she was like 13 or 14.

Jeff and I had just gotten a VCR, and we'd found a video store near us that had old rock'n'roll performances on video. We had a very early videotape of the *T.A.M.I. Show*, and we used to watch it all the time, especially The Rolling Stones' performance. We just thought Brian Jones was like the coolest dude on Earth; he wasn't a shredder, but he had this whole vibe. We decided we needed to get our own Brian Jones in the group, and Tracy Marshak was our equivalent. Somehow we got up the nerve to ask her if she wanted to play guitar with us.

JEFF: She looked like a young Elizabeth Taylor, and she was as cool as James Dean. And she said sure, she'd do it. But Tracy didn't really play guitar very well; I was struggling to learn how to play lead guitar, and she was kind of struggling as well. Fortunately, Steven and John were pretty good, so whatever Tracy and I slopped on top of it just kind of made it interesting.

STEVEN: Tracy had a mid-sixties Fender Duo-Sonic, and this loud as fuck little Music Man HD130 amplifier, and it was such a great combo. She was just always game, and we'd teach her the songs, but she would have these bouts of insecurity where she would cry and didn't think she could do it. And I would have to try and talk her through it.

JEFF: We started playing out a lot as a four-piece with Tracy, but at the time it was really popular to have these shows at places like Godzilla's, which was this miserable venue in some industrial warehouse in North Hollywood, where they'd have ten bands and it would just be a battle of who gets to go on before three o'clock in the morning. It was just a nightmare, but we did those shows for a while. It was kind of our Hamburg in a way, because it really made us gel as a band – and after playing those shows, we weren't afraid of anything.

86

These shows would be weird because it would be like death rock bands, junkie bands, hardcore groups, all these different groups on the same bill. We played one time with this flashy group from Chicago who had expensive amps and a real professional attitude; they were like these fake skinheads from Chicago called The Effigies, and I remember feeling so betrayed because Tracy was like, 'Oh, they're so cute!'

The LA scene was completely unfocused at that time. I guess it made it interesting on a certain level, the fact that you would have like all these weirdo misfit groups kind of happening together at the same time, having little or nothing in common with each other but having to coexist. You would have groups like Kommunity FK, which were one of the first LA goth groups ever, playing with people who would be in, like, Suicidal Tendencies. It was like a very dysfunctional version of what Bill Graham was doing in the sixties; if I'd just been an observer, maybe I could have seen it that way. But having to be in the middle of it, it was just dog eat dog.

Our rehearsals were good, and we were coming up with new songs, but the available gigs were just annoying. So we figured, 'If we can make a record, we can get to the next level where we can headline the Whisky or something.' That was the goal.

After recording demos for what would become the *Born Innocent* album, Red Cross sent a tape to Frontier Records, a local indie label that had recently released albums by Circle Jerks, Adolescents and T.S.O.L. But when Frontier proprietor Lisa Fancher passed on it, the band began recording individual tracks at Reels of Sound, a 24-track studio in Simi Valley where their friend Felix Alanis – frontman of punk band RF7, who had just launched his fledgling label Smoke Seven – had a connection.

JEFF: We just started recording with Felix, because he'd first asked us to do some tracks for the album called *Sudden Death*, and for a comp called *Public Service*. And then we recorded a few more songs because he would just invite us over to get stoned and record, and at some point we figured we might as well just keep going and do an album.

STEVEN: I think we met Felix at Godzilla's; he was just this dude from the Valley that was encouraging to us and wanted us to record for him. He was the only person we knew that was interested in doing an album with us.

Unfortunately, by the time the recording sessions for *Born Innocent* finally began, dysfunction had once again reared its head in the Red Cross ranks. John Stielow was losing interest in the band due to girlfriend pressures, and Tracy and Jeff were experimenting with pharmaceuticals that occasionally rendered them far less than reliable.

STEVEN: It was really awkward, because John didn't know how to say he didn't want to do it anymore. I'd see him at school and he kept saying he would come to rehearsal, and then he wouldn't show up; it felt like his girlfriend, who was my age, was now controlling him and didn't like our band. My brother was undependable – you didn't know if he was going to show up wasted – and Tracy was taking too many pills. We had the album sessions coming up, and I was a neurotic mess trying to keep it all together; it was like the Whack-a-Mole game at the fair, impossible to stay on top of it. Here we finally have this opportunity to make a record, and we're falling apart.

We recorded *Born Innocent* over two weekends, and I remember we showed up one of the mornings to Tracy's house and there was no answer at the door. I think we might have even snuck around the back and knocked on her window, and finally her dad just opened the door and barked, 'She's not coming! She's not coming!' She must have had a party the night before, and couldn't be roused to come out for the session. She did come out for another one, though, because she's on like half of the record; I can always tell what song she's on, because there's a very specific kind of tone to her Duo-Sonic and Music Man combo.

A 13-track affair clocking in at under twenty minutes, *Born Innocent* was even snottier sounding than the first Red Cross EP, with briefly explosive songs like 'White Trash', 'Burn-Out', 'Pseudo-Intellectual' and 'Kill Someone You Hate' packed full of gleefully skittering guitar runs and smart-ass lyrics. But a burgeoning pop sensibility was also evident, along with full-blown pop cultural aesthetic that – with the notable exception of Raymond Pettibone's illustration of Joan Crawford on the record's label – seemed worlds away from what was currently happening in the LA punk and hardcore scenes.

The album's opening track paid tribute to troubled seventies starlet Linda Blair, who had starred in both *The Exorcist* and the 1975 juvenile delinquent TV film that gave the album its name. 'Look On Up At The Bottom' was a cover of a song originally sung by The Carrie Nations in Russ Meyer's 1970 psychedelic satire *Beyond the Valley of the Dolls*; 'I'm Alright' was a Bo Diddley song that The Rolling Stones covered on the *T.A.M.I. Show*; and the album also contained not one but two tributes to infamous cult leader Charles Manson: Jeff and Steve's original composition 'Charlie', and a hidden cover of Manson's own 'Cease To Exist'.

And then there were *Born Innocent*'s hand-scrawled liner notes, which saluted a wide array of female celebrities, actors, musicians and film/TV characters while also dropping references to *The Partridge Family*, *The Brady Bunch*, Timothy Leary, and televangelists Jim and Tammy Faye Bakker. *Born Innocent*'s music may have retained the anarchic rawness of punk rock, but the album was clearly the work of a band intent on carving its own joyfully warped path.

JEFF: Linda Blair was a big influence – not just *The Exorcist*, which I snuck in to see when it first came out, but all of her teen films like *Sarah: Portrait of a Teenage Alcoholic* and *Born Innocent*, about a juvenile hall for girls. And that all kind of fit in perfectly with The Runaways and that whole aesthetic that I was so into, these mysterious, troubled girls who were a little bit older than me. So I paid homage to that world, The Runaways and Linda Blair via the song.

STEVEN: Linda Blair was a real rock chick – if you look back at the pages of *Teen Beat* or *Tiger Beat* from the 1970s, there are pictures of her hanging out with Jim Dandy and Black Sabbath. I think she posed nude for *Oui* magazine around the time our album came out; she definitely had this 'don't give a fuck' attitude that we totally related to.

JEFF: 'White Trash' is a song I regret writing now because it's very racist and classist. But it was about some of the people we had to deal with living in the neighbourhood that we lived in, and being able to write and record a negative song about them felt like kind of a one-up at the time. But I would never use that term today.

STEVEN: We got a lot of shit from this one family, these three or four teenage boys, for being into punk rock. And Jeff and I went through a juvenile prankster phase where we'd vandalise stuff, and late one night we drove past their stupid pickup truck that was like their prized possession, and we bashed out all its mirrors with a baseball bat. I think we really thought we were going to get away with it, but then at some point our house was descended on by all these Hawthorne stoners with feathered hair, who were like, 'We got the tip, McDonald! We know who did it. We're gonna kick your ass!' And Jeff came out and just lied to them, like, 'I don't know what you're talking about.' So yeah, we were super judgemental and harsh on this song, and perhaps we could have come up with a more sophisticated criticism than saying, 'You're just white trash/And your brother can't even read.' But we're kids in Hawthorne, you know?

JEFF: 'Burn-Out' is probably autobiographical. None of the punk rock people we'd met in Hermosa Beach smoked pot – they all drank beer and did acid. Weed was considered hippie shit. But we'd started hanging out with these witchy girls from Inglewood, Janus and Jeanie, who were obsessed with Jimmy Page and were total potheads, and we just kind of became potheads with them. I think I smoked every day from age 17 to 22; I finally had to go into a treatment centre to stop smoking.

Pot definitely did a number on me. On some levels I was very motivated – I was insanely motivated when it came to like, wanting to play music, or trying to find people to sell us pot. But as far as being motivated to do anything I didn't want to do, nope. I would just shut down.

STEVEN: Yeah, we're probably talking about our weed intake getting a little out of hand, although maybe not necessarily realising that that's what we're saying. I'd experimented with smoking weed when I was stupid young, like 9 or 10; I was really curious about it and wanted to try it. But around the time of *Born Innocent* was where Jeff and I really got into weed as a lifestyle, and it added to our general weirdness. It was an interesting time, because on the one hand we're getting more ambitious about our career, but at the same time we're becoming these stoner flakes.

JEFF: The Manson stuff on *Born Innocent* was all about getting on our parents' nerves. I mean, we're definitely overlooking the dark side of the whole thing – it was more an homage to foxy girls in cults, done for shock value purposes. We weren't *into* Manson, and didn't think he was cool; but growing up with The Beach Boys being part of our legacy living in Hawthorne, and the whole Dennis Wilson–Manson connection, we just thought

91

that all was pretty fascinating. Manson's record *Lie* was very rare at the time, and I heard 'Cease To Exist' for the first time on Rodney's show, when of course he played it alongside The Beach Boys' 'Never Learn Not To Love.' We tried it at rehearsal once just for fun and we loved it, so we just decided to put it on the album.

STEVEN: For all of Jeff's lack of interest in academics, he did a lot of his own self-motivated studies. He's a pretty avid reader, and his reading of *The Family*, Ed Sanders' telling of the Manson story, probably informed a lot of his desire to sing about it. But around this time we've also discovered the films of John Waters, and Jeff was really into his book *Shock Value*, where Waters is basically laying out his philosophy about how to maximise your potential through your differences – like, if you are a weirdo, then get even weirder, and if you really want someone's attention, shock the shit out of them rather than please them. So when you have a mentor like John Waters, you write songs like 'Charlie.'

But we didn't include 'Cease To Exist' on the track listing of the original album, because we were worried that we could actually piss off some Mansonites. And as much as we wanted to get involved with the shock of it, we were also aware that if you put enough energy into something weird and bizarre, you can usually will these people into your life. We didn't necessarily want to go that far.

JEFF: *Beyond the Valley of the Dolls* was one of the very first cool movies that ever came out when video stores first opened; there'd just be a bunch of crappy movies, but then there would be like a little weirdo section, and Russ Meyer films were in it right from the start. We'd already been to see his films in theatres at various Russ Meyer marathons, but *Beyond the Valley of the Dolls* was one of the first ones we were able to really just watch a million times on home video. So we were able to go in deep with that, and then actually learn The Carrie Nations' songs.

STEVEN: *Beyond the Valley of the Dolls* is such a great rock film, and it felt like it was custom-made for us: it takes place in Los Angeles. There's an all-female rock group. It's psychedelic. There's great clothes, sexual intrigue, bizarre rituals and all kinds of crazy, freaky things. And of course, John Waters loved it and talked highly of it. 'Look On Up At The Bottom' has kind of this Wrecking Crew-adjacent, rockier Partridge Family kind of vibe, so when it came time to come up with a cover song for the album, I think it was something we thought no one would know.

JEFF: I love *Born Innocent*. I kind of think it's our best-sounding record, sonically, because Mike Smith, the guy who engineered it, was an older dude who looked like he could have been in one of those seventies bands like Orleans or Exile. He didn't use any special effects, or try to make us sound like any of the other punk records that were being made at the time. He just used really good equipment to capture our sound in a really dry and organic way, and that's really hard to achieve.

STEVEN: Yeah, there's no big, hollow reverbs or super-compressed, blown-out sounds on it that would really date the record. If anything, it's probably a precursor to a lot of indie records from the nineties that have a similar vibe. But the perfectionist control freak in me would ruminate on *Born Innocent* for years, and on how much was wrong with it.

I really would have liked our record to have been as tight as the ones Circle Jerks or Bad Religion or T.S.O.L. put out that year, bands that were getting big then or are now considered seminal of the genre of that moment. Jeff's more of a contrarian, but I'm more of a conformist – at least in the sense that I wanted to compete and succeed within my own environment. I wanted us to somehow fit into a space and then just be the best we could possibly be. And maybe *Born Innocent* would have been that if our drummer had not decided to ghost us in the weeks before the recording sessions, and if we hadn't had all the other moving parts that I couldn't make behave according to my plan.

It's funny, because Pavement used to cover 'Pseudo-Intellectual', and Stephen Malkmus told *SPIN* magazine that we'd 'lost the plot' after *Born Innocent*. This was at the time when we were on hiatus, and I just thought, 'Oh my god, fuck you. I never even liked your stupid band!'

JEFF: Creating the record cover and the insert was a lot of fun, because it was an opportunity to do something really weird, and have total freedom in creating our own image – that's when Red Cross really started to gel in that sense. We had our friends Stephanie and Sherry pose for the front and back covers, and then we brought in some Linda Blair imagery, like 'The Broom', which was very heinous and un-PC; but we were teenagers at the time, enjoying the freedom to express ourselves by throwing in all these Easter eggs and weird, inside things.

We were kind of like Russ Meyer in a way, in that our superheroes were always, like, really cool women. We had musical heroes that were men, but that was about it; I didn't really like sports, so I didn't care about any of those people. The male heroes I have are all musicians, but as far as popular culture heroes are concerned, not many of mine are men. So it was natural for us to give a shout-out on the album to all these women that inspired us, whether it was Patty Hearst, Annette Funicello, Penelope Houston or Hayley Mills.

STEVEN: I think Jeff and I have always been in touch with our feminine side, and we always responded to that feminine energy; it just seemed cooler, you know? Like, Cher was always cooler than Sonny, and Addie in *Paper Moon* is way cooler than her dad. And the first band we ever saw at a nightclub was the Avengers, who were fronted by Penelope Houston, and the other band that was on the bill that night was X with Exene Cervenka, who was every bit John Doe's equal on that stage. Female heroes like Poison Ivy were just as valid to us as the Lux Interiors of the world.

But I think that there was something else about us including the names of these women on our record, which was a rejection of the overt jock mentality. I felt alienated from that energy even before I got beat up in PE class, and the more the punk music scene became overtly masculine – and by 1982, hardcore shows were all about dudes and their violent mating rituals – the more we felt alienated by it and wanted to explicitly reject it.

The 1982 Red Cross lineup with Tracy Lea and Janet Housden. (Photo by Ed Colver)

Chapter 9

WHAT ARE WE DOING HERE?

Red Cross would get even more in touch with their feminine side in 1982, when John Stielow left the band for good and was replaced on drums by Janet Housden, giving the band's lineup a 50/50 girl-boy split. *Born Innocent* was released in June 1982, and though it didn't elevate the band to Whisky-headlining status as they'd hoped, it did further increase the band's profile, leading to several memorable gigs in Los Angeles and San Francisco.

The next two years would be a heavily transitional period for the band, one in which their hair got longer, their clothes got flashier, their live performances got tighter (at least when drugs weren't involved), their lineup went through still more changes, and they distanced themselves even further from the LA punk scene that they'd come up in. This was also the period in which Jeff and Steven first encountered an all-girl group called the Bangs, who would make a huge impact on their personal and musical lives; and, thanks to the American Red Cross, this was when they were forced to come up with a new spelling of their own band name.

STEVEN: We were on the cover of *Flipside* when *Born Innocent* came out. Looking back, that might give the impression that we were one of the bigger bands of that moment, but that was probably more of a function of us being veterans in the scene at this point – we'd been around for, like, two and a half years. It wasn't like we were now selling out bigger venues so they had to put us on the cover. It was more like their own quirky choice.

JEFF: John had already left the band before the album came out, which is why he's not pictured anywhere on it. It was the first time we'd lost a band member because of a girlfriend, but it wouldn't be the last. So we were out of a drummer, and we kind of disintegrated for a while, but then we got our friend Janet Housden to play drums for us.

Around the time that Steven was gone, our friends Janus and Jeanie had this weirdo group called The Disposals. I was trying to position myself to be their Kim Fowley, and I was going to produce them. So when their drummer left, I suggested that Janet play drums for them. She didn't know how to play, but I had a drum set and could kind of keep a beat, so I gave her a couple of quick lessons.

I recorded The Disposals on an old Sony reel-to-reel machine, the same kind that the Germs recorded 'Forming' on. It was the only recording of them ever made, and it was really raw, but it was so cool. This guy Gary Kail from a band called Anti was going to put it out on this experimental art-punk label he had, but it never happened and I never got the tape back; he has since passed away, so that tape will probably never see the light of day. But that's how I taught Janet to play drums, and when John left we gave her a try. Our first gig after *Born Innocent* came out was with Janet on drums.

STEVEN: Janet had been a friend since the Church days; she grew up in Hermosa Beach, and she was one of the many wayward teens that we met through hanging out with Black Flag. Janet was just this amazing character who walked around in this leather jacket with this, like, Joan Jett hunch. She'd gotten kicked out of Mira Costa High School, where even the members of Black Flag had managed to graduate, and ended up at another school where somebody literally tried to drop a cinderblock on her from a two-story overhang, just because her hair was a weird colour. She understandably had a real chip on her shoulder.

JEFF: We started working and practising with her, and Janet turned out to be way more of a taskmaster than even Steven was. Janet was a full-on intense person who was very serious about practising and not being loaded at shows.

One of the more memorable early Red Cross gigs with Janet was playing at the City of Santa Monica's Beach Litter Walk event, which was both the only morning show the band ever played, and quite probably the only one where three out of four Red Cross members wore shorts onstage.

JEFF: That Beach Litter Walk gig was just one of those things where someone called on the phone and said, 'Do you wanna do this?' We didn't know what it was – some kind of garbage collection event on the beach, and I guess they wanted to have bands to lure kids out to it – but I just remember saying yes. We didn't have a manager at the time, so people would just get our phone number and call us.

STEVEN: There were often times where someone would call our parents' house to book us for some random show, and one of us would take the call and make the decision and forget to tell the other. And then the other would book something else on the same date, and then we'd have to alter the plan somehow. Jeff and I would go back and forth playing hot potato with the phone, not wanting to make a decision, or bickering about, 'Well, you call them, *I'm* not gonna call them.' That whole kind of trip.

JEFF: The Beach Litter Walk show was at 11 a.m. and I remember basically just rolling out of bed and having to get ready to do that gig. And I remember Steven was barefoot, and we were wearing short, short cutoff jeans that were almost like hot pants; it was terrible. I don't recall that there were very many Red Cross fans there, because it was way too early for rock'n'roll people, and I remember that the city councilwoman or whoever was emceeing the show was really *not* into us being loud. Jordan Schwartz took the famous photo of us playing the show, so I guess it was worth it for that single photo. At least people weren't throwing garbage at us; the next time we played Santa Monica, it was much more fraught.

STEVEN: That was also around the same time we played an outdoor show at Wilson Park in Torrance with the Minutemen and The Salvation Army. Someone saw the flyer and contacted both organisations, the Salvation Army and the American Red Cross, and sort of blew the whistle on us. So The Salvation Army became The Three O'Clock at the same time as we changed our spelling.

I don't know how they found me, but I got a note in my ninth-grade class at Hawthorne High to go to the principal's office, and I had this letter waiting for me from the American Red Cross. It just sort of said, 'This has been brought to our attention...' and they just didn't want any confusion in the world. And they offered some spelling suggestions, like R-E-D-K-R-O-S-S, which was what we originally changed it to for a few seconds, though we never made that official. But then Jeff refused to go with the flow on that one, and decided we should add a second D.

JEFF: It was our homage to the comedian Redd Foxx; plus, two Ds looked better than one with the two Ss.

STEVEN: In terms of rising our rank among the LA hardcore scene, I wasn't sure if that spelling was gonna make our mission any easier. But it did succeed in making sure that our band name would be spelled wrong about 50 per cent of the time from that point on.

JEFF: Once we got it together with Janet, we started going up to play in San Francisco about once a month. They had a really interesting scene happening, very arty and freaky, although everyone up there was way more advanced in their drug taking.

STEVEN: Chi Chi, who was the manager of Dead Kennedys, had this big loft in downtown San Francisco, right across from the Greyhound station. It was a bit of a punk rock crash pad; bands from out of town would stay there, and once a month they would have a big rent party in the loft. So we were up there for one weekend in '82, opening for 45 Grave for two sold-out nights at On Broadway, and we're booked to play Chi Chi's rent party after the Saturday show, and we're also staying there. It's San Francisco, where crystal meth reigned supreme for years, so you know the party's gonna go all night.

For some reason, even knowing that we've got this party to go to, we had the bright idea of taking acid on the second night after we played at On Broadway. It started off fun; we walked over to one of the peep shows in North Beach. We put in our quarters and we're having a gas watching all these girls dancing. Mostly they were just looking at themselves in the mirror, but sometimes they could see the person watching them, too; they see five or six goofy punk rockers crammed into this booth meant for one pervy dude, and all of sudden they start yelling, 'Frank! Stop! Stop! Get these jokers out of here!'

We get kicked out right as the acid's coming on strong, and suddenly the trip goes from being fun and goofy to very self-conscious. By the time we get to the loft where we're staying, there's more people there than there were at On Broadway, and everyone's excited that we're gonna play. And Jeff and I can't even finish a sentence or a linear thought at this point, so we find our way out to the car to smoke a joint and cool out, and we're both like, 'We're not going back in there!' People kept coming out of the party and being, like, 'How you guys doing?' 'Oh, you know, we're okay.' 'Well, you wanna come back in and play?' 'Oh no, we're fine.'

JEFF: It was a nightmare. Suddenly we realise that we're parked in front of the Greyhound station, and there's nowhere to go to the bathroom because we're in this really gnarly part of town. So we go back in, and everybody's on crystal meth, and we're trying to avoid eye contact with anyone because you don't want to get stuck in their world. The bathroom is just completely unusable at this point, so I just try to find a place in the loft to curl up and go to sleep, and this celebrity – I don't want to say his name, but he was a famous skateboarder – just starts talking to me. He's on speed, and he just keeps going on and on and on, and there was no escape. Someone who's on speed and someone who's on acid, it's not a good combination for a good conversation.

On November 21, 1982, Redd Kross played a show at the Santa Monica Pier with K.I.A. and SIN 34, a true trial by fire performance wherein they managed to both antagonise and ultimately win the respect of a Venice street gang known as the Suicidals.

JEFF: We met our friends Dave Markey, Jennifer Schwartz and Jordan Schwartz through their *We Got Power* fanzine, which they interviewed us for. Dave was in the band SIN 34, and he was filming bands with this plastic Super 8 camera when we first started hanging out; he's the one who filmed us playing The Partridge Family's 'Somebody Wants To Love You' at the Santa Monica Pier, when we're getting garbage thrown at us.

We were already starting to dress outrageously; Steven was wearing cutoff shorts, a ripped-up Sgt. Pepper jacket and platform boots, and that's when we were really into making our hair big like Johnny Thunders. The members of the Suicidals gang and their friends – they were a gang before Suicidal Tendencies was a band – they were throwing kiwi fruits at us and going, 'You suck!' And we were just coming back with more insults.

STEVEN: I think Dave and Jennifer must have told us about the Suicidals and Mike Muir, the frontman of Suicidal Tendencies. Because they'd gone to high school in Santa Monica, and that was their world, and they'd had to deal with these people. There was a hippie selling kiwi fruits at a stand on the pier, and these Suicidals guys are grabbing all of them and pelting us with them. I didn't even know what they were – in 1982, I'd never had a kiwi fruit before. But we played the Partridge Family song, and Jeff said something into the microphone about Mike Muir's mom – 'I learned this song from a record I bought at Mike Muir's mom's garage sale!' I mean, it's not like he said, 'I fucked your mother,' but it still could have been really bad; I mean, what if Mike Muir's mom was dead, or something?

JEFF: Some of the Venice hippies also tried to fuck with us, and we were coming back at them with insults as well; and then the hippies started fucking with the Suicidals, and the Suicidals started fucking with the hippies. It was like a prison yard fight.

STEVEN: It just turned into this whole food war in the crowd. But we didn't back down, didn't leave the stage until we were ready to. And we won their respect; one of the Suicidals went up to Jeff afterwards and was like, 'If anyone ever fucks with you, let me know.'

JEFF: I mean, we were booed on our very first performance, so we knew how to handle that kind of thing. We knew we were smarter than them and we knew we had loud electric guitars as our shields, so there was nothing to worry about. But I do remember having to clean gross kiwi fruit gunk out of the pickups of my guitar the next time I took it out of the case. But it was a success.

STEVEN: Yeah, it was a success – except I also got a ticket later that day for smoking pot in the parking lot. I had to go to a court over a pot fine; the Suicidals couldn't help me out with that.

Tracy Lea amicably parted ways with the band in early 1983, and Dez Cadena – who had recently left Black Flag – joined Redd Kross on guitar for the second time. Though his playing further bolstered the band's musical attack, Dez's enthusiasm for joining Jeff and Steven in their chemical adventures only aggravated the tension that was already growing between them and Janet Housden.

JEFF: Tracy lived in Hollywood with her parents, and the rest of us were in the South Bay, so it was just becoming too difficult to keep it together and function right. I don't know if Dez quit Black Flag or was fired or what, but he was free. He'd been in our band for about five minutes when Chett Lehrer was in it, and we were happy to have him back.

One of the first gigs we did with Dez was when Madame Wong's started booking bands from our side of the tracks again, like The Pandoras. The only time we played the Wong's in Chinatown, it was Janet on drums, Dez on guitar, and me and Steven. We all took LSD before we went onstage, except we didn't tell Janet. We wouldn't dare; she was like our den mom at the time. I remember we were playing and everything was fine, and then all of sudden we're just standing there looking at each other; we'd all forgotten that we'd taken acid. There's an audience looking at us, and we're just like, 'What are we doing here?'

STEVEN: The show got very psychedelic, with some unplanned jams that went into some spacey places, typical acidic behaviour – I don't remember anything too crazy happening. But Janet was really angry at the way the set had gone, except she felt like it was *her* fault, and that we were somehow blaming her for what happened. She took it really hard. So Dez and I had to tell her that we all had taken acid before the show.

JEFF: And then she was absolutely furious at *us*. And rightfully so. She was automatically blaming herself for us being so terrible because she had the least amount of experience, as far as being a musician; she took it really hard. And I was like, 'Look, you didn't know; you were good, and the audience loved it.'

That show taught me that if you take LSD, you have to have a plan for your whole journey – you don't just take it casually to get high. I think about all the sixties psychedelic bands that would play on it, and I'm like, how did they *do* this? Like, Carlos Santana turned in a blistering set at Woodstock while on LSD, and I'm like, 'No way.' Because when we did that at Wong's, it was just complete confusion. Like, 'What is this thing I'm holding on to? Ugh, get this guitar off of me!' And I'm looking at the audience, and it's like, 'Ah... bye!' Lesson learned!

STEVEN: We loved sixties psychedelia. LA's thrift stores were such a gold mine at this time – not just for clothes but for rare records. LA had had such a vibrant underground scene in the sixties, and we were finding all these old record collections with things like Love, The Seeds, The Standells and all these lesser-known garage rock and psychedelic groups. But we also loved that point where folk rock met psychedelic pop, especially like The Mamas & the Papas. We loved their harmonies and the way those songs were structured. So when I heard the Bangs, their music immediately ticked a lot of boxes for me.

JEFF: Bob Forrest, who was later in Thelonious Monster, had this after-hours club called After Everything Else, and he hired me to be like the local guest celebrity DJ. That was the first time I ever guest DJ'd in a club, so of course I played Partridge Family and Yoko Ono, all this kind of stuff that no one had ever heard on the discotheque floor.

The band that was playing there that night was the Bangs. And I didn't know them at all because we weren't from the same scene or anything. But I loved poppy music, I loved vocal harmonies, I loved The Beatles, I loved The Mamas & the Papas; I loved all the music that they were really influenced by, and you didn't ever see that on the LA scene at the time – you never heard people singing perfect three-part harmonies in garage bands, being perfectly in tune vocally while being ragged at the same time musically. They were, like, custom-made for my taste. And I didn't know them, I didn't have any friends that were even friends with them. So I went up and introduced myself, and we just became friends immediately.

STEVEN: That was the first time I remember seeing them. They were very retro, but they were also really polished; this was when they were first doing their original thing as a four-piece band, before they became The Bangles and all the producers and outsiders got involved, and they were doing it so well. And they were all rock historians and probably knew more about the LA scene in the sixties than I did at that point. I'm younger than them, but I immediately got what they were doing. I was enamoured with them musically, and I was enamoured with them as women, as well.

I think that might have been when Jeff first asked Vicki Peterson out on a date or something. And then those two paired off, and so I was immediately accepted into the Bangs' inner circle, and got some nice attention as this 'cool teenage rocker kid.' They were just another band on the scene at that time, but I wound up having a front-row seat for their whole experience in the music industry. It was something that I watched closely and was definitely affected by.

JEFF: Vicki and I were an item for like five years. It's weird; from the surface, we had nothing in common. I love pop culture, but she didn't care as much about that stuff; she loved music, but she was coming from a more strait-laced place with it than I was. But I guess that just made it more fun for both of us. I learned a lot about sanity through her, and she learned a lot about craziness through me. We were certainly never bored...

Redd Kross didn't really have a scene at that point; we kind of came from whatever was left of the Hollywood or South Bay scenes. But their whole group of friends were people like The Dream Syndicate and The Long Ryders and Green On Red, people who were a little bit older, more educated, and more ambitious with their careers. I still didn't think of music as a potential career at that point; I was just living day by day. And before the Bangs, I'd never met anyone who wanted to be on a major label or had the ambition to be on mainstream radio. It was fun to be in a scene where people actually took pop music very seriously. It was inspiring; if we hadn't met the Bangs when we did, I don't know if we ever would've taken our music, our attitudes and our ambitions to the next level.

On the afternoon of May 16, 1983, Jeff and Steven helped their parents move the last boxes out of 5259 W. 115th Street. The 105 Freeway, an east–west auxiliary interstate highway project that had been in the works since the 1960s – but had changed course numerous times due to lawsuits and neighbourhood opposition – was finally ready to obliterate the house and street where Jeff and Steven had grown up, and where Redd Kross had been born.

JEFF: I remember us doing the final move the day of the *Motown 25* TV special, the one where Michael Jackson did his 'moonwalk' for the very first time. The city had started vacating the houses in our neighbourhood like ten years prior to that, but they kept changing the routing, and our block stayed pretty much untouched for years. And then when they came down with the final routing, the 105 actually went on *top* of our block, so they were paying off people to leave. We lived on a normal grid street, probably a quarter of a mile or half a mile from one end to the other, and slowly but surely all the people there started moving out and leaving their houses vacant.

STEVEN: The city finally bought our parents' house in 1983, and we were like the last-stand holdouts on the block. We were five years into Redd Kross at that point, and for the last six months we were there we rehearsed in our garage with the garage door open, because there were no neighbours left to call the cops on us. It wasn't lost on us, this weird feeling of suburban decay.

JEFF: It had been great for us, having this whole block to ourselves. But at the same time, all the kids that we grew up with were gone, and all the houses were vacant or being torn down. So it was like living in a real ghost town, where actual ghosts from your past exist with you. It was very surreal. But it worked out well for my parents, because the longer you held out, the more money they gave you. So in the end, they got double or triple what the house would've been worth.

STEVEN: Jeff and I moved with our parents to their new house, which was only a mile away. But he and I stayed in the old house for a couple of nights, and I think he and Vicki stayed there for a while after the water and power got turned off. It was like their own degenerate palace.

Not so innocent pre-*Teen Babes from Monsanto*: The 1983 Redd Kross lineup with Dez Cadena and Janet Housden. (Photo by Dina Douglass)

Chapter 10

TEEN BABES FROM MONSANTO

Through their friendship with the Bangs, Jeff and Steven began hanging out with Dave Peterson, the younger brother of Vicki and Debbi Peterson. Like Debbi, Dave played the drums, and he also had a home recording setup in his music room at the Peterson family's townhouse condo in Rancho Palos Verdes, an upper-middle-class enclave in the South Bay. Like Jeff and Steven, Dave was obsessed with a wide array of sixties sounds, so it was only natural that they would gravitate towards playing together. Unfortunately, this would lead to a less than amicable split with Janet Housden.

STEVEN: I'd been playing with Dez in an early incarnation of his band DC3. Kurt Markham was the drummer at the time, and he had these massive Ludwig drums with this outrageous kick drum that was even bigger than John Bonham's. Kurt was this wacky, slightly older guy who was having a gas playing with punk rockers, but whose foot was still pretty firmly rooted in seventies rock. We were jamming, doing stuff in the vein of Mountain and Grand Funk, and it was the first time I'd ever played with people that could improv freely in these realms. I was doing my best to keep up, but there was also something really thrilling about feeling that freedom for the first time, that freedom to surprise yourself. It really upped my game.

I love Janet, and I've always loved her, but I think that I never took her very seriously as a drummer. From my perspective, bringing her into the band always was sort of a 'placeholder' decision, but she took drumming with us a lot more seriously than we expected her to. She also had her own vehicle and we didn't, so there was plenty of room for her to feel taken advantage of by us. But as hard as it was to reject her, I always took the band deadly seriously – and if I felt like someone was holding me back as a musician, that was going to be a big problem for me. Dave Peterson was much more fluid as a drummer, and had a much more sophisticated palate that he could pull from, musically. Playing with Dave was one of the first times where I was like, 'Whoa! I'm ready for this!' But then we had to break the news to Janet.

JEFF: Janet was a very solid, primitive punk drummer. Not in the hardcore sense; she was more like our Moe Tucker, which was great in its way. But she couldn't do a lot of the drumming stuff that we wanted her to do. Plus, she was kind of like our crazed, angry den mother, and we were all totally afraid of her. She was very serious at a time when we were still being kind of flaky; and if you did anything wrong, you'd get *the wrath*.

Janet was mad for years and years and years after we decided not to work with her anymore. And still to this day, she thinks we kicked her out of the band because she lost her truck and could no longer give us rides. And it wasn't the truth, but I let her believe that it *was* the truck, because I didn't want to tell her that she wasn't good enough to play with us anymore. But it's really just a case of people going in different directions; she's stayed a musician; she's played bass and drums in other groups, and got really good at both. She even taught herself violin, and she continues to have a real passion for playing music. But at the time, drums was just something she played because no one else was playing them.

Dave, on the other hand, played in kind of a Keith Moon style, and he was way more versed in the kind of sixties stuff we loved. He was the next level up as a drummer, and he was kind of a 'Radio Shack Phil Spector' with his home recording setup, so we asked him to join.

STEVEN: Dave was always a bit on the fence about us – it was like we were always on probation or under consideration or something. But he was probably having his own identity thing, trying to figure out who he was underneath the weight of having the Peterson sisters as his older siblings; joining his sister's boyfriend's band wasn't gonna be good enough for him, and I think we felt a little bit of resentment about his attitude. He had another band at the time with a friend, a good power pop band, but I think we were probably secretly dismissive of them.

Though hampered by the lack of a reliable rehearsal space, now that they no longer had an abandoned neighbourhood to play in, the Jeff-Steven-Dez-Dave lineup of Redd Kross began to conceptualise their next recording project: a collection of favourite cover songs from the sixties and seventies. While covers albums have become a dime-a-dozen in the 21st century, this was a fairly radical concept in the early-mid eighties, especially coming from a punk rock band led by brothers who had yet to reach their 21st birthdays. But since the McDonalds had lovingly covered songs both classic and obscure since their Tourists days, this felt like a natural progression – and their friend Bill Bartell thought such a project would be a perfect fit for his new indie label Gasatanka Records.

STEVEN: Before Dave played with us, we did a recording with Janet and Dez of Blue Cheer's 'Out Of Focus' for a New Underground Records compilation called *Life Is Boring So Why Not Steal This Record.* Dez sang lead on it.

JEFF: I remember hearing that Rick Rubin was a fan of our version of 'Out Of Focus' – he thought it was a Redd Kross song. I thought it'd be a really great idea to do an album of deep tracks from groups that we loved. We cited a lot of our influences on *Born Innocent*, so this was kind of a continuation of that. Our friend Bill Bartell was just starting his Gasatanka Records label; he had kind of a subsidiary deal with Enigma Records, and he wanted to put it out.

STEVEN: Gasatanka was right along the lines of Smoke Seven, in the sense that it was just like the person that was the most energetic about wanting to put something out by us, and we were like, 'Okay!' Jeff might tell the story more like it was all intentionally planned, but the truth of the matter is probably that Bill started grinding on us that he wanted to put out a Redd Kross record, and we probably didn't have any new songs. And then Jeff would've put together this mission statement of us delivering a lesson in the history of rock as we saw it. It was just like, 'Yeah, let's do a *Pin Ups*!'

JEFF: We thought of it as kind of like a cultural exchange – a way to turn people on to what we were into, but they maybe didn't know about. It was teaching the youth about what they *should* know. I mean, it's hard to imagine now, but a lot of people in the punk scene at the time were completely oblivious to, like, The Stooges or early David Bowie.

STEVEN: Jeff was always exposing me to weird music, and he's only three years older than me. And he brought that same mentality to this record – he's barely 20 himself at this point, but he wants to school everybody else.

JEFF: We became friends with Bill Bartell in the early eighties, in the same way that we all made a lot of our friends at the time – somebody would get your phone number and they would just call you, and then you would end up becoming friends on the phone. Someone would call and say, 'Oh, I'm a big fan of your band, and I play guitar too.' And then you'd end up talking for hours and you'd become friends. I don't really ever remember meeting Bill, but we just started chatting on the phone, and he became one of my best and most notorious friends.

STEVEN: Bill had formed Gasatanka to put out records by his own band, White Flag, but he wound up forming this really solid relationship with Enigma Records, which was kind of a happening indie label at the time. He was always very industrious; Bill was already scamming his way backstage to KISS concerts when he was a 16-year-old in Riverside, California. He intuitively understood how to sound official and how to appeal to people. His story is so wild, because he had the skills and the smarts to become one of those super-duper success stories, but his agenda was never necessarily to have traditional success; he wasn't fetishising greenbacks, he was more about fetishising the absurd. He loved getting attention, and not always favourable attention.

JEFF: One of the first times we ever hung out with Bill, he got us into the press conference KISS did for the *Creatures Of The Night* album. I didn't really know what an insane prankster he was yet. KISS were like politicians that day – all their answers were so pat and rehearsed, like, 'This is the greatest record we've ever done,' and all this stuff. This was supposed to be their big comeback record. There were all these annoying plants in the audience, with people asking things like, 'Hey Gene – how long is your tongue?' But Bill was standing up and challenging them with all these questions about why *The Elder* had tanked, why *Love Gun* was out of print, and why no one was going to see KISS anymore. Ace – who was basically already out of the band at that point – was standing there chuckling, and Paul looked startled and annoyed, which was even more hilarious with his makeup on. Bill loved KISS, but he also knew Gene and Paul were total control freaks, and he couldn't resist making them squirm. This was the first time we'd kind of met our match with someone who was a prankster like us, but even worse.

As the band mulled over which songs to record for the new record, it became clear that Dez was coming at the project from a different angle – not wildly so, but it was divergent enough from Jeff and Steven's increasingly well-honed vision that he ended up parting ways with the band before they headed into the studio.

JEFF: It was getting a little off-kilter, because we were trying to be fair and let everyone have a say, but Dez was very much into his older brother's music, and he wanted to do songs by Mountain and Grand Funk. I can't remember which ones, but we tried rehearsing them, and it just wasn't working. I liked stuff like that for its power, but I could never get behind, like, Mark Farner's interpretation of the blues. I would've had no trouble interpreting The Rolling Stones' version of that, because the British bands always seemed to take that stuff to a different level. But for some reason, the American hard rock version of the blues felt very inauthentic and less adventurous to me.

Really, when it came down to it, Steven and I were never open to anyone else's suggestions. Bill had suggested one of the really great *Runt*-era Todd Rundgren songs, and maybe something by Traffic; and they were good, but they weren't *us*. We just had to pick the songs; that was the only way this was going to make any sense. So with Dez, it wasn't like anyone was kicked out; it was just like, 'Okay, you want to do that, and we want to do this. And that's fine.' It was decided that I'd do all the guitars on *Teen Babes*, kinda like Keith Richards on *Let It Bleed*.

Redd Kross adjourned as a three-piece to Kitchen Sync with producer Geza X, already legendary for his work with the Germs,

Black Flag, Dead Kennedys, MDC and other punk bands. *Teen Babes From Monsanto* wouldn't be a punk record, however, but rather a middle-finger salute to eighties punk orthodoxy in the form of speed-fuelled, irreverent yet also deeply affectionate romps through songs by the diverse likes of KISS ('Deuce'), The Rolling Stones ('Citadel'), The Shangri-Las ('Heaven Only Knows'), The Stooges ('Ann'), David Bowie ('Saviour Machine') and Tommy Boyce and Bobby Hart ('Blow You A Kiss In The Wind'), along with a revved-up reworking of 'Linda Blair' from *Born Innocent* thrown in for added fun. Released in late 1984, *Teen Babes* was the first Redd Kross record to receive decent distribution outside of California. It would serve as a sort of warped bat signal for like-minded weirdos across the country, and set the stage for the band's first US tour.

JEFF: Geza X had produced all our favourite California punk bands, all the good Dangerhouse Records. I didn't know him, but I just cold-called him and we hit it off. We did *Teen Babes* in two sessions, and I think we paid him $300 for it. He did it more because he was really into the idea. He was a genius, and it was super fun to get a lot of work done in a short period of time with him, because he had this manic, crazed energy.

STEVEN: Geza X later complained that the monitors were off at Kitchen Sync, and that it wasn't his fault that the record sounded as thin as it sounded. But the other part of that story is that Jeff and I were on massive amounts of speed when we made that record. We didn't tell Dave Peterson; we just worked him into the ground while we were like flying high all night, just playing with manic enthusiasm and zero inhibition. We did let Geza in on it, and he was all too willing to get on that train with us. It wasn't like a Marc Bolan cocaine session – it was like straight-up dirty biker speed. Obviously, that wasn't the sort of behaviour that we could sustain for very long, and we stopped doing that shit pretty soon after.

I *will* blame Geza somewhat for the way it sounded, because we really didn't know what we were doing. We were just like, 'Yeah! Turn it up!' All we knew was that the guitars were really crunchy. Jeff was mostly using a Tom Scholz Rockman, this early amp modelling gadget, in the studio; it was like the size of a Walkman cassette player, but it was a mini-amplifier that you plugged your guitar into. You can really hear that Tom Scholz chorus effect on 'Saviour Machine' – it's not an over-the-top early eighties chorus sound, but more of a tasteful, smooth seventies sound.

JEFF: I think the whole thing cost about $3,000 in total. Steven had a job at the time, so he contributed some of it, and I think our parents gave us like a thousand bucks. And Bill Bartell had got an advance for his label through Enigma, so I think he paid for like a third of it, which I guess he thought gave him a right to have an opinion. He came to the studio at one point when we were all really out of our minds; he listened to the playback and said, 'I'm just a little disappointed. I was kind of hoping it would sound more like Dio.' I was like, 'What? Get out!' I kicked him out of the studio for saying that, and wouldn't let him back in. He always denied saying that, and he can't defend himself now because he's no longer with us, but it's the truth.

STEVEN: Everybody wants to be a Kim Fowley, you know? Like, the cassette of *Teen Babes* has 'Saturday Night' by the Bay City Rollers in the track listing, but it doesn't exist; we never even recorded it. That was a song Bill wanted us to do; he had this 'idol maker' fantasy of moulding and shaping us, but Jeff wasn't interested in any input from him, other than a thumb's up and his unconditional approval of what we were doing.

JEFF: We had a few guests on the album – Bruce Duff played lead guitar on 'Deuce' at Bill's suggestion, and Sid Griffin from The Long Ryders played harmonica on 'Blow You A Kiss In The Wind.'

STEVEN: I'd forgotten that Sid played on that. What a fun fact. Yeah, we were like, 'Can you play harmonica on this song that we know from the TV show *Bewitched*?' 'Yeah, man, sure – you guys are crazy, ha ha!'

JEFF: And then, of course, that's Vicki and Debbi Peterson singing the uncredited backing vocals on 'Heaven Only Knows.' It wasn't like they were ashamed of us and didn't want to be credited, but they were the only band any of us knew that were on a major label, and they were on Columbia Records, which was like the most ultra-conservative and mainstream of them all. Today, anyone can sing or play on anyone else's record without asking for permission from their label, but at the time they were dealing with all sorts of insane pressure from Columbia, and it was a whole scary world for them to navigate. Having their voices on the record ultimately meant more to us than having their names.

STEVE: I mean, it would have been great to have the bragging rights – by the time *Teen Babes* came out, The Bangles were just starting to blow up. The fear of a 'no' inspired us just to not ask at all. We didn't want to chance being told that they were exclusive to Columbia and couldn't appear on a record from another label, or whatever other obstacles Columbia's lawyers could have thrown at us.

JEFF: The entire album title is *Teen Babes From Monsanto: A Rock'n'roll Retrospective, Vol. 1* – it says that on the spine. Monsanto's a Chemical company, but we were also referencing Disneyland's Adventure Thru Inner Space presented by Monsanto; for Southern California kids who grew up going to Disneyland, that was the ride you could smoke weed in, because it was dark inside and it didn't have cameras. It was like a psychedelic journey from full-size to atom-size; total Disney psychedelia.

STEVEN: I don't think we even understood at the time just how controversial Monsanto was. They're still being sued for contaminating baby formula, lakes, rivers, soil, this whole plethora of horribleness that you generally don't cross-pollinate with the kind of *Teen Beat* magazine thing we were going for.

JEFF: We were presenting ourselves as teen idols – kind of the anti-Henry Rollins, like we were like these teenyboppers within the realm of our punk rock roots, which was already kind of bizarre. And Monsanto being an evil chemical company that's supposedly responsible for all this pollution and mutation, we were like *mutant* teen idols.

STEVEN: *Teen Babes* was very much us forming this idea of who we were. In a way, it was done out of necessity, but it was also a good idea at the right time. Later on, people like Buzz and Dale from the Melvins and Mark Arm from Mudhoney told us that the album really kind of helped to set in motion what would become the grunge explosion, because we included things like The Stooges and early KISS on the same page.

JEFF: People don't realise now just how uncool and un-punk it was at the time to say you liked KISS, and here we were saying, 'We love KISS – and we love The Stooges and Bowie and The Shangri-Las, too!' It was like making a mixtape or public playlist for your fans, or fans you don't have yet. We didn't announce *Teen Babes* as an album full of covers, and a lot of people didn't even know that the songs were covers when they heard them. But the people that *did* know were the people we became friends with once we started touring; once the record started to reach outside of California, we were going out and meeting these like-minded people, and started building our network of friends, most of whom were musicians and artists and weirdos. *Teen Babes From Monsanto* gave us a way to find *our* people.

Flyer for the Lhasa Club premiere of *Desperate Teenage Runaways* — later changed to *Desperate Teenage Lovedolls* — July 13, 1984. (Courtesy of Geoffrey Weiss)

Chapter 11

LOVEDOLLS

Also helping Jeff and Steven find 'their people' in the mid/late eighties were 1984's *Desperate Teenage Lovedolls* and 1986's *Lovedolls Superstar*, a pair of delightfully trashy, supremely low-budget feature films directed by Dave Markey. Shot guerrilla-style by Markey with a single hand-held Super 8 camera, the films – which follow the career of an all-girl band as they claw and kill their way to stardom – featured performances from the McDonalds, as well as numerous friends and fellow musicians from the LA music scene, including Jennifer Schwartz, Jordan Schwartz, Janet Housden, Tracy Lea, Dez Cadena, Annette Zilinskas, Phil Newman, Michael Glass and Vicki Peterson.

Heavily influenced by Russ Meyer's *Beyond the Valley of the Dolls* and the early films of John Waters – and filled with campy improvised dialogue and hilariously awful special effects – Markey's *Lovedolls* films were embraced by underground music fans and psychotronic film aficionados who found them a refreshing alternative to the slick and soulless product of eighties Hollywood. Though these films didn't have any dedicated national distribution at the time, copies nonetheless made their way around the country via various tape-trading networks and in-the-know video shops. Interest in the films was further stirred by their soundtracks, released on SST and Gasatanka, which featured contributions by Redd Kross, Black Flag, White Flag, Nip Drivers, SIN 34 and other Southern California punk bands. (Sonic Youth, big fans of both Redd Kross and the first *Lovedolls* film, contributed a cover of Alice Cooper's 'Hallowed Be Thy Name' to the *Lovedolls Superstar* soundtrack.)

Markey would go on to direct *Macaroni and Me*, a surreal eight-and-a-half-minute short starring Redd Kross that was occasionally shown before the band's late eighties headlining appearances, as well as the acclaimed 1992 alternative rock documentary *1991: The Year Punk Broke*. Jeff and Steven's appearance in the *Lovedolls* films would likewise lead to a higher cinematic profile, first in Lucas Reiner's 1990 film *The Spirit of '76*, and then in several films by Allison Anders. But four decades later, the *Lovedolls* cult remains as fiercely devoted as ever.

JEFF: In the early eighties, we had one of the early VCRs, and there was a cool video shop that was about 10 miles from our house, run by this guy named Lance Lawson. We became friends with him, and he would loan us all these bootleg music films and videos that hadn't officially been released yet. It was like our YouTube at the time; a huge resource for us. We would go to his store all the time, and the one he opened later called Video Archives – which was the one Quentin Tarantino worked in, along with our friend Chuck Kelley.

STEVE: Lance saw that we were into John Waters and Russ Meyer, so he started turning us on to all sorts of other cool and weird films.

JEFF: There was also a weird film scene happening in LA at the time, with revival houses like the Nuart showing all these really insane movies on the big screen, and places like EZTV, which was this gallery in West Hollywood where local independent filmmakers and video artists could show their things. Which was so great for us, because that gave us something to do whenever the music scene wasn't really happening here; a lot of times, the things we saw at these places were more inspiring to us than the music we were listening to or the bands we were seeing in the clubs. So when Dave Markey and Jennifer Schwartz started making *Desperate Teenage Lovedolls*, it was just kind of in keeping with all of our love of weirdo movies. It was like, 'We can really do this. Let's keep going!'

STEVE: We were up in San Francisco opening for 45 Grave again, this time at the Elite Club, which had actually been the Fillmore West but now was pretty dank and in disrepair. Jeff and I announced from the stage that, 'If anyone knows where to get some Quaaludes, we'll be backstage!' Just typical between-song banter. And that's how we met Hilary Rubens, who became my first girlfriend after the Dee debacle. I was like 14 or 15 at this point, and she was probably four years older than me, but it was at least a little more age-appropriate.

Hilary moved down to LA, and she and Jennifer Schwartz became good friends immediately. Dave Markey had a camera and was into making films, and he and Jennifer had just started collaborating on a movie that they were then calling *Desperate Teenage Runaways*; Jennifer was playing Kitty Carryall, who was the lead singer of the band, and Hilary played the bassist Bunny Tremelo, so that kind of became my social world. We would spend weekends shooting scenes all over Santa Monica and LA. My first scene in the film, where I'm playing the talent headhunter Johnny Tremaine and I find the girls busking in the Santa Monica Promenade, that was the first scene I shot with them. It was all very spontaneous, and we probably cut the shots in order; there wasn't a script – there was just like an outline of an idea for each scene.

125

JEFF: Whenever Dave got $20 together for a couple rolls of film, we would think about what we would film, and it just became kind of like our fun thing. And Dave was really good at seeing things through; I mean, if I'd had the camera, we would've never got around to any of it. But then, I was really good at kind of like helping out with ideas for scenes and feeding dialogue to the people. I especially loved collaborating with Jennifer. But those projects were a couple years of fun. Everyone got so enthused, and all the people we knew wanted to be in it; the *Lovedolls* films were like home movies of our little friend group.

STEVEN: We would just get together the morning of the shoot and discuss what we were trying to accomplish, and how we're trying to push this story along that day. We would come up with our own dialogue on the spot – and when you look at it, you can tell – but we were all weaned on subversive and DIY underground films, as well as TV sketch comedy like *Saturday Night Live* and *SCTV*, so that's kind of what we were going for. And we just did that every weekend for a year or so, and eventually there was enough footage for Dave to cobble together a cut of *Desperate Teenage Runaways*.

Dave first showed the film at this little art space called the Lhasa Club, and Kim Fowley showed up at the screening. He was really angry; he said we were ripping off his story and the story of The Runaways, and told us that if Joan Jett were there, she would kick all our asses. It was pretty hilarious. I mean, there *were* scenes where the girls were lip-synching to Runaways songs, so I don't know what Dave was thinking there. But really, we were referencing *Beyond the Valley of the Dolls*, and the whole 'meteoric rise of an all-girl band in the dangerous city' storyline in that film.

Anyway, that's why the movie's name got changed to *Desperate Teenage Lovedolls*. This was all happening around the same time as we were making *Teen Babes From Monsanto*, so we went back and recorded a bunch of songs that they could use in the film, like 'Ballad Of A Lovedoll', which we later re-recorded for *Neurotica*, and 'Legend', which we recorded with our friend and later co-manager Spock singing, and which Jennifer lip-synced in the film. But there was no original or authorised music in the film until after that first screening.

JEFF: When I first started going out with Vicki, she was sharing a house with a bunch of her friends on Crescent Heights in West Hollywood. The lease holder on the place was Joanna Dean, aka Spock, who had played bass in Backstage Pass, a power pop band from the original seventies LA punk, power pop and new wave scene. They had a great trashy song called 'Legend (Come On Up To Me)' that was on *Saturday Night Pogo*, an early punk compilation that Rhino put out in 1978. I only knew them from that song, but I loved it – so meeting her was like, 'Oh my god! Spock!'

STEVEN: That Crescent Heights house was kind of like The Church equivalent to what would later be known as the Paisley Underground. Steve Wynn from The Dream Syndicate lived there for a while, and Johnette Napolitano who was later in Concrete Blonde, and Michael Steele from The Bangles moved in there at one point. The Long Ryders and Green On Red hung out there a lot, and I slept on the couch there a lot in like '83, '84.

We weren't really a member of that scene; we were never members of any scene, at least once we graduated from Black Flag mentorship. We were more like 'Paisley Underground Adjacent.' We would play with those bands – we played a lot with The Salvation Army, who became Three O'Clock, and there's a flyer out there from 1983 where The Bangles are playing with Redd Kross and Black Flag at the Cathay de Grande – but we kind of did our own thing. We were respected and allowed to hang out, though. The Long Ryders probably wouldn't have expected me to be able to keep up on a conversation about

The Flying Burrito Brothers; but at the same time, they got our references, because they were probably at a KISS concert in 1974 before they'd rediscovered Chris Hillman.

JEFF: I think the recordings of 'Legend' and 'Ballad Of A Lovedoll' that we did for the first film were the first things we ever recorded with Dave Peterson, and we did it on his little Radio Shack 4-track setup at his parents' townhouse in Palos Verdes. The other tracks we did for it – those things like 'Purple Haze' and the best part of 'Stairway To Heaven' – were done at Spinhead Studios, this little 8-track studio that Dave Markey and Phil Newman, the bass player from SIN 34, had out in the Valley. It was a very creative time; we were always filming, recording, playing shows, doing something fun.

For a while there was only one copy of *Desperate Teenage Lovedolls*, so you could only see it locally. But sometime right after we finished *Teen Babes*, it started getting around the country. Dave and Phil also had a band called Painted Willie, and they toured with Black Flag – so they may have shown the movie on that tour, and maybe sold video cassettes of it. But like *Teen Babes*, it got a lot of people's attention. No one else from the punk scene was doing trashy underground movies or concept records at that time, so it was easier to get noticed, at least by the people who were your potential fanbase.

STEVEN: At the end of the first *Lovedolls* movie, Johnny Tremaine, my sleazy, Kim Fowley-esque character, dies after the Lovedolls slip me some acid and I jump off a building. And then in the second film, I play Rainbow Tremaine, Johnny's twin brother who lives at a freedom school in New Mexico – total *Billy Jack* – and then, pre-'Welcome To The Jungle', comes to Hollywood and is jumped into the horrors of living in the evil city. Eventually I am so distraught over the corrosiveness of the toxic city that I morph into Chemical Warfare, lead singer of the hardcore band Anarchy 6.

I actually wound up doing a whole Anarchy 6 record, *Hardcore Lives!*, with Dave Markey, Phil Newman and Mike Glass of SIN 34, which eventually came out in 1988 on Bill Bartell's Gasatanka label. It's all done tongue in cheek, and we wrote and recorded the whole thing in a weekend. I did my best to ape Henry Rollins and Mike Muir, or at least whatever I knew of them. But those other guys had all been in actual hardcore bands, and I think their hearts were in it way more than mine was. I think a lot of people thought Anarchy 6 was a real band; I still get people telling me that they seriously liked that record – the unspoken message being that they liked it better than anything Redd Kross ever did, and that we could still be out there doing it along with the Cro-Mags or something.

JEFF: I'm not really in the first movie that much; I'm only in it for a second, but I'm more featured in the second one: I play this character who gets possessed by a Gene Simmons doll and assassinates Bruce Springsteen onstage. This was around the time that we met Dave Nazworthy, whose family rec room would later become our social and music home base, and we were shooting in his neighbourhood in Beverly Hills.

The *Lovedolls* movies were total guerrilla films; in LA, if you were filming with a tripod, cops would stop you and ask for permits. But since we were filming with Dave's little plastic hand-held camera, we could get away with it – we just had to do things really fast. Lucille Ball lived right by Dave Nazworthy; her house was on the corner, with a big, long driveway that led to the back yard. I was like, 'Oh, let's use Lucy's house for an exterior shot!' I suggested we do something where I was escaping from the cops, and I'm coming through the backyard and on to the sidewalk. Lucille Ball was still alive at the time, so we had to do it really fast, because we didn't want Lucy to catch us and yell at us. Plus, I'm dressed in rags and I'm in full Gene Simmons KISS makeup, and it's all smeared because I'm supposed to have been running from the cops and hiding out all night after assassinating Bruce Springsteen.

So it's daytime now, and I'm just dragging myself past Lucille Ball's driveway, across the yard, and they're getting the shot they needed – you can see it in the film, too. That part of Beverly Hills is just a fancy version of any other tree-lined neighbourhood; it's 'The Flats', I think they call it. So I walk out of the shot and stop on the corner, which is just a normal corner. This car pulls up at the stop sign, and it's Michael Jackson driving a completely beat-up 1965 Mustang. His passenger seat window is open, and he sees me standing there in KISS makeup. All I can think to say is, 'Oh, hi Michael.' And he goes, 'Hi.' That's our entire exchange. And then he drives off.

No one else witnessed this because they were all back behind me at 'the set.' I ran back and was like, 'Oh my god! I just saw Michael Jackson! I just said hello to Michael Jackson!' And they're like, 'What?!?' I'm like, 'Yeah, he was driving a really thrashed Mustang, and I said "Hi, Michael." They all thought I was hallucinating.

STEVEN: Nobody ever believed him. I tend to believe the story is true; but you know, Jeff was such a prankster that that's kind of his karma. He had this thing where he would always claim to have seen Charlene Tilton from *Dallas*; there were lots of false Charlene Tilton sightings. So the idea that he would have met Michael Jackson while standing on some random corner in Beverly Hills and wearing beat-up Gene Simmons makeup just seemed too absurd. '*Suuure*, Jeff, you saw Michael Jackson. Uh-huh.'

JEFF: A couple of years later, I read Michael's autobiography *Moonwalk*, and in it he talks about how he used to love driving around in cars from Rent-a-Wreck, which a lot of celebrities did at the time, because no one looks at you in LA if you're driving a beater – and if they do see you, no one will believe it's you, because what would a famous person be doing driving around in dented, primered, towing trash?

I was kind of out of my mind at the time, in general; but I know now that at least I was sane in the moment. He didn't seem confused by me at all; it was a nice little exchange. He was much nicer to me than Madonna was in the same situation; years later, I was walking across Sunset, and Madonna was just sitting there in a car on her phone. I said, 'Oh, hi Madonna,' and she just glared at me.

But it's true, every time I saw a blonde in those days, I would say, 'Oh, there's Charlene Tilton!' Everybody would be like, 'Jeff, that's not Charlene Tilton!' And then I finally *did* see Charlene Tilton at a yoghurt place, when I was by myself. Seeing Michael Jackson and Charlene Tilton in person with no one there to witness it – maybe those were like wishes that I blew on weird things.

1985 Redd Kross lineup with Robert Hecker and Dave "The Rave" Peterson. (Photo by John Scarpati)

Chapter 12

HAVE FUN OR START CRYING

In late 1984, Redd Kross re-expanded to a four-piece with the addition of lead guitarist Robert Hecker. A record-setting track star in high school, Hecker applied the same rigorous intensity to practising and playing guitar, and his slim frame, eccentric sense of humour and granular knowledge of both The Beatles and KISS catalogues almost made him seem like a long-lost third McDonald brother. Hecker would hold down the band's lead guitar spot into the nineties; the Redd Kross drummer situation, however, remained frustratingly unresolved.

JEFF: I'd done all the guitars on *Teen Babes*, but we knew that we wanted to have another guitar player, because it was going to be hard to sing and play everything live. We'd met Robert Hecker through the South Bay scene – he'd gone to high school with Janet Housden and Bill and Frank from the Descendents – but we didn't really know him that well.

STEVEN: He'd grabbed our attention because he never conformed to the hardcore code of having short hair. He was always this the crazy hippie dancing wildly at the Black Flag show, and we were like, 'That guy is a real freak!' And when he put on his guitar, he was amazing.

JEFF: Robert came over to our house to audition. He lived in Hermosa Beach, and he rode his bicycle the entire way – which is like 5 or 6 very hilly miles – with his Gibson SG strapped on his back. He walked into my bedroom and just started playing our version of 'Deuce' without even plugging in; he was dancing wildly, jumping up and down on the bed, just full-on performance mode. It was the best audition ever, and we didn't even think about anyone else.

STEVEN: Robert is a real character, and definitely his own person; he always had this really hardcore hippie thing going on. He's one of those guys that you would think was completely out of his mind on psychedelics but has never even, like, had a sip of coffee his entire life. He was just naturally straight edge, and extremely judgemental of any drug-taking behaviour.

JEFF: We were in a very insane, druggie, crazed party state at the time, and he had never tasted alcohol or taken a drug in his life. But he was by far the most eccentric and crazed person that we had ever met, so it was perfect. We connected on just about everything other than chemicals. We were both heavily into The Beatles and KISS on a nerdy level, and we could go down these deep rabbit holes on them where other people would have no idea what we were talking about. And Robert also liked to gossip; our rehearsals would often go on and on where we we'd be gossiping about, like, Perry Farrell or Bret Michaels.

STEVEN: Robert's maybe a year younger than Jeff, but he didn't get hip to KISS until the *Creatures Of The Night* album – the same album that Bill Bartell took us to the press conference for. His love of eighties KISS just seemed so eccentric and bizarre to us; I think we would have preferred it if Robert had been an Ace Frehley obsessive, and we were probably horribly withholding with him at times because he didn't play like Ace at all. But Robert completely worshipped Paul Stanley, especially the high notes that Paul would hit on, like, 'I Was Made For Loving You.' So at least we had the good sense to realise, 'Robert's obsessed with Paul – let's run with it!' If things were going really poorly at a show, we would break into that song, or 'God Of Thunder.' If you heard 'God Of Thunder' at one of our shows, that meant something was going really wrong.

At the beginning of the Robert era, we were still doing shows with punk and hardcore bands. There was a gig in March 1985 at the Olympic Auditorium with Social Distortion, who were now one of the bigger punk bands in LA, and Goldenvoice, the show's promoters, offered us the gig with Social Distortion and said we would be direct support. So we arrive at the Olympic Auditorium for soundcheck, only to find out that all the other bands had been also told that they'd be playing just before Social Distortion. We confronted Gary Tovar from Goldenvoice, and he was like, 'Oh yeah, I'm sorry – I was hoping you guys could work that out.'

I remember having a very shrill argument with the members of SSD Control; they were explaining to me how they were having a reunion and they had just got back together and they'd flown out from Boston for the show. I think my diplomatic response was, 'I don't give a fuck – I don't even know who you *are*.'

And then of course, karma bites me on the ass; SSD Control plays before us, and the crowd – which is mostly hardcore kids – really enjoys them. Then we get onstage, and Jeff is wearing an American flag as a cape, and I'm wearing Daisy Dukes and platforms; Jeff's guitar won't stay in tune, my amp blows up and the hardcore kids are booing us, and by the third song of the set we're already doing 'God Of Thunder'.

JEFF: We had so many crazy gigs with Robert, like the Gila Monster Jamboree, which was just maybe a month or two after he joined. It was this concert at a secret location out in the middle of the Mojave Desert; it was put on by Desolation Center, which was an arts collective that some of the early Goldenvoice people were involved with. Sonic Youth and Meat Puppets were also on that bill, along with Psi-Com, Perry Farrell's pre-Jane's Addiction band.

STEVEN: We had a manager at the time named Carmel Moran, and she was in with the Desolation Center people and they were in with the Sonic Youth people. I think that was Sonic Youth's first West Coast tour. That's when we became friends with them – I remember they borrowed our gear for some LA shows.

JEFF: We had a big show in San Francisco that weekend, and I remember to one of the Gila Monster organisers telling us, 'We'll have someone pick you up at the airport, we'll have gear for you, blah blah blah,' because we weren't able to fly with amplifiers; we just had our guitars. So we do our show in San Francisco, fly in to the Ontario Airport with no sleep, and some punk girl picks us up in like a 1968 Ford jalopy. And she was nice enough, but she got us so insanely lost in the desert that we didn't get to the secret location until well into the night's festivities.

STEVEN: We were driving back and forth on these unmarked desert roads, looking for some kind of paper-plate sign on the side of the road with an arrow on it to tell us which dirt road to go down next. The sun went down, and we were still driving around for hours. It finally looked like we were about to run out of gas, and that we were gonna have to resort to cannibalism or die, but we eventually made it there. And the rumour was that we had purposely stalled so that we didn't have to open for the

Meat Puppets. I mean, we *were* very competitive, and it was a fair accusation – I'm the guy who told SSD Control that I didn't even know who they were – but it was not the case.

JEFF: It was the middle of winter, so it was freezing cold, and our guitars would not stay in tune. And by this time the promoters were gone, everyone was on acid, there weren't any amplifiers for us, and the Meat Puppets wouldn't let us use their gear because they thought we showed up late on purpose. So we cobbled together some gear, but there was no stage – we were standing on raw dirt, so every time we moved it was like Pigpen from *Peanuts*, with big clouds of dust billowing around us. The guitar I used that night still has dirt in it from that show.

STEVEN: It was kind of the opposite of the Madame Wong's show where we were on acid and nobody else was; this time we were the only ones who *weren't* on acid. We jammed it out the best we could, but all I could think about was that it was freezing cold, this girl with the mohawk nearly killed us all, and what the hell was Carmel Moran thinking when she booked this show for us?

JEFF: There was no heat, no firewood, no water, no food, no bathroom facilities, and the buses that everyone had taken out to the desert were just rickety old school buses. I managed to hitch a ride home with D. Boon of the Minutemen; he probably saved me from dying out there, because suddenly people were leaving on the buses, and we found out that the person who drove us to the gig didn't have plans to get us out of there. We were lucky to have had friends there with cars, but it was a total afterthought. We were all at the age where we hadn't realised yet that people actually die out in the desert in these kinds of conditions.

After all was said and done, though, it *was* really fun. I remember walking way out on this plateau and hearing Sonic

Youth's music floating through the desert; there was no light pollution, and the night sky was beautiful. We later became friends with tons of people who were there that night, and for many of them it was like this Woodstock scenario, this mystical religious experience. But, you know, they were out in the desert on acid; for us, it had just been this stressful, terrible day. We did have fun with it, but there was no other choice; it was either that or start crying.

Though cool enough to fit comfortably on a bill with Sonic Youth, and still retaining enough punk credibility to open for Social Distortion, by early 1985 Redd Kross were also finding themselves on bills with metal bands. By early 1985, the LA 'hair metal' scene was in full flight; local acts Mötley Crüe, Quiet Riot and Ratt had achieved multi-platinum success, and swarms of spandex-clad, Aquanet-misted hopefuls were descending upon the Sunset Strip and San Fernando Valley in hopes of following in their footsteps.

With their long hair, flashy stage clothes, love of KISS, Alice Cooper and the New York Dolls, and – thanks to the addition of Robert Hecker – a shredding lead guitarist, there were many places on a Venn diagram where Redd Kross and eighties hair metal might have crossed; and the fact that *Teen Babes From Monsanto* was being distributed by Enigma Records, which had recently scored a surprise hit with the debut EP from Christian metal band Stryper, further linked them to a scene that they had deep misgivings about being associated with. On January 26, 1985, Redd Kross played a bill at the Country Club in Reseda, California with fellow Enigma metal acts Leatherwolf and Poison, the latter of whom would quickly become the very bane of Jeff and Steven's existence.

JEFF: The LA metal scene was actually really fun at the beginning. I would occasionally go to the Troubadour to see the heaviest of these bands, knowing full well that they were kind of braindead,

138

and that there was a certain kind of filthiness you would feel from being exposed to such moronic presentations. It would still deliver on a certain level; like, back when W.A.S.P. was only drawing about a hundred people, they were kind of fun to watch.

STEVEN: We thought of a lot of the metal musicians as far beyond us, technically. We'd actually asked the drummer from W.A.S.P. to play on *Teen Babes*, because we used to always see W.A.S.P. at the Troubadour around '83; they put on this crazy KISS kind of show, and they were really kind of aggressive and weird, not at all like their records.

JEFF: And Ratt were hilarious; people forget that Ratt were one of the first LA metal bands to have a radio hit, with 'Round And Round', even though Stephen Pearcy's voice made Vince Neil sound like Paul Rodgers. Guns N' Roses kind of toyed with the glam thing, too, but they were a tough band that loved Aerosmith, so I got it with those guys. And there were bands like Jet Boy who had one foot in the punk scene, so they were acceptable. But all the glam bands seemed completely moronic, or just really weak.

STEVEN: People would say to us, 'You guys like the New York Dolls? Well, you gotta check out this new band Poison. You're gonna love 'em!' And I'm sort of sceptical, but also interested. But then we play that show with them at the Country Club, and we're just kind of standing there watching them with our jaws hanging open.

JEFF: It was the Coco Smith-era Poison, before they got C.C. DeVille, so they weren't huge yet. But they'd rented these big prom limos to take them to the gig, and they'd hung this hand-drawn sign on the dressing room door that said, 'The Glitter Glam Slam Kings of Noise.' And then they get onstage and it's just this terrible, terrible Van Halen impersonation.

STEVEN: They sounded nothing like the Dolls; there was no danger in the music at all. CoCo Smith was wearing a Sex Pistols T-shirt, which was like the edgiest thing about them, but the rest of them were wearing sparkly clothes, which was more in the vein of like the women from the TV show *Dynasty* than the Dolls' 'beat-up transvestite' look. And I just felt myself leaving my body over the very idea that people would think that we would feel a kinship with them, that we would somehow be comrades-in-arms with these clowns. It was just total humiliation.

JEFF: We'd grown up loving the New York Dolls and The Runaways, and we'd paid for it – we'd had to take all this shit at school for liking them. And now all these glam bands are showing up on our turf pretending that they're influenced by them, and people are loving them… It was just too much for us to take.

Between the desert expedition and the Poison associations, it was all definitely too much for Dave Peterson to take, and he tendered his resignation in order to concentrate on his own musical endeavours. Glenn Holland, former drummer of metal band Pandemonium, joined Redd Kross, but abruptly left the band in the summer of 1985 on the eve of their first US tour.

JEFF: Glenn had a full-on Mötley Crüe double kick drum kit and a Vince Neil hairdo, but he was a really talented drummer. He knew a lot of our punk friends from Orange County, but he was trying to make it big in the metal world. We did some great shows with him; it gave us this new power, having this crazed, Tommy Lee-quality drummer in the band.

STEVEN: The thing about musicians from the metal world is that they were all very career oriented. They'd all taken business classes at MIT that were like, 'How to Get Signed.' And it was like, if you're a drummer, stick with a band for six months; if they don't get signed by then, move on to the next group. And that was definitely Glenn's mentality with us. He was a really nice guy and a great drummer, and I felt really confident playing with him. But he had a girlfriend who was not into us; she would come to our practices and just sit there with her arms folded, glaring at him; I don't think she thought we were his ticket to success. He wound up pulling out of the band like two nights before we were supposed to go on tour. He was like, 'I forgot to tell you – I can't go.'

JEFF: It was the weirdest thing on earth. Enigma had even given us a couple thousand dollars to go on this tour, because we were supposed to make our next record with them. Steven and I had looked for a week trying to find a used van; we didn't know what we were doing, but we finally found this incredible 1970s Ford Country Squire station wagon, exactly like the Brady Bunch used to drive, with the wood panelling and everything. So now we were finally about to go out on our first tour, and Glenn completely ghosted us. Luckily, Dave was totally into going. At this point, Dave was kind of my unofficial brother-in-law, so it wasn't like he'd left the band on bad terms; if he was able to do it, we were really happy to have him come along.

STEVEN: It's the summer of 1985, and I had just graduated high school. We left for the tour on the day of Live Aid, and we were listening to the live simulcast in the station wagon. We hadn't finalised the deal on the station wagon and the U-Haul trailer until 24 hours before our first show, and then we got a bubble in our tyre in Arizona, and none of us know how to change a tyre. So right away we're off to a great start; we wind up cancelling the first few dates, but finally make it to Houston in time for our show there.

Robert's father was this enigmatic character, this political hippie who was very counterculture but not at all based in rock'n'roll. When Robert explained that he was gonna go on tour, his father told him, 'If you leave the house to go do that masturbatory bullshit, don't come back here.' Robert didn't have a home to go to on the way back, so he came on tour with all of his worldly possessions in three gigantic Glad bags, all of which were stuffed in the trailer along with all of our stage clothes – which was basically entire Salvation Army drop-off containers emptied into the trailer – and our amplifiers. It was complete chaos back there.

JEFF: Black Flag had kind of written the book on DIY touring, putting together a network of underground clubs and promoters, and SST had started their own booking agency that was run by Chuck Dukowski. He kind of reluctantly agreed to book our tour, but they didn't really know what they were doing yet, because there weren't that many bands on our level touring at the time. And none of us knew what to do; we didn't know anything about routing – we had about six weeks' worth of dates written down, and we just showed up to them. We didn't know you had to call and make sure the show was going to happen.

STEVEN: We quickly learned that our itinerary was like a book of lies, a book of false hopes. Half the shows would be like, 'Oh, you're here – we didn't think you were going to show up! Yeah, I guess we can do a show.' But sometimes it would be, 'Oh, the show was cancelled two weeks ago.' And there was one show where they were like, 'Oh wait, your singer plays guitar? We don't have a microphone stand.' So someone taped a microphone to a broomstick, and then held it in front of Jeff's face while we played the show.

JEFF: The shows would be like, half-empty, and we'd have to make these long drives between them in the Country Squire, with no real plan of where to stay whenever we got where we were supposed to be going. Dave was driving through

Louisiana one night at four in the morning; we wake up and the car and trailer are just zigzagging all over the highway.

STEVEN: Dave had closed his eyes for a second and fallen asleep on that long, terrifying stretch of Interstate 10 that goes over the swamps. Luckily, Dave Travis, our friend who went along on that tour as our roadie, was in the passenger seat and grabbed the wheel before we jacked up the trailer hitch or flew over the side of the highway into the bog. That would have been the end of us, right there.

We were always afraid to sleep on people's floors. Like, we knew that it was part of the code, a very Black Flag thing to do, but I didn't ever want to sleep next to someone's cat box. I'm still like a suburban kid, and if we can find a Holiday Inn that we can afford, I want to do that. And of course, we weren't budgeting anything properly, so we couldn't afford anything.

But there were some high points. When we played in Raleigh, we met these people Bill Mooney and Barbara Herring, who told us we could crash at their place. It turned out they'd rented this big old house in downtown Raleigh, and they had just got this silk screen set up and were making silk screens of the Madonna pictorial that had just come out in *Penthouse*. Instead of sleeping, we stayed up all night making nude Madonna shirts with Bill and Barbara, and kind of became friends for life. A few years later, they started a legitimate merchandising company, Tannis Root. It's still going today, and we're credited as their first artist.

JEFF: We played at the famous Danceteria in New York, which Madonna had been haunting just a year or two earlier – the 'Into The Groove' scene in *Desperately Seeking Susan* was shot there. We had a big guarantee there, like $3,000, because all those shady, mafia-type clubs paid really well.

STEVEN: Much to our surprise, the show was packed, and everything really landed that night – with New York, it was love

143

at first sight. I remember we met Ann Magnuson that night, and she was losing her mind like we were The Beatles; she actually jumped up on stage in the middle of the set, grabbed Robert and made out with him. And Thurston Moore was hanging out with us backstage, raving about how we'd brought sunshine to the New York darkness.

JEFF: That Danceteria money was supposed to pay for the rest of our tour. Robert was the one in charge of handling the money, because he was the most responsible. The next day, we're driving in to Boston to play The Rat, and we get completely lost. So Robert gets out at a payphone to call the club and get directions. He comes back to the car, and we take off, and then he's like, 'Dudes, I think I left the money in the phone booth.' We went back, but of course it was gone.

STEVEN: We did have a great show at The Rat that night, so the good news was that we played two great shows in two important cities in the Northeast; the bad news was that we'd lost all of our money. I think we had a week of shows left at that point; we did one or two more, and then just said, 'Fuck it' and went home. Chuck Dukowski was out on tour with SWA, so we had no communication with him at all for weeks; we didn't even bother calling to let him know that we were cutting three or four dates at the end.

JEFF: When Dinosaur Jr. opened up for us a couple of years later, and J Mascis told us that they'd gone through the same thing as us when they were touring in '85, because they were also being booked by SST at the time. I think our parents wired us like five hundred bucks; along with the $500 we made at The Rat, it was barely enough to get home. It was gnarly, but we still had fun, and we made it back alive.

STEVEN: And we all came home with nude Madonna shirts.

Flyer for the band's May 21, 1986 gig at The Whisky a Go Go in West Hollywood. (Courtesy of Geoffrey Weiss)

Terry and Jeff McDonald, 1965.
(Courtesy of McDonald Family Archives)

Janet McDonald in front of the family's house on W. 115th Street in
Hawthorne, late 1960s. (Courtesy of the McDonald Family Archives)

Steven, back home in Hawthorne following his kidnapping ordeal, 1981. (Photo by Jeff McDonald)

Images from the Beach Litter Walk free concert in Santa Monica, 1982. (Photos by Betsy Devine)

Lost in the desert: A flyer for the legendary Gila Monster Jamboree. (Courtesy of Geoffrey Weiss)

Somewhere in America with Dave Peterson and Robert Hecker on the *Teen Babes* tour, 1985. (Photo by Chuck Kelley)

An alternate photo from the *Neurotica* cover photo session, 1987. (Photo by John Scarpati)

Redd Kross rock UMASS Boston, 1989. (Photo by Michelle Smith)

Atlantic Records promotional postcard for *Third Eye*, 1990. Original artwork by Vicki Berndt. (Courtesy of Geoffrey Weiss)

In London with pal Mike Dalke for the 1992 Finsbury Park festival. (Photo by Ella Black)

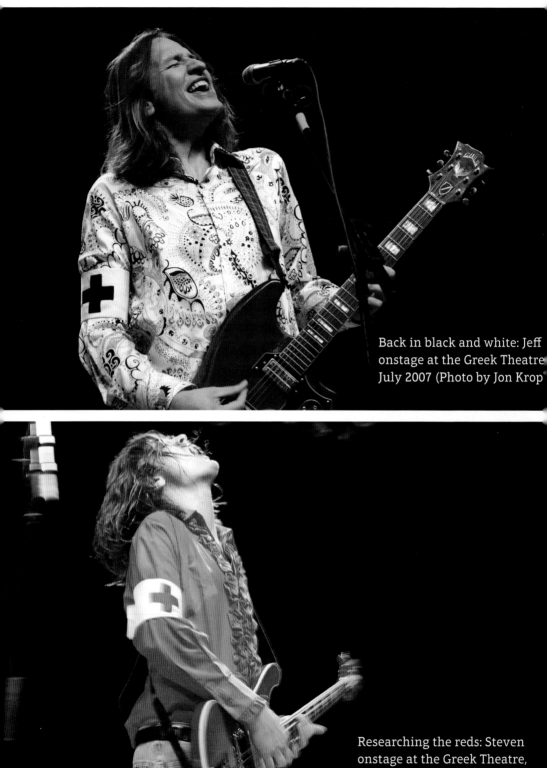

Back in black and white: Jeff onstage at the Greek Theatre July 2007 (Photo by Jon Krop)

Researching the reds: Steven onstage at the Greek Theatre, July 2007. (Photo by Jon Krop)

The *Neurotica* lineup, reunited and looking sharp for a November 2007 show at Slim's in San Francsico. (Photo by Jon Krop)

With longtime inspiration John Waters at the 2017 Mosswood Meltdown. (Courtesy of Jason Shapiro)

Beyond the Door lineup with Dale Crover and Jason Shapiro, 2019.
(Photo by Julian Fort)

The 'Candy Coloured Catastrophe' video shoot, April 2024, with Astrid McDonald
filling in on guitar. (Photo by Gilbert Trejo)

Chapter 13

A WASTE OF GOOD BRAIN POWER

Having successfully weathered their first cross-country tour, it was time for Redd Kross to start thinking about the follow-up to *Teen Babes From Monsanto*, and a rock opera seemed like the obvious next move. With competent new managers in their corner and an agreement for a new record in place with Enigma Records, it seemed as if the band were poised to take things to the next level. Unfortunately, drugs and a penchant for absurd (and potentially self-defeating) pranks were taking precedence at this point for Jeff and Steven over things like songwriting and musical development.

STEVEN: We'd first met John Silva in San Francisco when he was Jello Biafra's roommate. He moved down to LA at some point and started managing The Three O'Clock, and he was really persistent about wanting to manage us.

JEFF: We always managed to make records, we managed to play shows, but there was only so much we could do on our own. And we also were, like, being stupid druggie teenagers, so we were kind of stalled. John was starting a management thing with Spock from the band Backstage Pass, and they slowly started handling all of our affairs, and things started becoming more organised and together.

STEVEN: John had a lot of 'new guy in town' energy, and I think he needed to put it somewhere. Jeff and I weren't born into our connections, but we were very social people, and I think we were always viewed from afar as people who were connected to something, who had our finger on the pulse, so I think John was attracted to that. And Spock was definitely connected; she'd worked in and around the music business for a while, and was friends with a lot of A&R people. We would have thought she was cooler than John, but John eventually seemed more competent. Not that we deserved more competence.

JEFF: After we did *Teen Babes*, I was thinking that our next record should be a concept album, like a rock opera. We were still on Enigma Records, and we were to the point of talking about which producers we wanted to work with; we told them that our dream was to work with Sonny Bono. The album was supposed to be called *The Shroud Of Laurie Bono Christ* – the title is part of a poem that came with the original *Teen Babes From Monsanto*. Laurie, of course, was Laurie Partridge from the Partridge Family; and Bono was Sonny, not the Bono from U2. I commend Bill Hein at Enigma for completely taking this concept seriously, even though we weren't in any condition to see it through.

STEVEN: Kim Fowley was kind of keeping tabs on us; we would do a Runaways song at a show, and then we'd get a call from him at our parents' house the next day. Like, 'I heard you played 'Neon Angels On The Road To Ruin' last night. Well, I've got three others just like it, but better!' He was so funny, but so crazy; we would be laughing at him as much as we were laughing with him.

JEFF: Kim would always give us this whole spiel about how he had 250 published songs and eleven gold records, and that he had all these great unrecorded songs that we should record. And I'm like, 'I think we're good; we're putting a rock opera together.' He's like, 'Well, I *have* a rock opera!' I'm like, 'Really?!?'

And we're thinking, 'Wow!' I mean, the idea of writing the music to a Kim Fowley rock opera that's produced by Sonny Bono? That's where our heads were for our next record. But then he sent it to our house, in manuscript form, and it was just *so* bad. It was called *Roommates*, and it was just this really bad kind of theatrical piece. I was like, 'Oh my god, how are we gonna tell him that we are *not* gonna do this?' Because it was so terrible.

It just got pushed under the rug for a while; we weren't ready to make a record, anyway. Later on, he called and wanted me to send it back to him, but I couldn't find it. And the weird thing about it is, I was recently going through this one upper closet at my parents' house that still has stuff in it from when we lived there, and I found the envelope for it – addressed from Kim Fowley to me at my parents' house – but it was empty. I looked everywhere, and I still can't find it. So that's one of my holy grails, to find the manuscript to *Roommates* by Kim Fowley.

STEVEN: Kim wanted to produce us, but I think Enigma had only promised to give us like $8,000 to make a record. By today's standards, that's actually a pretty decent budget, especially with inflation, but by 1985 standards that wasn't much. And then Kim told me that Enigma had given Poison $25,000. And oh man, that just sent me through the roof. I was outraged. Having to watch the rise of Poison was so painful for the teenage Steven McDonald; to be labelmates with them, and have people think we somehow had anything in common with those assholes, was just mortifying.

JEFF: I mean, now I'm like, 'Good for them, they found their thing.' But at the time, because we had close ties and we were considered peers – even though we never exchanged a single word with them – it was really annoying. And I have to say I prefer Vince Neil's voice over Bret Michaels', any day.

STEVEN: At some point I actually marched into the office of Bill Hein, the president of Enigma Records, and said, 'Kim Fowley told us you're giving Poison $25,000. And I just want to tell you that you're wasting this company's money. That band's not going to amount to anything!' I was probably 17 at the time. Flash forward a year later to when *Look What The Cat Dragged In* comes out and is getting a lot of MTV airplay; by then, we're actively destroying our reputation with our own record label by crank calling them on a daily basis.

JEFF: We were always into playing pranks and making crank calls, but I think we probably pushed it to the edge a bit by targeting Enigma while we were still on the label.

STEVEN: Stryper was doing really well at the time, and both them and Poison were both on Enigma. We used to call Enigma, pretending to be various members of those two bands, and we would make complaints about how much attention they were giving to the other band. It would be like, 'This is Michael Sweet from Stryper. Poison's getting so much support, and we can't get any love from the label. This is bullshit – and it's pissing both Jesus *and* us off!' Or then it would be like, 'This is C.C. DeVille from Poison – I'm seeing all these Stryper albums in the record stores, but I can't find our records anywhere. What the fuck is going on?' We were literally calling our own project manager, and saying this shit to them in our whiny, recognisable voices.

JEFF: We also crank called Gloria Bennett, who was famous for being the vocal coach of the worst singers in Los Angeles – she advertised that she worked with Vince Neil and Bret Michaels. And she later worked with Anthony Keidis, so that's quite the trifecta right there. Steven and I actually took classes with her a few times, and it was absolutely horrifying; she was this big, heavyset opera lady who had this whole classical approach of yelling at you if you weren't doing it right, and forcing you to put your hand on her abdomen so you could feel her diaphragm move when she sang properly. So we left some messages on her machine where we pretended in hoarse voices that we were Robert Sweet and Bret Michaels, and that she'd blown out our vocal cords with her bad instruction.

STEVEN: 'You've destroyed my voice and ruined my career! I'm going to sue you!' So she gets all upset and takes the tapes to Enigma and plays it for them, and the same project manager we've been crank calling goes, 'That's not Robert Sweet. That sounds like Jeff McDonald.'

JEFF: I remember John Silva calling us in a panic – 'What did you guys *do* to Enigma?' We didn't admit to him that we'd done it, but he knew we did; he knew us. He was like, 'How are we going to explain this to the A&R person at Enigma?' So rather than come clean, we threw a friend of ours under the bus. I called our friend Paul Koudounaris, aka Paul K from the band Imperial Butt Wizards, and said, 'We don't know what to do. Can we blame it on you?'

STEVEN: We told Enigma, 'Oh, that was our friend Paul. He's a really mischievous character, and he somehow got ahold of our Rolodex. We're sorry.'

JEFF: It was such bullshit, such a sad lie. But in order for Enigma to save face, we had to make it look like *we* were the victims, too. It was the ultimate act of passive-aggression.

STEVEN: But then the A&R person at Enigma told us, 'I want you to write an apology to the Stryper organisation and the Poison organisation,' and there were all these other stipulations and conditions about what we needed to do to gain redemption.

JEFF: We told Paul we had to write apologies to Poison and Stryper, and he goes, 'I'll do it. I'll write an apology on a tortilla with a sharpie and send it to them.' That was the first thing that came to his head.

STEVEN: I always thought it was going to be a ballpoint pen on a tortilla. But either way, I remember thinking that it was a really funny idea. I don't think we ever executed it, though.

JEFF: It was all kind of dropped once we were able to find a scapegoat to blame, someone that they didn't know. It just kind of went away. But it would've been a great ending to the story if there really was documentation of the Poison and Stryper organisations receiving apology letters on tortillas.

For some reason, our relationship with Enigma wasn't ended by that fiasco. I think our relationship just kind of fizzled out because we never got around to making a record for them; and by the time we *were* ready to make another record, we were already talking to another label and Enigma was busy shipping out millions of copies of *Look What The Cat Dragged In*.

That whole incident should have put the kibosh on our pranks, but that's the thing with being a habitual prankster. Getting caught that time should have been like, 'Oh my god, I'm an adult – I can't be doing these things.' But of course it kept going; like, later on, we'd be on tour and we'd be calling our road manager from the back of the van while he was driving, pretending to be the promoter calling to cancel shows. I mean, you're bored – what else are you supposed to do? But it's such a waste of good brain power, I will say that. I mean, we could have been putting that energy into writing really creative songs.

Redd Kross only played about a dozen shows between the end of their 1985 tour and the beginning of 1987, largely due to Jeff's intensifying addiction issues. Thanks to the efforts of their parents, Steven and Jeff's girlfriend Vicki Peterson – the latter of whom would later appear with Jeff in a sweet yet cringe-inducing TV spot for the RAD ('Rockers Against Drugs') campaign – Jeff was finally able to get clean. In typical Redd Kross fashion, however, his rehab attempts were not without humorous incident.

JEFF: There were so many great things that happened in the period between *Born Innocent* and *Neurotica*, but that period is sometimes a little foggy for me, because that was kind of the 'trashcan drug' era. We were hanging out in Hollywood, all kinds of drugs were easily available, and just about everyone we knew still had the Darby Crash philosophy of drug taking – you know, just take anything someone hands you. So it was starting to influence everything, and the thing it influenced most was our ability to function as a band. It would occasionally lead to these incredibly magical moments, but it eventually took its toll to where everything came to a stop.

STEVEN: All these ridiculous shenanigans have been going on for a couple years, and they're just getting out of hand by the time we started talking to Big Time Records about making the record that would become *Neurotica*. We'd gone from experimenting with things like psychedelics and psychotropics, smoking a lot of pot and taking a lot of acid, to getting into heavier things like opiates. I was always the 'good boy' – I would be Jeff's partner in crime on the weekends, but I also always made sure I could get my homework done. But by 1986, the year after I graduated from high school, Jeff had taken that sort of ridiculous, fun, loose party vibe way too seriously, and gotten himself into a really nasty habit.

It was really scary. He was like 30 pounds underweight, and constantly lying to us or giving us some lame excuse so that he could go get drugs; it was like Jeff had left the building and something else had entered his body. We came to blows so many times. The one that sticks in my head the most is the time where he wanted me to take him down to the Crenshaw/ Adams district to score drugs, and I refused. I was driving and we were on the 101 Freeway; he was in the backseat, and my girlfriend was in the passenger seat. I was like, 'No, fuck you.' And he grabbed my hair and pulled my head down behind the passenger seat, while I was driving at five o'clock in the afternoon in moderate traffic. And that was the kind of shit that was going down – violent, scary, horrible shit where we all should have died.

JEFF: When you're taking opioids, you become physically addicted to them, and it's kind of hard to hide it. I was in big trouble. My parents knew what was going on, and they were just like, 'You *have* to do something about this.' It was horrible at home, and my girlfriend Vicki was very straight edge. I was about to lose everything.

I was ahead of the curve, in a way. Everyone knows about AA and treatment centres now, but at that point in the mid-eighties, I didn't know a single person who had ever been to AA or rehab, so I didn't know a thing about any of these programmes. And the first one I went to was hilarious. I had seen a flyer for this drug programme that had Melanie, one of my favourite singers, and Nicky Hopkins on it, saying, 'I got control of my life through Narconon!' I figured it would be like a rock'n'roll centre.

So my mom takes me to do the intake thing, and I meet with the administration before I agree to sign up. And this guy hands me *Dianetics* and a glossary to go with it. I'm like, 'Wait – is this Scientology?' And he goes, 'Oh no, no, no – we just use some of the *principles* of Scientology!' I knew about Scientology on a cult level because I was so fascinated with cults, but I didn't know how they operated. But the guy was like, 'I used to be like you, but now I can drink wine!' They tell you what you want to hear, so I'm like, 'Okay, I'll be open to it.'

The problem was, I signed up as an outpatient, and everyone else there was in-patient. I would have to drive halfway to Hollywood every day from Hawthorne, and the place was such a dump, and everything we did was so stupid. They tell you, 'Oh, you'll do sauna therapy where you stay in the sauna for eight hours, and all the drugs will be released from your fatty tissue and you become very, very high and experience all these repressed memories.' And I was waiting for that, I *wanted* that, but they never got around to that with me. Instead, we had to do all these confrontation exercises where you insult another person while looking into their eyes; and if you messed up and started laughing, you had to start over. The idea of insulting people to their face sounded fun, but it got boring pretty quickly.

They had a clay table, where you're supposed to find your inner child by working with clay. And while we were sitting there doing that, our instructor was being audited. These people would come in and tell her, 'Confront the room! Confront the ceiling!' And she'd be like, 'I've confronted the ceiling.' 'Confront the saltshaker!' 'I've confronted the saltshaker.' It was all this insane shit.

And then they took me in to be audited. Well, I know now that it's called being audited, but I didn't at the time. When you see pictures of the Scientology e-meters now, they're all high-tech. But at the time, the e-meters were, like, soup cans and a battery tester. The guy's being really serious, handing me these cans, and I'm like, 'Oh wow. These are like soup cans and a battery tester!' And they're really pissed.

They were trying to pretend like they really believed in what they were doing, but they were asking me all these really stupid questions while I was holding these soup cans, and I was just laughing at them. I think I was impervious to their influence, because on the way there every day, I always got loaded. So I had that shield of protection; for me it was just entertaining, and it got everyone off my back for a while because I was 'in treatment.' But I just eventually stopped going. They called me a couple years later to check in on me. I was like, 'I'm fine.' And they were like, 'Okay, we're done with you.' They didn't even want me; I was rejected by Scientology.

STEVEN: That was Jeff's first foray into recovery, and it made me very embittered about the Church of Scientology. Before, I would have just been like, 'It's innocuous, just avoid it.' But then to know that they had lured innocent people like my parents into it under false pretences, and that they would deny they were affiliated with Scientology even while working out of the *Dianetics* workbook…

So, that didn't work for Jeff, and it took him another year or so before he ended up in a facility that actually worked for him. It was a harrowing time; I've blacked out much of it, but I just remember trying to stay on track with our band, and feeling like I just didn't know what was going on with him, or whether or not I could trust that he would show up to anything. And whether or not he was gonna be safe. It was really scary. He finally went to the Daniel Freeman Hospital in Marina Del Rey, where Kurt Cobain famously went several years later, before he escaped and killed himself. Fortunately, it worked for Jeff.

JEFF: We found it through our family doctor, who had worked at the hospital and told us about their treatment centre. I was there for thirty days. I was one of the only white guys in the place, so it was an interesting cultural exchange to hang out with all these Black dudes. I was wearing an Oingo Boingo T-shirt one time, with all these skulls on it, and they were like, 'Hey man, what's with the skulls?' And I was like, 'Oh, I believe in Satan.' Even if they were gang members or scary crackheads, these guys had grown up going to church and were very superstitious, so that really freaked them out. They thought I *was* Satan. But eventually we all became friends.

There was a famous baseball player in there with us named Ellis Valentine. He was famous for having the most powerful arm in baseball, but drugs had ruined his career; according to him, a lot of guys in baseball at the time were freebasing on airplanes, and it was a really drugged out scene. He was a big guy with a big personality, and he was always the star of the show at our group therapy meetings. I got along with him okay, but he was a real flexer; he would be like, 'As soon as I get out of here, I'm gonna buy a boat!' One day, he started hassling me for not participating in group. I was really messed up on speed and opioids when I went in; I was just a zombie, and it took me some time to come out of it. I could barely talk, but when he started hassling me, I snapped out of it and told him, 'Fuck you – all you ever talk about is what a big star you are and your fucking boat.' I thought that was an honest exchange, but when the session was over he waited for me outside the door and sucker-punched me as I left the room.

The funny thing was, it didn't hurt. His hand was so huge, it was like it was padded; and I hit the floor so fast that at first I didn't even know what happened. He was kicked out of the programme immediately, but we ran into each other at a meeting a couple months later; he'd gone to another treatment centre and got clean, and he completely apologised. So we were totally good. I found him on Facebook a few years ago, and he was running a youth recovery centre and seemed totally happy; I hope he's doing well. Maybe he had to get kicked out to get humbled; because he wasn't humbled at all when we were in treatment together, and I was just, like, not having it. But the place worked for me – after thirty days and being punched by Ellis Valentine, I was fine. I stayed sober for many years before I'd have any other run-ins with that behaviour.

The Rock Against Drugs ad that Vicki and I did together was truly an embarrassment, though. Not because of her – she was great, because she was always so supportive. She drove me to rehab when I finally got clean, after she had already dealt with a lot from me. I was completely out of my mind, and she was this very studious, smart, talented, focused, very intelligent person who put up with me for years. How did she do it?

Miles Copeland had the idea for this project about drug awareness, and I think he was coming from a very good place, but all the other people who did the spots – people like Vince Neil and Belinda Carlisle – were all still completely out of their minds on drugs. I was the only one who wasn't. I had gone through rehab; maybe Vince went to court-appointed rehab, but I don't think he ever got clean. And I know it took a while for Belinda to get clean; she definitely wasn't at that time.

The director didn't have much of a prompt for us; they just kind of wanted us to talk, so we babbled for a bit and then they took like ten seconds of it and put some sad music on it. We looked like we'd been through hell and high water by that point, which we had, but it was just super embarrassing. And then it aired, and people kept saying, 'I saw you on MTV!' And it was like, oh god…

One thing about the treatment centre was that, in order to keep us focused, they didn't have any radios or televisions in there. They had a common room with a TV in it, but people were always watching religious programmes on it – the kind of things I watched for fun when I was on drugs.

And then, near the end of my stay, they had a picnic for us out in Marina Del Rey, and someone had 'Strawberry Fields Forever' playing. I hadn't heard music in a month, and it was so inspirational; I realised at that moment how desperate I was to make music and play guitar again. Steven and I wrote 'Peach Kelli Pop' together the day I got home from treatment.

Steven with Kim Shattuck and Melanie Vammen of The Pandoras, Cavern Club bathroom, 1985. (Photo by Dianne Carter)

Chapter 14

PURPLE ELECTRICITY

As the Hollywood music scene continued to shift, morph and mutate, by 1985 a dedicated segment of its denizens were looking back to the 1960s for inspiration. Rejecting the synthetic sounds of eighties rock and the big hair and big shoulder pads of eighties fashion, Southern California bands like The Unclaimed, Thee Fourgiven, The Pandoras and The Tell-Tale Hearts were sporting vintage paisley shirts, hip-huggers and miniskirts, strapping on vintage guitars and playing tough, three-chord garage rock as if 1967 had never happened, much less 1977.

For these bands and their fans, the centre of the LA scene was the Cavern Club, a weekends-only nightclub operated by Greg Shaw, proprietor of the indie labels Bomp and Voxx. Though Redd Kross technically weren't a 'Cavern band' – their music drew from too many diverse post-'67 influences for them to be considered as such, to say nothing of their seventies-centric fashion sense – it was through Shaw's club that Jeff and Steven would make some crucial connections, as well as back one of their idols, former Seeds frontman Sky Saxon, on 'the worst record ever made.'

JEFF: We were friends with a lot of the regulars from that scene, as well as Greg Shaw, who we had a lot of respect for. The Cavern Club was home to the sixties garage band movement that was happening in LA at the time, and it was kind of centred on a handful of bands that were on Voxx Records, and these girls that did authentic go-go dances like The Pony, and people who were very dedicated to the historically accurate look of the day. The Rolling Stones were like the gods of that scene, especially Brian Jones, but nothing after 1966 – those were the rules. But we loved that music, too, so we hung out there. We were like the honorary freaks, because we didn't have the chilli-bowl haircuts or adhere to the rules of the uniforms for that movement, but we ended up having a lot of fun there.

STEVEN: The Cavern was in an old dance studio on the second floor of a building on Hollywood Boulevard, which you entered through an alley off Cahuenga. Coincidentally, we rehearsed for a while at an old bank building one block down on Ivar. I started hanging out at the Cavern when I was in eleventh grade, and it was a pretty magical time. The place could hold about 150 people, and it was a place for bands of a specific retro ilk. It wasn't like groovy sixties beads, peace signs and granny glasses; it was like the girls all looked like *Hullabaloo* dancers from a specific September 1965 episode. I was never as narrow as that – like, I had written CRAMPS STOOGES SEEDS on my denim school binder at the time— but I loved the music, and I was accepted into the scene.

JEFF: We were there the night Sky Saxon made his return to the Cavern Club, which was like the most insane thing. Because The Seeds were total gods of this scene, but Sky had been living in Hawaii for years with a cult called the Source Family, where he had a hundred dogs and changed his name to Sky Sunlight Saxon. And for some reason, he had suddenly come back.

STEVEN: He showed up with Lee Joseph, who was like the elder statesman of the Cavern Club scene. My memory is that Sky was barefoot and wearing a blanket, and he looked like Lee had literally just fished him out of the waves at El Porto Beach or something. It was like this *Close Encounters* moment, where everyone is making contact for the first time with the legendary leader of The Seeds, but being careful not to make too many fast motions that might scare him away. And I think about what it must have been like for Sky, who had been lost in the South Pacific Island chain wearing a K-Mart blanket for who knows how long, and professing that dog love is the only thing that matters, and now he's back in Los Angeles being swarmed and worshipped by these 16-year-olds who look straight out of 1965. It must have been like a *Twilight Zone* episode for him. I remember loving the moment, but also appreciating just how insane it was.

JEFF: He was just this bizarre, eccentric hippie dude, and everyone was tripping out. I actually drove him home that night. He was like, 'Could you drive me home, man?' And I remember talking to him during the drive, and he just seemed really spun out, and then he had me drop him off at some giant mansion in Bel-Air.

STEVEN: Very soon after this very timid meeting moment, Sky went from being a shy beach hippie to marching into the club and making a beeline straight for the stage. He'd get up there, and people would be excited at first, but then everyone would quickly realise that Sky '85 is not Sky '65. He was just kind of winging it, but not in a very happening way. And his ego was just insane – he just kind of assumed that everybody would have 'Pushin' Too Hard' on boil, just waiting for him to show up. But before he wore out his welcome, we got to be his backup for the *Sky Saxon Purple Electricity* live album, which Jeff likes to call 'the worst album ever made'. He likes to take credit for being a part of that.

JEFF: Greg Shaw asked us to back Sky for a show, but we didn't know that they were going to be recording it. Sky would never rehearse with us, and we weren't the kind of musicians at the time that could just play anything, so we just kind of winged it.

STEVEN: Just dealing with Sky's ego was insane. I could probably pathologise him in a much more articulate way now, but I couldn't then; I just remember thinking, like, 'What is *wrong* with this dude?' I love his music; I was a huge fan of everything that I knew. But I remember Jeff interviewing him on KXLU and asking him questions like, 'What do you think of The Rolling Stones?' And he went down this whole rabbit hole about The Seeds playing the Hollywood Bowl, and his final statement was like, 'All I can really say about The Rolling Stones is that we never outsold them, but they never outsold us.' It was such a weird, fragile ego crack, you know? And as an ambitious young musician, it was confusing and disturbing, and I didn't quite understand what was at play.

JEFF: We opened by jamming on 'Dazed And Confused' until Sky came out, and all these bowl-haircut kids and girls in miniskirts were like in mourning; they were so bummed out that we were playing Led Zeppelin. And then we did a couple of Seeds songs, but Sky wouldn't come in at the right time and he would have his back to the audience; we were doing the ones that we knew, which were mostly very heavy and weird songs from *The Future*, The Seeds' concept album, and then we ran out of songs, so we did 'Cherry Bomb' by The Runaways, and some KISS song I can't remember, and Sky just kind of free-formed it and made up the lyrics. All this stuff we're doing actually comes out as an album without us even knowing it was being recorded, and it's credited as 'all songs written by Sky Saxon.' It really is the worst album ever, but I kind of love it, knowing that we were kind of there to freak out all the Cavern people for being so ridiculous, and then Sky was being so weird.

STEVEN: We did do some other recordings with Sky that I would love to find. It was another Greg Shaw thing – he put us in the studio with Brett Gurewitz of Bad Religion and Epitaph Records behind the controls, and it was Jeff, me and Debbi Peterson on drums; this was right around the time of The Bangles' first album, with 'Hero Takes A Fall.' And Mars Bonfire, who'd written 'Born To Be Wild' for Steppenwolf, was on keyboards. I remember Sky saying to Jeff, 'Hey man, can you play more like Robbie Krieger?' Which was probably a decent suggestion, but that's not what we were doing.

JEFF: We met Roy McDonald at the Cavern Club. He was playing drums for a band called The Things, and he was kind of the Keith Moon of the Cavern scene, a flashy, really powerful drummer. We had a lot of mutual friends, and by the time we got back from our first tour, where Dave filled in for Glenn, we asked him if he wanted to come over and jam with us at this cool old Raymond Chandler type of office building up the street where we were practising.

STEVEN: When we went out on that tour with Dave, I already knew that I was going to call Roy McDonald when we got home and see if I couldn't tempt him away from his band. But it was hard because, just like Dave, he had skin in the game with a band with his friend, and he didn't wanna let them down, even though they didn't have nearly as much going on as us. And we would've been really rolling our eyes at that because any kind of entity that wasn't all about us and valued anything other than us on anywhere near the same level would have been worthy of nothing but just severe eye rolls. But at any rate, we got him to join.

JEFF: Roy was very much like us, in the sense where he was a record geek, a music history buff. He didn't have the same David Bowie/Iggy Pop knowledge that we did, but otherwise

165

his knowledge at the time was even more advanced than mine. I remember Roy really turned me on to The Kinks; I loved their greatest hits, of course, but I didn't know their deep cuts. Roy gave me their late sixties albums, and I became a fanatic. When we started to go on tour with Roy and Robert, it was such a special time because we'd all play mixtapes for each other in the van and turn each other on to all this other great music. It was such a wonderful kind of a communal experience.

STEVEN: Jeff has always really vibed off of Roy in a great way. They both have the mentality of collectors, even though they might not necessarily have the most complete collections, and they're both extremely well-read in the rock-bio world. Just listening to those two kind of like ramble on about obscure points of reference in rock'n'roll is very soothing for me, and fun. And then Jeff's banter with Robert is unique and funny, more kind of a playful and teasing kind of relationship, but funny and loving. So that was all part of the unique dynamic of that lineup. At the time Roy joined, I would say he had a foot more in the *Magic Bus* era of The Who, while Jeff and I would have been gassing more on The Runaways than anybody else in the group, while Robert was obsessed with all things George Harrison. We all loved different things, but there was this crossover.

JEFF: Fan fanaticism has always fuelled our group; if you can't go toe to toe on some kind of musical influence, it's not gonna work out with us in the band. Everybody in the band was a fanatic about something, but what Roy really had in common with me, Steven and Robert was that we were all big Beatle fanatics. When it comes to songwriting, focusing on other people's music can be such a great learning experience, like, 'Oh – this is how you do this,' and then it just kind of comes more natural. We didn't feel like it was going to advance our abilities by spending most of our rehearsals jamming hundreds of cover songs both great and terrible, but that's what we did because it was so much fun. There were so many times with the Robert and Roy lineup where we'd be in rehearsal and I would think, 'No one will hear this, but this is the greatest thing in the world.'

STEVEN: We'd been having problems with rehearsal spaces, but then we met Dave Nazworthy at the Cavern Club. He was 16, and he was sort of like a talent scout – he would scout for bands that he wanted to hang out with, and he'd offer them a place to rehearse.

JEFF: Dave Naz, as everybody called him, lived with his mom in Beverly Hills, but he had a little soundproof rehearsal studio in the back. At first I was like, 'I don't want to rehearse at someone's house again,' because we'd had a lot of bad experiences with situations like that. Plus, we still lived in Hawthorne, and the thought of schlepping our gear up to Beverly Hills all the time just seemed like too much to deal with. But Dave had had the studio professionally soundproofed, so we could play there at three o'clock in the morning and no one would hear us. And we did – we ended up rehearsing nearly every day there for six or seven years. It turned into this magic period in our lives. That was when we were truly able to put our nose to the grindstone, thanks to Dave and his mom Maxine being so generous to us.

STEVE: Just before us, Hillel Slovak's pre-Red Hot Chili Peppers band, which was called What Is This?, had rehearsed there. And then The Pandoras started rehearsing there, and a little later L7. And of course Dave's band, Chemical People. We found ourselves hanging out with The Pandoras a lot, which was so much fun.

JEFF: That ended up being another whole weird period because, when we weren't rehearsing, Beverly Hills became our playground. Dave lived near all these old Hollywood stars, like Lucille Ball, so all of a sudden I'm playing 'ding dong ditch' at Buddy Hackett's house, or I'd be devising pranks that I would be too chicken to pull off myself. Like, Bob Dylan's ex-wife and kids lived over on Bedford, and I dared Melanie from The Pandoras to ring her doorbell and claim she was their new neighbour just dropping by to see if she can borrow a cup of sugar. And she did, but there was no sugar.

STEVEN: Jeff had inherited the station wagon that we took on our first tour, and I remember one night we stole this effigy from a Halloween display on someone's front lawn near Dave's house, and went driving around Beverly Hills trying to figure out what to do with it. Finally, we drove up to Cielo Drive and found the Sharon Tate murder house. We pushed the intercom button, screamed 'Happy Halloween!', then threw the effigy over the security fence and took off. Hopefully that didn't seem *too* disrespectful.

Jeff was sober by then, and I'd more or less stopped indulging as well. So if the Beverly Hills cops pulled us over, which was always a possibility, they weren't gonna find any grass or even like a half-drank bottle of Kamchatka or anything. We stunk like cigarettes, that's for sure. But all they were going to find in that car was cigarette butts and candy wrappers.

JEFF: I really wanted to find out where Prince lived, because we knew that Prince had rented a house in the neighbourhood, and that he was over at Sunset Sound or some other studio manically recording nonstop, like 24 hours a day. Vicki Peterson, who was my girlfriend at the time, had actually been there, because Prince had invited The Bangles over. And she goes, 'I will *never* tell you where Prince lives.' And I'm glad she didn't tell us. Because that would've been really bad.

The *Neurotica*-era lineup with Robert Hecker and Roy McDonald, 1987.
(Photo by Greg Allen)

Chapter 15

NEUROTICA

With Roy McDonald firmly ensconced on the drum throne, and Jeff and Steven finally free of chemical distractions, Redd Kross were ready to concentrate on making their first new album of original material since *Born Innocent*. Now that Enigma Records and the band had mutually parted ways, the path was open for Big Time Records to offer them an album deal.

An Australian label started in the late seventies by Lance Reynolds and Fred Bestall, co-managers of soft rock hitmakers Air Supply, Big Time had distributed Slash Records' releases in Australia in the early eighties, and then gained recognition in America via a diverse artist roster that included mid-eighties college rock favourites such as Hoodoo Gurus, The Jazz Butcher Conspiracy, Dumptruck and the Turbines. Redd Kross seemed like a perfect fit for the up-and-coming label, and vice versa.

JEFF: Big Time had a real cool roster of bands, very eclectic but all aimed at a certain demographic. It seemed like they were going to be the next IRS Records. This was at the height of the 'college rock' era, before it had been rebranded as 'alternative rock.' R.E.M. were the gods of college rock and were getting huge, and all these other groups were kind of coming up through the college radio charts, which actually meant something. The Hoodoo Gurus were very much rising in those ranks, and they were on Big Time, and I knew Brad from the Gurus from when they toured with The Bangles.

A major label wouldn't have touched us at the time, even though we'd got to the point in LA where we were headlining the Roxy. The Go-Go's had opened things up a lot by having hits for IRS, but major labels were still super-fearful of bands that had come from out of the punk scene. We would go out with The Bangles sometimes on their dinners with their record company, and I remember one person from Columbia talking about what a terrible singer Exene was – and this was at a time when X was already considered the second coming by critics all over the country. That's how 'head in the sand' major labels were then; so that world was not open to us, at all. Big Time had a really good A&R guy named Geoffrey Weiss, who was our champion over there.

John Silva and Spock were our co-managers at that point, and they got Big Time to give us $25,000 to make a record. We did the demos for *Neurotica* ourselves at Spin Head Studios, Dave Markey and Phil Newman's 8-track studio in the Valley; we'd come up with all the arrangements ourselves, and the songs were already really well-rehearsed. But Big Time wanted us to have a real producer for a record. Sonny Bono wasn't available – I think he was just getting into politics at that point – and so Flo and Eddie were our next choice, but we met with Howard Kaylan and Mark Volman and it didn't seem like that was going to work out, either.

STEVEN: There weren't many recent records that we really liked the sound of, but we'd heard that Tommy Erdelyi – aka Tommy Ramone – was available to produce us. We really liked

Too Tough To Die, the Ramones album he'd co-produced a few years earlier, and he'd recently done *Tim* by The Replacements.

JEFF: We loved the Ramones, especially their records that Tommy had produced. Like, my all-time favourite Ramones album is *Leave Home*, their second album, which is this great, weird, reverbed-out hybrid of sixties pop and seventies punk; it's actually more of a Phil Spector record than *End Of The Century*. So we thought Tommy would be perfect.

Recorded in all-night sessions at American Studios in Woodland Hills, a spot owned by Steppenwolf co-producers Richie Podolor and Bill Cooper, *Neurotica* was a 12-song statement of purpose, transporting the listener *Oz*-style to the band's private world via a thrift store cyclone of punk rock, psychedelia, bubblegum pop, seventies-style hard rock and a veritable encyclopaedia of pop cultural references.

An Olympian leap forward from *Born Innocent* in songwriting and instrumental proficiency, tracks like 'Play My Song', 'Peach Kelli Pop', 'Frosted Flake', 'Janus, Jeanie And George Harrison' and Robert Hecker's George Harrison-esque 'Love Is You' further refined the band's unique vision while ably capturing the 'Robert and Roy' lineup's personality on wax. ('It's The Little Things', a cover of a Sonny & Cher duet sung by Jeff and Vicki Peterson, would be shelved until later reissues of the album out of a reluctance to get The Bangles' and Columbia's lawyers involved.)

But while *Neurotica* would massively influence the burgeoning Seattle music scene, and is still widely considered a classic by Redd Kross fans today, Jeff and Steven were deeply disappointed with how the finished album sounded.

JEFF: We were always in our own world, very insular – like, we wouldn't even let people come to our rehearsals most of the time. So bringing someone in as a collaborator was always going to be a challenge. We had fun with Tommy; he was a grouchy New Yorker, but being such Ramones mega-fans, we had a great time asking him all the questions and pumping him for stories. We loved a lot of the same music, though we had very different opinions on certain things. Like, he thought the *White Album* was terrible, because there are no finished songs on the record.

He also had a much different sonic vision for the album than we did – we wanted to have a really clean recording, like AC/DC. We knew our songs weren't like AC/DC songs, but we wanted something with minimal fussing like those records. And those records never sound old; we know that now, like forty years later. I was like, 'I want a John Bonham drum sound, and I want my guitars to sound like Angus Young.' And Tommy was like, 'Those are old records. Why do you want to make an old record?' And he was right, but I still would have preferred a Led Zeppelin drum sound.

STEVEN: I think as a producer, and in his peer group that he was in competition with, Tommy was trying to break new ground and be a part of the current musical landscape. He was trying to find the connection between what we were doing and, say, the college success of a band like R.E.M., while we were trying to find the sweet spot between The Partridge Family and *Live At Leeds*. We had no interest at all in the current musical landscape. We *hated* the current musical landscape – which, in retrospect, I think we were kind of right about. But the guitars on *Neurotica* aren't mixed as up front as we would have liked, and the drums have weird eighties reverbs on them that we didn't really relate to.

JEFF: It's such a weird-sounding record. It's, like, thin and heavy at the same time, while missing something in the middle. But as a band, you're never fully happy with records when you're done – especially in those days, when they mixed down on tape, because by the time you heard it on vinyl it was several generations down from what you heard in the studio.

STEVEN: We didn't have a lot of experience in the studio. We knew how we liked to be mixed live, but performing live and making records are such different processes, and then there's the whole thing of getting used to what it sounds like in the studio versus what it sounds like at home, and knowing how to trust your ears and articulate what you want to hear to the engineers. No disrespect to Tommy, but he'd co-produced *Too Tough To Die* with Ed Stasium, and in retrospect I think we were responding more to Stasium's sonic influence on that record than Tommy's.

JEFF: We were also having real difficulty with the mixing because we mixed the record at this place in North Hollywood called George Tobin Studios, and the owner was kind of nuts – he wouldn't let us take cassettes of the mixes home to listen to, because he thought we were gonna steal the mixes and master 'em from the cassette and then put out the record and not pay him. But the dude was running hot because he had just produced Tiffany's first record; it hadn't been released yet, but he knew it was going to be huge, and the secretary in the studio was listening to it all the time while we were there mixing the record. Maybe it slightly influenced us.

STEVEN: I mean, don't get me wrong – I love *Neurotica* all the same, and I don't want to talk shit about it. And I think the album title is perfect; it always felt to me like a cross between 'neurosis' and 'erotica', those two things together, which still seems like kind of a timeless concept. But I will definitely remix the album one day, just because I'm a control freak.

JEFF: Tommy's production input on the record was more about mixing and engineering, saying yay or nay on takes, and

175

making suggestions here and there. But he didn't sit down and dissect our songs and go through arrangements – those were already completely together before we went into the studio with him. Except for 'Love Is You.'

STEVEN: When we started doing 'Love Is You', Robert just had the verse; it was basically 30 seconds long. Our A&R guy, Geoffrey Weiss, knew it had the potential to be a great song and kept trying to convince him to write more of it. And Robert, who is like the George Harrison hippie of the punk rock era, had all this integrity about it, like, 'Oh, it's beautiful just the way it is!' Finally, Geoffrey was able to bribe him to flesh it out. 'It's beautiful as it is!' 'Here's fifty bucks.' 'Okay!'

JEFF: Robert has since re-recorded the song with his band It's Okay!, and restored it to its original 20-second version.

STEVEN: We would extend it when we'd play it live. Jeff would play bongos, and then we'd have this middle section that was inspired by the African American cheerleaders at Hawthorne High – all those cheers like, 'My name is Yolaaaanda, I like to boooogie' – and would go from there to, 'Oh Mickey you're so fine/You're so fine you blow my mind/Mick Taylor!' It was just another chance for us to throw out some pop cultural references to the people, and see what comes back.

JEFF: I don't like talking about specific meanings behind our songs, because so many of them have always been about a combination of weird people we knew, weird stories or stream-of-consciousness references, more than me trying to communicate my inner feelings. Which I do a bit because you have to have some reality attached to it, but it's a fine line. It's more fun to just throw in some abstract decoration that can lead the listener down any path, because the listener's interpretation is really the only important one.

That's kind of how 'Neurotica' and 'Janus, Jeanie And George Harrison' were written – abstract word-association, but coming from a mischievous place. Like, the 'long-haired friends of Jesus' line in 'Neurotica' was definitely plucked from C. W. McCall's 'Convoy', but that other line, 'Get that salami sandwich out of here (it's just a concept)' came from a story Jennifer Schwartz told us about a Lovedolls rehearsal where one of them pulled out a salami sandwich and Janet didn't like the smell, and she goes, 'Get that salami sandwich out of here! Oh my god, it's just a *concept*!' And we thought, that is so great – let's throw that in there!

People have all kinds of interpretations of what 'Janus, Jeanie And George Harrison' is about, but that one's literally about our friends Janus and Jeanie, these cute witchy stoner girls who were in this garbage punk band called The Disposals and were always finding themselves in these weird situations. They had a friend who was selling a boat to George Harrison; they got invited to this get together at the boat storage place, and George was there. And the line, 'When Jesus Christ Superstar was crucified/The Beatles were still making noise,' we heard an old hippie homeless guy spouting that exact line when we were sitting in a Denny's-type restaurant on Market Street after a show in San Francisco. And then we changed 'Beatles' to 'Disposals' the second time it came around in the song.

STEVEN: There's a lot of references to our environment on *Neurotica*. 'No metal sluts or punk rock ruts for me' from 'Play My Song', that was us rejecting the hair metal scene that was happening, but also saying, 'Don't box me into a punk rock scene, either.' At this point, we felt that playing shows with SST bands was just as limiting for us as playing with the hair metal bands.

JEFF: The line from 'Play My Song', 'Play my tambourine and there you go/Your open minds are so closed' – that goes back to when we did 'Puss 'N' Boots' for the *Hell Comes To Your House* compilation album, and all these punkers that thought we were just the biggest freaks for using a tambourine on the track. We got hassled for that, but then we didn't fit in to any of the other things that were happening at the time, whether it was pop radio, heavy metal or college rock. So we just chose to do what we wanted to do, and sing about what we wanted to sing about, even if people didn't get it. Like, 'Peach Kelli Pop' – a lot of people think it's some kind of power pop statement, but Kelly Pops were like these Mexican popsicles that our mom would bring home, and Peach was the best flavour. And then the verses were various scenarios from our lives – 'Laughing at all the assholes at the Rainbow, flying so high on coke.'

STEVEN: 'Frosted Flake' was inspired by this girl I used to do drugs with, but there was also an element of, Is this real life, or is this some kind of cautionary tale from a Russ Meyer film? We're coming out of the drug era for ourselves, and we're now kind of speaking judgementally of someone who does a lot of cocaine; we're moralising now, but we're also trying to encourage ourselves to stay on a good path, and keep away from anyone who wants to make us stray from our path, whether that would be with sex or the promise of some kind of chemical-based altering of our boundaries.

In our teen years, our mischievous sense of fun was connected or conflated at some point with getting wasted. So now by *Neurotica*, Redd Kross is sober – Jeff has cleaned up his act, and I have too, because I want to support him. And it was scary, like, are we still gonna be able to have fun and be crazy? Where are we going to be able to seek inspiration? It turned out that it wasn't a problem because we could clearly still get into all kinds of ridiculous situations when we were bone-sober.

JEFF: 'Ghandi Is Dead (I'm The Cartoon Man)', I got that from a Bollywood movie I was watching. The girls in those movies are always singing in the same super-high pitch with this crazy slap-back echo with long tails, like way beyond the first Elvis Presley records. And I could swear I kept hearing this girl singing, 'Gandhi is dead, I'm the cartoon man. Gandhi's dead, I'm the cartoon man.' And then there were other lines in the song that were just made up of things that I heard people saying in person, like 'I hate paintings' — that was something Paula Pierce from The Pandoras said, and I thought that was like the most absurd thing for someone to say; it made no sense to me at all.

A lot of that song was about hanging out with The Pandoras while they were going through this hypersexual period. They were among our best friends at the time. They weren't being sexualised by, like, men, or the media, or by their record label; they were sexualising themselves, and they were just like on this *tear* during that period. Anything that's sexual in that song, like 'She jerks off to rock'n'roll,' that's about them.

The most literal thing on *Neurotica* is probably Robert's other song, 'What They Say.' It's about Robert hanging out with us for the first time outside of a band situation, right after he joined; we were snorting crystal meth off the album cover of *Teen Babes*, and we asked him if he wanted any. And he was so horrified, so offended, appalled and disgusted by that; but we never knew he was horrified until he wrote that song, and then he told us what it was about. We loved that – it was like when The Beatles wrote songs about each other.

STEVEN: It's a very Jeff McDonald thing to kind of work in code, or in a collage style. He's always feeding the listener these self-referential clues, which I think originally came from us just kind of riffing on our own inside jokes because we didn't know what else to write about. But by *Neurotica*, the songwriting has kind of moved into this idea of indoctrination into our cult – identifying who we are and figuring it out in front of everybody, and picking up cohorts along the way. But it's a *safe* cult, one that you're actually free to leave anytime. The only sort of requirement for group membership is a desire to relate to us on this level, and an ability to appreciate and identify with the sort of references and clues we're putting out there. If you pick up on, say, an *H.R. Pufnstuf* reference, well, 'Now you're one of us.'

In the internet age, it's easy to find a community for any interest you can think of, as obscure as you could dream up. But in the days before that, finding your tribe was more difficult, and maybe more meaningful. At the end of *Neurotica*, there's 'Beautiful Bye-Byes', which is kind of like our Beatles 'Her Majesty' way of ending the record, but it's also singing this song of inclusion for all the beautiful misfits out there. I guess it's another one of those moments where we're kind of crystallising this indoctrination concept for this cult of ours. But once again, it's one that you are free to leave. We promise.

JEFF: On the original release of *Neurotica*, there was a tiny message on the inner sleeve advertising the 'Redd Kross Flaming Neurotica Starter Kit', which was like our equivalent to a fan club package that you could send away for. For $15 or something ridiculous, you'd get a personalised copy of the record plus everything you needed to perform the 'Neurotica Purification Ritual', including a special incantation – this long and super-funny poem-slash-spell that we all wrote together – and instructions on how to use it. It was a very witchy thing; you were supposed to chant it aloud while listening to the album. And then, when the record was over, you had to bury it in the backyard. Plus, there was all this other stuff we'd put together for the package, like stickers, and photos of Jim Dandy and Yoko Ono.

We were never really clear, however, on who was going to put the packages together or do the mailing, and a lot more people ordered it than actually received it, so that became part of the folklore, too. If anyone has the Starter Kit envelope with all the stickers and photos in it, that's like the rarest of all Redd Kross collectables.

Housed in an eye-catching cover featuring a John Scarpati photo of the band lurking mysteriously among some giant, garishly painted heads, Neurotica was released in April 1987, and Redd Kross celebrated the album's release with two headlining nights at the Whisky with Painted Willie, The Pandoras, Frightwig and The Lovedolls opening. The album got the band some of its first national coverage in the mainstream music press – including a rave review in *CREEM* – and set the table for two extensive North American club tours that year. Unfortunately, just as Redd Kross's star was beginning to rise, their record company was collapsing.

STEVEN: John Scarpati was an LA photographer we worked with a lot back then, who became quite successful in the hair metal world. We had a little bit of a budget and we were in Los Angeles, so we were able to rent things from various movie studio prop departments, like those heads that we're posing around. I've seen them turn up since then in the weirdest places, like old episodes of *Laugh-In*, or some seventies TV variety show where people will be performing some kind of dance number around those same heads.

I'm not sure what they were originally supposed to be for, but I know we rented them again for some of our LA shows. This was around the same time that we were also into renting dry ice machines to get that classic seventies rock show fog on stage – or like on *Bewitched*, where there was dry ice fog on the floor every time they were in an alternate witch universe. That's basically where we were coming from at the time, just being colourful and wanting to put our unique style up front, and taking advantage of whatever assets we had.

JEFF: We didn't know Big Time was in trouble while we were making the record, but it became apparent almost immediately afterwards; even before the record came out, there were issues, problems, unpaid bills, and everything was getting really chaotic. But at the same time, they weren't letting any of their artists go; some people had to sue to get up their contract.

STEVEN: It was one of those things where they had this bustling office full of people before we left for tour. And then when we came back, it had been whittled down to a secretary and like one or two people. We didn't really understand what it meant, but we got the sense it wasn't great.

JEFF: We just continued to play live and just do our thing. It didn't really devastate us, because at the time we were more concerned with, 'Okay, what's next?' We were having so much fun going on tour, and our fanbase was growing. At the same time, *Neurotica* wasn't showing up in stores, and we would have had to sue Big Time in order for some other label to pick it up and put it out, so it just kind of had to exist in the 'used' realm as a collector's item. But it really became like a cult record; it continued to find new fans, even years after we recorded it.

Jeff gets down at San Francisco's Fillmore Auditorium, 1989. (Photo by Vicki Berndt)

Chapter 16

DEFINITELY NOT WHAT THEY WANTED TO HEAR

By just about any metric, Redd Kross's two 1987 North American jaunts were enormously successful. The band spent nearly three months on the road in total, playing in front of ecstatic crowds and headlining hip venues like the 9:30 Club in D.C., Maxwell's in Hoboken and Cabaret Metro in Chicago. Their May 23 show at Tacoma's Crescent Ballroom saw them top-billed over Soundgarden, Green River and Malfunkshun, while seemingly every other leading light from what would soon be dubbed 'the Seattle grunge scene' was there to pay homage. And that October, the band opened several Midwestern dates for their friends Sonic Youth, who were out promoting their new album *Sister*. But as the year drew to a close, Redd Kross once again found themselves in a familiar position, with no label to support them and – more importantly – no drummer.

JEFF: The tour was really great. We were solidifying our fan base, and it was really fun. We did some of the major cities in Canada and the US, and some 'fly-in' shows where the promoters would fly us out to New York or Boston for a single show. Because it was such chaos with the record label, and there was no one there to help us and no promotion, it didn't feel like we were supporting an album. It just felt like we were supporting our band. And the idea that we didn't come home in debt meant a major success to us.

STEVEN: We weren't thinking that much about what had happened with Big Time. From our perspective, we were doing better than we expected. We were playing our second major US tour; the first one had been pretty disastrous, but now we were having really good crowds in most towns, and we got to play some dates with Sonic Youth, who we loved.

At the same time, I was always highly competitive, and I remember being in New Orleans around the same time that Guns N' Roses was opening for The Cult at some big theatre there, and feeling really pissed off about that. We'd had a couple hundred people at our show, and that was respectable, but *Appetite For Destruction* had just come out, and I was coming to grips with the fact that this band was likely going to skyrocket. Not that I wanted to sound like them, but up until that point they had just been another LA band who could sell out the Roxy. We were moving up incrementally, but they were moving up exponentially – and watching something like that can sometimes encourage you to reframe your experience in a negative way.

JEFF: Big Time was going under, but we had to wait around for them to officially do so before we could go looking for another label. So that meant there was no rush for us to come up with a follow-up record. Which was fine; we always kind of took our dear old time about things, anyway, and it's not like we were the most prolific songwriters. And Roy had left the band, so we had to regroup, anyway.

STEVEN: In some ways, I guess you could say the *Neurotica* tour went on for three years, because we didn't make another record until 1990. But really, the *Neurotica* tour ended when Roy left the band. It was a real mind-blower. I felt very abandoned when Roy left, and very bummed.

Roy always seemed truly interested in doing what we were doing; he was a great drummer, and we had a lot of amazing times together. But at the same time, it always felt like he was overextended, and there was always one entity or another that was trying to drag him away from us. He was a very responsible, job-holding individual, which is great, and he was always working one or two jobs while living 25 miles east of LA with his parents in Walnut. And I was always asking too much of him, wanting him to rehearse five times a week. He'd be like, 'Well, I've got a morning shift, and then I have an evening shift.' And I'd be like, 'Okay, I'll take the afternoon.' It's so weird – I can't walk up to a neighbour's house and ask to borrow a cup of sugar, but I never think twice about asking way too much from any band member.

JEFF: Roy had a girlfriend that he eventually married and had a child with, so it was a classic rock'n'roll 'me or the band' situation. I guess that's an age thing; at some point, you have to set your life up in a sense where you're thinking of your future, and if you're gonna get married and have that sort of existence. And we were just oblivious to that, but he wasn't, and his girlfriend wasn't. So, Roy disappeared for several years, moved to Texas, and we just lost touch until he started playing with The Muffs in the nineties.

STEVEN: That was my first time experiencing that sort of mentality of, 'I'm going to be a grown-up and quit playing music.' I didn't understand it, at all; to my mind at the time, playing music is what you *do*. I can't remember how he broke it to us, but I'm sure I didn't handle it well. And, I mean, it's hard to imagine being in a band with young adult Jeff and Steven while also trying to handle adult responsibilities. I'm sure that was really difficult for him.

JEFF: We put ads in the papers for a drummer, and we auditioned a lot of people from the Musicians Institute, all these people who could play like Neil Peart from Rush, but they couldn't handle a simple Ringo shuffle.

STEVEN: We'd had a lot of luck finding people for the band through our friends or through the scenes that we were part of. I'd found Roy at the Cavern Club, but Roy had been the best drummer of that scene, and the Cavern Club didn't exist anymore. So where do we go from here? We were well known enough by this point that we could put an ad in *Music Connection* or the *Recycler* and people would send us their tapes. And that's how we found Victor Indrizzo.

JEFF: We were still based in Beverly Hills, with our whole social scene centred on Dave Naz's house, and Victor came down from Simi Valley to jam with us. We instantly bonded over The Beatles; we just started jamming Beatles covers, and it was so much fun. He was a brilliant musician, and very musical; he's kind of a multi-talented Dave Grohl type. Victor definitely took us to the next level; we had so much fun rehearsing and hanging out with him that we accidentally got really tight.

STEVEN: It was right around the time when we started getting really into *Jesus Christ Superstar* – the brown, original album. And he was really into that, so that was another thing we really bonded on; we even did the 'Superstar' song live, and Victor sang it. He also went really deep into some seventies muso stuff that we were always suspicious of, like LA session players like Russ Kunkel, but we found that kind of endearing, kind of how we loved that Robert Hecker loved everything George Harrison did, no matter how questionable. The one bridge that was maybe a little too far with Victor was that we were always worried that he was going to slip in some white boy funk, because he *loved* early Red Hot Chili Peppers; it was just like, 'No – we can't go there.' But we had more in common than not, and we really focused on the stuff that we all loved. We first started doing shows with him in 1988, and those were some of our most exciting shows yet.

In November 1988, Steven and Victor Indrizzo participated in the infamous Tater Totz performance during the annual Beatlefest convention at LA's Bonaventure Hotel, wherein they hijacked the battle of the bands with an extended version of Yoko Ono's 'Don't Worry, Kyoko.' One of Bill Bartell's many loopy projects, Tater Totz was a high-concept band with a rotating membership that included members of LA bands like Redd Kross, The Pandoras, Chemical People and The Three O'Clock, as well as the occasional C-list celebrity like *The Partridge Family*'s Danny Bonaduce.

The first Tater Totz album, 1988's *Alien Sleestacks From Brazil (Unfinished Music Vol 3)*, featured gleefully warped covers of songs by The Beatles, The Rolling Stones, Yoko Ono and legendary Brazilian band Os Mutantes, the latter of whom were all but unknown in the US until Bartell began proselytising about their music. Though it was predominantly Bartell's baby, Redd Kross's involvement with Tater Totz further bolstered Jeff and Steven's reputation as weirdo visionaries.

JEFF: Tater Totz was Bill's thing, though I did record with them a bit, and it was kind of my idea in the first place; I would always throw out insane ideas to Bill, and if he thought it was funny, he would run with them. I said, 'How about a tribute band that just pays tribute to Linda McCartney and Yoko?' And he's like, 'Oh, that's incredible!' Then he took it to the next level, getting all his friends to come out to his studio in Fontana to record with him. Fontana's just like the armpit of the Inland Empire, but Bill somehow got Cherie Currie to drive out there and cut a version of 'Instant Karma', which was actually really good.

STEVEN: Beatlefest was this longstanding event, an entire weekend at the Bonaventure Hotel with vendors selling Beatle paraphernalia and rare records, and screenings of Beatle movies and live footage, and that sort of thing. This was 1988, years before the Beatles organisation was legitimately releasing that stuff. Bill and I loved The Beatles, but the rigidity of the Beatles fan community at that time was really annoying to us; they were all about nostalgia, especially for the pre-psychedelic era, and at the time, there was no easier way to bait a bunch of middle-aged Beatle geeks than to praise Yoko Ono in their presence. This was way before most people were willing to accept the idea that Yoko wasn't evil, she hadn't broken up The Beatles, and that she was actually quite brilliant in her own right.

Bill and I had a sincere love for Yoko's weird perspective – in fact, he was the one who really got me into her records – and he somehow got Tater Totz booked onto the Beatlefest main stage, where the final day of the convention would culminate with a battle of the Beatle bands. It was always a bunch of bands with names like The Fabs or P.S. I Love You or whatever, but this time there was also Tater Totz, with a lineup that included a bunch of our friends from the *Lovedolls* films like Dave Markey and Jennifer Schwartz, and special celebrity guest Jimmy McNichol of Kristy and Jimmy McNichol fame on floor tom. Victor was on drums, Bill was on guitar, I was on bass and Jennifer was in a bag, and we did a cover of 'Don't Worry, Kyoko', which is basically like a 10-minute blues jam that Yoko screamed over the entire time; it was her performance piece about her estranged child from her first marriage. There were maybe two thousand people in the hall, and this was definitely *not* what they wanted to hear.

There was this loud roar of boos through the entire thing, and people were flipping us off and throwing things at us. And of course, being veterans of dealing with antagonistic punk crowds, we pushed it and pushed it, and wouldn't leave the stage until we were finished. It was just us turning the mischief dials up to 11. I remember afterwards, one of the organisers yelled at Bill for like a half an hour. Bill told him, 'I think John Lennon would have loved our performance,' and the organiser was like, 'Yeah, well, but John Lennon also loved Yoko Ono.' Like, that was his big comeback.

Of course, in classic Bill form, he managed to get the performance recorded and videotaped – it's up on YouTube – and he put the audio out on Gasatanka, his label, in a record he called *Live Hate At Beatlefest*. I suppose our justification at the time was just to have a gas and prank a bunch of uptight Beatles fans. But in retrospect, I can see why Sean Lennon became a Tater Totz fan, because our Beatles fandom was a little more irreverent, and our Yoko fandom was sincere. According to Bill, he had some kind of email exchange later on with Sean; I think Bill was asking Yoko to sign off on some Tater Totz artwork, a *Revolver* look-alike cover that had all four members redrawn as Yoko. Sean passed along her approving response. It read, 'Sean, Tater' – she called us Tater – 'has always been a big supporter of your Mother's work.' I always loved that... 'Tater.'

By late 1988, the band's affairs with Big Time were settled, and various major labels had begun sniffing around. College rock was now being rebranded as 'alternative rock', and – thanks in part to MTV's weekly show *120 Minutes* – was now seen by the majors as commercially viable product. Indie and underground acts who just a few years earlier might have worried about losing their underground credibility by signing with a major were now following the example set by bands like R.E.M., Hüsker Dü and The Replacements and doing just that. Meanwhile, Guns N' Roses' breakthrough success had Hollywood A&R people scrambling to find the next big edgy-yet-commercial metal band. Redd Kross's prominent LA profile and increasing national buzz was sufficient to lure numerous major label reps to their shows, but the band's joyously expansive musical approach often proved profoundly confusing to the uninitiated.

STEVEN: Every band and their mother in LA was getting signed, and it became like this ridiculous status symbol. We felt superior to so many of the local bands that were getting big, but at the same time, we too wanted to reach as large an audience as possible – so if, say, D'Molls could get signed to a major, why not us? We felt like we would do something better with major label resources than what those bands were doing. I don't know why I'm focusing on D'Molls, but there was a story going around at the time about how they had taken their signing advance and bought a yellow Corvette that they all shared; they would take turns going on dates with the yellow Corvette. That wasn't part of our plan.

We had enough of a hardcore following in LA that people in the industry had to take notice of us, but we didn't fit into an easily marketable slot.

JEFF: People from the major labels would come to our shows in LA, which were always sold out and really fun. But then they would pass because we would do, like, Side Two of *Sgt. Pepper's* live, and they just didn't get it.

STEVEN: Victor was really musical, and Robert was like a human jukebox, so sometimes our shows would break out into an *Abbey Road* medley or *Jesus Christ Superstar*, and our fans would love it. And we'd have platforms up behind us, where our friend Laura Lovelace – who later appeared as the waitress in the opening scene of *Pulp Fiction* – would do all these incredible go-go dances while we played. We seemed totally signable to me, but the label people were just baffled. I remember some lawyer who was working with us and trying to get labels out to our sold-out show at the Roxy. The show was great, and ended with everyone singing along to 'A Day In The Life', but then the next day the lawyer told us, 'No one will bite. I mean, you guys played *seven* Beatles covers.' I didn't know what to say.

JEFF: It was like, 'People were tripped out by us, and they signed Red Hot Chili Peppers?' But I think it was harder for us because no one really knew where we were coming from, as far what our point of view was. I mean, no diss to the Chili Peppers, but they had songs like 'Party On Your Pussy', songs that we would've never sang, but maybe that was a frat mentality that these A&R people and post-college people could relate to. We were just too weird, too cerebral and too bizarre for them.

STEVEN: John Silva and Spock had parted ways at this point, and we stayed with John. I'm sure Spock's feelings were hurt at the time, and I'm sure we probably didn't handle that situation well, either, but it's not like we went on to become Guns N' Roses. By now, John had partnered with Danny Goldberg and Ron Stone at Gold Mountain Entertainment, and Danny and Ron were these really successful guys who had a lot of industry connections going back to the seventies, so we were hoping that their muscle and influence could make a difference. But it was in no way a done deal; we were always hearing things like, 'Oh, this A&R person loves you, but they can't get their boss's attention.' All this industry crap. 'Oh, Rick Rubin doesn't dig you guys.' Well, you know, *fuck* that dude.

JEFF: Everybody who was anybody in LA totally passed on us, so we figured we'd just put the next record out ourselves. And then suddenly there was a little bidding war going on for us in New York. It was kind of an 'if you ask your mom and she says no, you ask your dad and he says yes' kind of situation. We spoke with a lot of labels for a while, and we eventually chose Atlantic.

STEVEN: We were a band that could draw a thousand people in New York. And even though no one in LA would touch us, it just so happened that, with some New York A&R people at various labels, it was 'their turn' to sign a band – that's basically how it went. Not that they were particularly inspired by us, or what we were doing; it was more arbitrary, like it was this person or that person's turn to sign someone, and we just happened to fit the bill.

JEFF: We went to play a show in New York, and all these record people were there. I can't remember the name of the venue, but it was horrifying; it was like an old church, and it was really dusty, there was no air, and it was like a hundred degrees onstage. We thought it was the worst show, but everyone loved it. We were literally gasping for oxygen up there, but maybe it was one of those sloppy disasters that people find endearing. And that started the whole bidding war.

STEVEN: It was some weird space that didn't really have shows often, in an old building that was really decrepit. But it had a pretty big room, and the room was packed. I remember my amplifier died twice. So it was a very stressful, miserable experience for me. But it didn't matter; the A&R people there had already decided that they were going to sign us. Anything could have happened; just the fact that there were a thousand people in the room that night, that was enough for us to pass the audition.

Young love: Sofia Coppola and Steven, 1990. (Photo by Chuck Kelley)

Chapter 17

AN OFFER WE
COULDN'T REFUSE

In early 1989, an out-of-the-blue invitation from film director Francis Ford Coppola led to an audition of a different sort, which resulted in Jeff and Steven making their big-screen debut in *The Spirit of '76*, a film comedy written and directed by Lucas Reiner. Though extremely low-budget by Hollywood standards, the film – an intentionally campy send-up of science fiction flicks and seventies pop culture – was a huge step up from the *Lovedolls* productions, and presented Jeff and Steven with the surreal opportunity to act alongside David Cassidy, one of their childhood idols.

STEVEN: We got a call at our parents' house, on the classic kitchen wall phone. It was from Francis Coppola's office, telling us that we were invited to come with him to his home in Napa Valley – and that if we were interested, we were to meet him the following day at Van Nuys Airport. Of course we thought it was someone playing a prank on us; but once we realised it was legitimate, we weren't gonna turn down 'an offer we couldn't refuse.' When we were flying with him on this small jet up to Napa, Francis told me that he'd asked his daughter Sofia if she wanted him to bring anything home with him from Los Angeles, and she'd requested Redd Kross.

JEFF: We used to play about once a month at the I-Beam in San Francisco's Haight District, and the shows were always like these big happenings. Sofia and her brother Roman had seen us there, and they were big Redd Kross fans.

STEVEN: In fact, Sofia had even already befriended our roadie, Mike Dalke. I remember there was one night when we were staying at a motor lodge in San Francisco, all of us jammed into two rooms to save money, and Mike asked if his friends could sleep on the floor after our show. We were like, 'Uh, okay, whatever,' and three teenage girls slept on our floor, because Mike had a crush on one of them or was being nice or whatever. We only found out months later that it was Sofia and her girlfriends. She would've been like 17 at the time; nothing happened, but it could have been a dangerous situation, because we didn't find out 'til later that they were underage. But it was pretty hilarious.

So anyway, it was a two-part thing. Sofia thought that Redd Kross were, you know, the coolest, foxiest dudes, or whatever. And Roman had ambitions of being a cigar-chomping, wannabe Roger Corman, a B-movie auteur. So he basically pitched us the idea of this movie, and the idea of Jeff and I being in it or getting involved with it on some level. And of course he didn't have to twist our arms.

JEFF: We had family Sunday dinner with them, and we were hanging out with the kids. Roman discussed what he wanted to do with us; I think Francis was starting a small film company for making genre films, like inexpensive science fiction and what have you, and this was going to be their first project. It was kind of created as a business, but also a way for the kids to start working in film and doing their own thing. At that point, Sofia was still in high school, and she was going to be doing the costumes for the film, which Roman had co-written with their friend Lucas Reiner, who was Carl Reiner's son and Rob Reiner's brother.

STEVEN: By then, SST had officially released the *Lovedolls* films on VHS. The whole SST thing seemed very passé to me by 1989, which maybe sounds arrogant to say, but remember that it had been a decade since we first started hanging out at The Church. The Coppola kids thought it was all very exciting and cutting edge, however. They'd grown up travelling the world with their parents, but they were also having somewhat of a normal experience going to a public school in a small town in Napa Valley, and cool American underground music was what they gravitated towards. Roman's dad had gifted him a production company for his birthday, and part of the inspiration for *The Spirit of '76* had been seeing the *Lovedolls* films, which was pretty cool. He knew about his dad's history, so he knew about Roger Corman films, and he was able to draw a connection between what we'd done and what his movie company could be – making low-budget 'genre' films that could be fun and profitable.

JEFF: We became friends with Roman and Sofia right away. It was very strange and very surreal, because they weren't 'Beverly Hills famous' – they weren't at all like the crazy, spoiled celebrity kids that grew up in Los Angeles. They lived in this very nice but very small town in the country, and hanging out with them was very comfortable, very normal. And then we got the call that the movie was actually going to happen, and suddenly we were part of the whole thing.

At that point, we had to do some audition stuff. I guess Francis always had this way of doing table reads for his films, where they would do 'radio play' versions of them in a recording studio and then listen back to it. And that was really fun. We passed the test, but they hadn't really cast any of the other actors yet.

STEVEN: We immediately became like collaborators, in a sense, because Jeff and I were definitely key to them reaching out to David Cassidy to be the star of the movie.

JEFF: We essentially moved to the Bay Area for a while to work on the film, and I remember driving up from LA with Lucas Reiner, and we kept telling him, 'David Cassidy, you have to get David Cassidy!' And he's like, 'Yeah, that's a good idea.' Because they were thinking about which seventies icons they could get to do it, sort of pre-Tarantino stunt casting. David Cassidy was our John Travolta, you know? Keith Partridge was our hero!

STEVEN: It was a real mind-blower for us that these people actually could just *reach out* to David Cassidy.

JEFF: We had to talk Lucas into dropping the idea of Donny Osmond for the Adam-11 role. We were saying it should be David Cassidy, but they were saying, 'No, Donny Osmond!' In retrospect, though, I think that could have been really good. I mean, Donny Osmond was damaged goods too, but I think it would've been more fun to get into that whole Mormon thing with him. But at the time I was like, 'Have you *seen Goin' Coconuts*? Donny Osmond's already made a horrible movie, and David Cassidy's never made a film!' I think he went on to do some film stuff later, but at that point he'd never done a movie. So they reached out to him about taking the role, and he eventually said yes.

STEVEN: Being in the film was intimidating and exciting at the same time. It was an exciting time. We had our Atlantic deal at that point, but hadn't made our record, and there was all this excitement about what was coming up for us.

Despite the lack of any formal acting training, Jeff and Steven eagerly jumped into their roles as Chris Johnson and Tommy Sears, a couple of dim-witted Bill & Ted types who help a time-traveller from the future (played by Cassidy) after he inadvertently lands in 1976 while trying to make his way to the signing of the Declaration of Independence. The film also featured such luminaries as Rob Reiner, Carl Reiner, Tommy Chong, Moon Zappa, seventies teen idol Leif Garrett, British actress Olivia d'Abo, and members of DEVO.

STEVEN: We didn't really have the discipline at the time that film acting requires, but we're both natural hams, and we had the enthusiasm for the job. We were doing our best to exaggerate our California-ness and give our characters a Cheech and Chong/Valley dude kind of flavour, along with our weird Redd Kross twang. I guess we kind of found our feet eventually.

JEFF: They just kept telling us that as long as we knew our lines and could hit our marks, we'd be okay; we were so scared that we made sure we were really well-prepared, and we knew all our lines for all of our scenes. When I'm performing with Redd Kross in a club or somewhere bigger, I never get stage fright, but filming a movie or a TV show, to me that's like doing an acoustic set – there are ten, fifteen people gathered around, and they're all watching your every move really closely. Any time I've done it with Steven, it's just been easier, because at least both of us are there.

The first scene they shot with us was really nerve-wracking, but it was great because it was our scene with Moon Zappa. She did the most incredible Cher impersonation, and that totally put us at ease. She was great, and we stayed friends for a long time after that. We became friends with Olivia d'Abo, too; she was really quiet, but it turned out she had a real sense of humour. Her dad was Mike d'Abo, a very cool singer-songwriter who was in Manfred Mann for a while, her mom was in the train sequence of *A Hard Day's Night*, and her boyfriend at the time was Julian Lennon, so we had a lot to talk about. She was like, 'I play music,' and when Bill Bartell found out, he was like, 'We should have her be in the Tater Totz!' She was into it, and she actually played keyboards with us at a Tater Totz show at the DNA Lounge in San Francisco; it was a real all-star Tater Totz lineup with Pat Smear, me and Steven, Rebecca from Frightwig, Roman and Sofia, and Olivia on two-finger keyboards. Bill later released the tape of it as *Tater Comes Alive!*.

STEVEN: The person we did most of our scenes with was David Cassidy. I think that was the only part of the film we had any real expectations about – the idea of bonding with Keith Partridge. But that was our first time dealing with someone who was so at odds with their place, their experience. And it was weird to us, because we had such reverence for something that was very painful for him at that point.

JEFF: He was kind of suspicious of everyone, like, 'Are you making fun of me?' He'd been trying to live down *The Partridge Family* for so long; it was like, 'I'll never be taken seriously because of *The Partridge Family*.' So it was kind of hard to get him out of his shell. I think we were sensitive to that, but we were instantly just wanting to let him know that, 'No, this isn't a joke to us. This isn't kitsch. We think you're great, and we think Partridge Family records are really great.' It just took forever because he was like, 'Yeah, sure.'

STEVEN: We knew that it was the Wrecking Crew musicians playing on all those Partridge Family records, and that a lot of their songs were written by the same people who'd written songs

202

for The Monkees. We just wanted to talk about all that stuff with him from kind of a record-collecting, *MOJO* magazine mindset, because we knew we were unique in holding it in such high esteem. We thought we might be able to bond with him over that, and that he would indulge us and share some stories with us.

I remember we asked him about the song 'Summer Days' from the *Sound Magazine* album. I guess you would consider it a deep cut, but it's one of our favourite songs – it's got this like 'Good Vibrations' flavour to it, this 16th-note cello thing, and it might have even been recorded in the same studio as 'Good Vibrations' with some of the same musicians. So we were like, 'Okay, it's 1971, and you're at Hollywood Western Studios or Ocean Way, and you're about to record 'Summer Days.' What do you remember?' And he just stood there looking at us open-mouthed, like, 'What? Are you fucking with me?'

JEFF: We were big fans, and our goal was just to really kind of validate him, you know? But he wasn't real open to it; he had a lot of Hollywood damage, a lot of show business diva damage. Like, if we did a scene with him and we were really good in it, he'd want the scene to be cut. We didn't know star protocol; we didn't know about not upstaging the star. We were just trying to do our best. But he was like that. And really, how would he know any different? I think about him in his superstar bubblegum icon days, doing *The Partridge Family* show during the week, then recording albums at night, and then doing his own stadium shows in England on the weekends, and then flying back. And being a serious musician with good taste in music, and absolutely nobody cares about that. I mean, anyone would go insane.

STEVEN: He was really embittered by how things had gone for him, and we didn't understand it at the time. It was later that I kind of realised that things had gone so differently than the way he wanted them to go, and that he was still trying to work it out and come to terms with it. Because in his mind, he'd wanted to compete with the big arena rockers of the seventies, but instead he'd been pigeonholed into a teenybopper world that was disposable. And he wasn't able to reframe it in his mind, like, 'These freaks right here really care about this stuff, so maybe there's a different way of looking at this.' I think he just thought we were nut jobs. 'I've gotta do my scenes with these guys? This is what they're going to be filling my brains with between takes? This is a nightmare. Get me outta here!'

JEFF: He was difficult; but looking back, though, I have nothing but compassion for him. The memories are mostly good. We asked him, 'How come Shirley's name is on the records. Did she really sing on them?' And he was like, 'Are you kidding? She never sang on any of those records!' And he told us that Bernie from *Room 222*, the guy with the big red afro, was his best friend at some point. Occasionally, you'd get those little moments of humanity that would pop through.

STEVEN: It was pretty magical getting to work alongside him, even if we were just getting hits of the Keith Partridge chops coming through. Ultimately, our take was like, 'David Cassidy is okay, but he's no Keith Partridge.'

The Spirit of '76 was released in October 1990 to a small array of theatres and wildly mixed reviews. But not unlike the *Lovedolls* films, it became something of a cult classic once it hit video. The film's soundtrack, released by Rhino Records, was made up largely of seventies rock and pop hits, though it also included Redd Kross's '1976', which was written for the film by Jeff and Victor Indrizzo. By the time of the film's release, Steven and Sofia Coppola were living together in Los Angeles.

STEVEN: Sofia and I were friends first for a long time, and nothing happened until after she turned 18; and then at some point during the film, we started this romance. Once the film was done, it turned into a long-distance thing, and then she moved to LA and lived with me at my parents' house in Hawthorne for a couple of months. Then she and I found an apartment together in LA, in a cool old 1920s building on the edge of Hancock Park. It was our first adult apartment; we basically moved out of our parents' houses together. I was 22, and she was 18.

JEFF: The film premiered at the Chinese Theatre, and that was so much fun because there were all these legends there who were involved in the film because their kids, or the kids of their friends, had been part of it. I remember meeting Martin Landau, whose daughter was best friends with Lucas and was one of the producers; and Anne Bancroft and Mel Brooks were there, because they were best friends with the Reiners. We got to meet a lot of 'Golden Age of Hollywood' people that night. The film kind of came and went, but it wasn't like we were expecting it to be a big hit.

STEVEN: We didn't grow up in show business, and I don't think we had a really clear picture of the difference between a big film and a small film, per se. But at the same time, we always understood the difference between mainstream and cult. If *The Spirit of '76* been made ten years earlier, it would have been the kind of thing that ran with *The Kentucky Fried Movie* or *The Groove Tube* at a drive-in theatre double feature. If it had been a surprise runaway hit like *Airplane!* or something, that would have obviously been great, but we were just enthusiastic about being in the film, regardless of what happened with it.

JEFF: Victor and I wrote '1976' specifically for the movie. Any time we wrote anything together, it was always kind of funky, and the Victor influence is very heavily there on that song.

STEVEN: The Dickies had written a song for the movie too, which made it into the movie itself but didn't make it onto the soundtrack. We were offended that they were bucking to get a song into a project that we saw as our territory. We definitely had some Dawn Davenport outrage about it, though our song was used over the closing credits.

JEFF: To this day, people think it's Paul Stanley singing in the middle of '1976', but it's actually Robert Hecker. Paul has such a weird voice, but Robert can do a brilliant Paul imitation. During long drives in the van between tour dates, we used to pass the time by getting Robert to sing any song we could think of in a Paul Stanley voice, songs like 'Wildfire' or songs by punk bands that we were friends with. My god, sometimes it was like, pee your pants funny.

STEVEN: When we did the original demos for *Neurotica*, Robert sang 'What They Say' in full-on Paul Stanley voice, but Tommy Erdelyi was kind of scratching his head over our KISS fanaticism and was like, 'Maybe we tame down the Paul Stanley for the record.' Fortunately, by the time we did *Third Eye*, we realised that you actually *want* to fan those flames.

JEFF: '1976' is on the *Third Eye* album as well, and because we thanked Paul Stanley on it, people think that must be him singing on the song. But we're always doing our little Easter eggs, like mentioning random people in the 'Special Thanks' section. We thanked Barbra Streisand on that record, too. Must people took it as the joke it was, but some still ask us about it. I wonder if Paul Stanley's ever heard that song.

JEFFREY McDONALD   STEVEN McDONALD   ROBERT HECKER

REDD KROSS

Between drummers: Atlantic Records promotional photo for *Third Eye*,
1990. (Original photo by Vicki Berndt)

Chapter 18

THIRD EYE

Redd Kross spent much of 1990 recording *Third Eye*, their first album for Atlantic Records. It had been three years since the release of *Neurotica*, but while much had changed in the music business in the meantime, plenty had not – for one thing, sterile instrumental tones, digital reverbs and rigid beats still dominated most major label releases.

In the fall of 1991, the unexpected breakout success of Nirvana's *Nevermind* would make it acceptable again – and even *de rigeur* – for rock records of the non-metal variety to sport distorted guitars, non-robotic grooves and a natural ambience. But just a year earlier, most of the college/alternative bands trying to reach a wider audience via major labels were still being pressured to contort their music, ideas and personalities to fit into the standardised sonic templates of the eighties. This would have been a tall order for Redd Kross to accomplish in any case, even if Jeff hadn't been completely obsessed at the time with the late-sixties bubblegum pop productions of Jerry Kasenetz and Jeffry Katz.

JEFF: Before we made the record, I was telling people that I wanted to make the bubblegum rock opera. That's what the whole idea behind *Third Eye* was, initially – a hard bubblegum concept album. And it *is* kind of a hard bubblegum concept album, but it was gonna be more in the vein of the song 'Bubblegum Factory.' But anytime you make those kind of announcements, they never happen. I've learned that lesson so many times.

STEVEN: We were staying in a swinging bachelor condominium apartment in the Alameda Marina while we were working on the film. We already had some songs for the album together at that point, but that's when we came up with 'The Faith Healer' and a few other things. I remember that Jeff was doing this deep dive into sixties bubblegum, Kasenetz-Katz, 1910 Fruit Gum Company, etc., and really going on about that stuff. And I was like, 'What are you talking about?'

I mean, I trusted his taste, but this gives you some insight into how different we are, and how our perspectives on making an attempt to break into the mainstream were so different, as well. Jeff is someone that, for whatever reason, turned out to be the kid that had very different interests than the other kids did, and was weird enough to pursue them. Whereas I, for whatever reason, was someone that actually could fit in and do well that way. So when I think about getting this opportunity to hit a note with the masses, my mind automatically goes to, 'Okay, how do we do that? Where do we fit in? What are the big records right now that have something in common with what we're doing?' But when Jeff talks now about *Third Eye*, he just goes, 'I went too bubblegum on it,' and that's it. He doesn't say, 'Oh, Guns N' Roses really hit right after *Neurotica*, and then Jane's Addiction hit a year later.' He was not looking for his place in it. He was actually quite literally thinking about Kasenetz-Katz at that moment.

JEFF: We basically wanted to produce the record ourselves, with help from an engineer. We didn't need someone to help shape or rearrange our songs.

STEVEN: We did meet with potential producers, though I think that it was more like our management just presented people to us to consider. In our minds, a producer was always a necessary evil, something that we never really viewed as a potentially cool collaboration.

JEFF: We met with Gus Dudgeon, the guy who produced all those great seventies Elton John albums like *Goodbye Yellow Brick Road*, and he was hilarious. He was like a flaming queen, wearing a jumpsuit and pink high-top Chuck Taylors, and he was telling us all these great stories. But we didn't feel like we were musical enough for him; we were punk musicians, so I think we were kind of intimidated by anyone who was too professional.

STEVEN: I remember Gus Dudgeon talking about how Roger Taylor of Queen couldn't play drums, and rolling his eyes about how frustrating he was to work with. And it was like, read the room, dude. It's such a stupid thing for a producer to walk in and tell you that someone you have mad respect for can't play, at least if that person actually wants to work with you and have a positive effect on the outcome of your performances.

JEFF: At one point, we were just like, 'Let's get Debbie Gibson to produce us!' She was on Atlantic, and she had actually produced half of her most recent album, *Electric Youth*. Also, her sister was one of our A&R people at Atlantic, so we set up a meeting. She was a super nice, smart, cool person, but the idea didn't seem as fun or crazy or out-there once we finally met with her. Plus, she was still really concentrating on her own career as a performer. It's interesting to imagine how that would have turned out, though.

STEVEN: We'd already heard all these stories from The Bangles and other bands about how the producer got 'their guy' to come in and play something – like, that iconic guitar riff on your friend's hit song that you thought your friend played was actually some session guy. So these were the kind of forces we felt we immediately had to take a hostile, defensive stance against.

JEFF: We wound up going with Michael Vail Blum, who had been an engineer on a lot of big records, like Madonna's *Like A Prayer*, but was just starting to produce. We thought, 'Okay, he's a solid engineer, and we'll just collaborate on it.'

STEVEN: Not that we were planning on making a record that sounded like *Like A Prayer*. But I think we just chose him because he seemed passive, and we thought we would be able to boss him around. That wasn't the most evolved stance we could have taken, but there you go.

JEFF: Ultimately, the problem was just the taste thing. We were such an insular band, and so clear about what we were into, and he was coming from a Phil Collins state of mind – you know, making references to Peter Cetera when you were recording.

STEVEN: He would obsess about the brilliance of the double-tracking of Peter Cetera's voice. And maybe there's some decent Chicago from the seventies, but Peter Cetera in 1990? Are you kidding me? We were just alien to each other.

JEFF: Michael heard things in a way that was very sequenced, very on the beat. Eighties music was so sterile because there was no swing to it. But all the music we grew up liking and playing, even the original punk stuff, was influenced by sixties-style players that played with a swing – the drums aren't all stiff, and the guitars kind of move in and out of the beat a little bit. That's what gives it its soul. But so much of eighties recording technology was all about being right on the beat. Perfect, perfect, perfect. That wasn't naturally the way we played, so he didn't get that.

STEVEN: Suddenly, we now have to be radio perfect on every take, and there's some dude telling us that we're rushing the beat or that we're sharp or flat. And we didn't have the confidence or wherewithal to be like, 'Yeah, I *like* that. Rushing the beat – you mean the part where it gets exciting? Too sharp or flat – you mean, like, Mick Jagger?' But I didn't speak that language at the time. And we're trying to sort all this out while also trying not to be overwhelmed by all the expensive studio gear, or the fact that it costs so much to be in there and the clock is ticking, or the fact that people are expecting you to catch lightning in a bottle.

Third Eye was recorded and mixed at Sound City Studios in Van Nuys, California. Famous for birthing such seventies classics as Fleetwood Mac's self-titled 1975 album and Tom Petty and The Heartbreakers' *Damn The Torpedoes*, and soon to become fashionable again thanks to Nirvana recording *Nevermind* there, the complex had become a favourite haunt of metal bands by the turn of the nineties, which only intensified Redd Kross's 'fish out of water' feelings. German metal band Scorpions were next door putting the finishing touches on their blockbuster album *Crazy World*, their presence lending an amusing, if somewhat bizarre, note to Redd Kross's daily grind.

JEFF: Sound City had this really terrible lounge. It was like someone's stoner pad in Lawndale, with a plaid couch, but they also had a vending machine. The Scorpions were at the studio next door for a couple of weeks while we were there, and we'd always see Rudy Schenker in there getting coffee – 'Hallo!' And it was like, how surreal is this?

STEVEN: The Scorpions were there when Victor told us, in the middle of our sessions, that he was quitting the band. His girlfriend A'me Lorain was a pop singer; she had lucked into a huge dance-pop hit with a song called 'Whole Wide World', and suddenly he'd decided to take over her career and lead her band.

JEFF: We were like, 'How are you gonna do both bands?' He goes, 'I could do it.' And then, all of a sudden, he couldn't do it.

STEVEN: I remember we were tracking and there was tension, because we knew things were getting weird. And I said to him, half-joking, 'Are you even gonna tour this record with us?' And he said, 'Oh yeah, I've been meaning to talk to you about that…' And I was like 'What?!?'

He breaks the news that he's going to finish recording his drum parts for the album, but then he's out. And I'm livid; I'm furious. And then, right at that moment, we turn around and there in the hallway is Klaus Meine, just kind of absentmindedly listening to the playback from our studio. He gives us the traditional heavy metal thumbs up, and it's just straight-up Spinal Tap. You're navigating the most tense, stressful moment, and then out of the blue Klaus Meine is there giving you a thumbs up, and all you can do is just say, 'Thanks, Klaus.' And he's like, 'Zounds great. Zounds great.'

JEFF: Victor leaving was a big bummer. We had a really tight unit, a really fun one on many levels, and it felt like it was more than just losing a drummer. But now we were going to have to find a new drummer, and we'd also have to wait until after the record was done to start looking.

The tensions in the studio finally culminated in an ugly incident in which Jeff kicked Steven in the balls. The brothers had often come to blows in the past, but this scrape was a bit much, even by their fractious standards.

JEFF: We would get into some gnarly fights, and nearly everyone who was in the band at some point has a story of having to break us up from getting into fistfights. When tensions would really get heavy, there would be a lot of button pushing; like, something I would do would just irritate Steven, and he would say something, and I would punch him. I always threw the first punch, but he was always the one to, like, push and push and push and push and push until I exploded. Those things would just happen in these brief bursts from like these long, secret relationship battles. I mean, to us it seemed normal, but now I just think in horror of what it was like for our friends to have to deal with it. It wasn't something that happened all the time, but it always *could* happen.

I actually did pretty well for most of the record; we got along fine through most of it because we were both trying to get through dealing with Michael and Victor. But there was one day where I was trying to record a part on an acoustic guitar, and I was just off a little bit. The producer was being super strict about timing, and Steven was standing over me, going, 'I can do it! I can do it!' And that's just like the worst thing you could do when is someone sitting there struggling with the part. You don't do that; I would never do that to him, and he would never do that to me now. But the stress of it all just kind of exploded in that moment, and I kicked him. I think that's the last time anything like that happened during a record. Coming down from that kind of rage, you're like, 'Oh my god, what did I do?' I felt horrible. I mean, he was not an innocent; but I have to say, yeah, my reaction was harsh.

Third Eye was released on September 12, 1990. Despite the difficulties involved in its creation, and the complete lack of rough edges on the final product, Redd Kross's major label debut contained a number of indelibly hook-filled tracks, especially the brilliant one-two-three opening punch of 'The Faith Healer', the MTV sort-of hit 'Annie's Gone' and the breakup ballad 'I Don't

Know How To Be Your Friend', all of which highlighted Jeff's impressive evolution as a vocalist and melodicist. The album's colourful cover, on which the three remaining members of the band (and a masked and naked Sofia Coppola) posed together in an oddly barren art gallery, reflected the weird but wonderful offerings within. Unusually for an all-male rock band of the era, there was a heavy feminine energy running through the record, thanks to the contributions of several female backing vocalists (including Susan Cowsill and Vanessa Bell Armstrong), and lyrical shout-outs to Debbie Gibson, Kim Gordon, Cherie Currie, *Planet of the Apes* actress Kim Hunter, and all-female Japanese garage band Shonen Knife.

JEFF: 'The Faith Healer' is a tribute to the Ohio Express and the 1910 Fruitgum Company – almost on an Oasis level – with a little nod to Brian Wilson thrown in. Michael Quercio from The Three O'Clock actually wrote the opening riff of that song, but because opening riffs don't always constitute songwriting, he didn't get a songwriting credit, which I regret to this day. It's only a couple of bars at the beginning, but that riff was the prompt for that song. I mean, monetarily it would have meant nothing to him, even to this day, but he should have got credit for it.

STEVEN: We wrote 'Annie's Gone' with our friend Michael Cudahy from the band Christmas. I wish that it had sounded more like the way we play it now, with crunchier guitars, but it still came out pretty cool.

JEFF: He sent us a tape of some half-finished songs he had, and for 'Annie's Gone' he had some of the melody, all the chords and the title; we fleshed it out and finished the lyrics, so that was a total collab. I think he had the Annie character from *Foxes* in mind – Cherie Currie's character who comes to a tragic end.

STEVEN: Michael had another song in consideration that we should have tried to do, which was called 'Teen God In An Oily Cocoon.' Michael should have produced *Third Eye*, frankly.

JEFF: 'I Don't Know How To Be Your Friend' was my attempt at a big breakup song: breakup, depression, trying to be friends with your ex-girlfriend, being really sad. I don't write a lot of relationship songs, but it just came to me; I was living on my own in a bachelor apartment on LA's Miracle Mile, and feeling kind of down, so I just wrote that.

STEVEN: That was Jeff working out his breakup with Vicki Peterson. 'I ate two candy bars for breakfast.' Those are good lyrics, and melodically it's somewhere in between 'You Can't Always Get What You Want' and John Denver.

JEFF: I wrote 'Shonen Knife' after a friend showed me this videotape of Shonen Knife and all their homemade videos that they had made for their first couple of records. I became obsessed with them, and I wrote to them and we became pen pals; and then we had a show at the Roxy, so I invited them to come to LA and open for us. They borrowed our gear, and the audience loved them, and that was their US debut. I felt like Diana Ross with The Jackson 5, introducing them to a wider audience. Naoko was the one I would always talk to on the phone, and she would say 'Only hobby!' – like, they weren't in it for a career. But they've been at it since 1981, and they're still playing. They also wrote a song called 'Redd Kross', which was very flattering.

STEVEN: 'Shonen Knife' is a really good example of Victor's prowess; he could do this really fast, fancy tom stuff like his wrists were rubber.

JEFF: We were giant Cowsills fans, so we hired Susan Cowsill – a friend of Vicki's who'd become a good friend of mine as well

– to come in and sing backing vocals on 'Bubblegum Factory' and 'Love Is Not Love.' It was so exciting to work with her; she's such an incredible singer, and The Cowsills hadn't re-emerged yet, so it was kind of fun to have her credited on our record. We also had Vanessa Bell Armstrong, who was one of the top gospel singers in the country, sing on Robert's 'Zira (Call Out My Name).' Robert always wrote really good songs, but they were not always Redd Kross songs, and I'd always feel weird singing them. That one always felt a little too Van Hagar to me, but I tried to sing it without the bluesy Sammy Hagar tone, to make it more like a hybrid of Van Hagar and The Beatles. Another thing that made the song interesting to me is that Robert's lyrics were like a love letter to Kim Hunter's character on the original *Planet of the Apes*.

STEVEN: 'Where I Am Today' is very emo, and a little embarrassing for me now. It was a case of me just trying to write what I know, which at the time was a lot of emotional confusion. I was living with Sofia, but at the time she was off making *Godfather III*, and it was all a little overwhelming to me. It was like, 'I guess this is the way this is supposed to go. I have no idea. I hope it works out!'

I actually did go and visit her in Italy for a couple of weeks while she was making the film. It was nice, but I was really out of my element. I was trying my best to roll with it, but it was stressful. I didn't come from a showbiz family, so I might as well have come from, you know, Wichita.

JEFF: 'Debbie And Kim' was another part of our bubblegum opera. It's kind of a 'what if?' song, like what if Debbie Gibson and Kim Gordon were two characters in the story?

STEVEN: I guess that song is sort of a female empowerment thing, where we're saluting and connecting the two archetypes: the Lesley Gore and the Anita Pallenberg of today. I mean, Kim was in Sonic Youth, and Anita wasn't in the Stones, but at that point we would have thought that Anita Pallenberg was cooler than Keith Richards. And then with Debbie Gibson, we're saying that she's pop, but she was kind of okay to like, because she seemed real.

JEFF: 'Elephant Flares' was kind of the climax to our bell-bottoms period. Because we had that image, but that whole late sixties/early seventies look was starting to catch on with other bands, and people would come to our shows dressed like that. We were always very conscious about that; and like Madonna, we had to change it up. So *Third Eye* was the end of that period.

STEVEN: I think at this point, we were making *The Spirit of '76*, and probably felt a little tired of the whole seventies fashion thing, and we were probably thinking, 'Well, the masses are always late to the party, so we'll just have to stomach that.' I mean, we had been dumpster diving at Goodwill since '82… but the bell-bottoms thing would follow us around for years to come, even after we'd moved on.

JEFF: Looking back, I still don't mind *Third Eye*. Any problems I have with that record would just be that it ended up sounding too clean. But it's of its time. I do think we would've made a more *Phaseshifter* version of that record had we had enough experience in the studio, though.

STEVEN: For me, *Third Eye* is still a sore subject. It was the wrong record for us at the wrong time. We had the wrong producer, and we shouldn't have had a producer anyway – just a great engineer that didn't fancy themselves a musician, and wasn't caught up in trying to advance their career. We were a garage rock band, like Crazy Horse, and we just needed to have a record that sounded as good as the first Crazy Horse album.

JEFF: The original album cover was like an altar of various products like Joy dish soap, Skippy peanut butter, a Marie Osmond doll and all these other products – it was our ode to popular culture that we grew up, this worship of products confusing sex and polarity and fashion. And then we commissioned our artist friend Vicki Berndt, who also directed the photo shoot, to do those Margaret Keane-style portraits of us, which went well with our demented view of what art was.

But the Atlantic lawyers flagged it and told us we didn't have the clearance to use any of the products, so the art department had to go in and airbrush them all out of the image. We have a couple of un-airbrushed versions of the cover, and it still looks so great; I wish we could have kept it.

STEVEN: We were trying to improvise without having the usual four lovable characters as our fantasy of the band, so that's where Sofia came in with the mask – this mysterious, half-naked girl with the long hair that matches mine. We thought that would really catch your eye.

JEFF: I kind of wish we'd stuck with the original album title, too: *Third Eye Paralyze*. We had recorded the album and were thinking of title ideas, and Robert and I had gone to Tower Records to flip through albums for inspiration. We found this Cher album where she's wearing red new wave glasses, and she has like a new wave haircut, and it's called *I Paralyze*. And I was like, 'Robert – what if we call it *Third Eye Paralyze*?' And he was like, 'That's incredible!'

No one would have made the connection. But then we decided, 'Well, we're being too clever here,' and just made it *Third Eye*. ''Third Eye' was already kind of a joke with us because of Laraine Newman doing Indira Gandhi on *SNL*; she was always saying 'Don't touch my third eye! Don't touch my third eye!' People think it was a George Harrison thing, but it was really more Laraine Newman.

Fashion icons in action, 1990. (Photo by Vicki Berndt)

Chapter 19

CROSSING PATHS WITH DESTINY

In October 1990, a month after *Third Eye*'s release, Redd Kross hit the road with Sonic Youth on their *Goo* tour, where Jeff and Steven regularly joined the headliners onstage to sing backup vocals on 'My Friend Goo.' Unable to find a permanent replacement for Victor Indrizzo, the band hired former Red Hot Chili Peppers/future Pearl Jam drummer Jack Irons to fill in for that tour, and their own subsequent headlining dates. Though *Third Eye* received mostly positive reviews at the time, and the Ann Magnuson-starring video for 'Annie's Gone' garnered just enough MTV play to pull in some new fans, many longtime Redd Kross followers were put off by the album's unexpected slickness. And when the album didn't sell enough copies out of the gate to even make the *Billboard* 200, Atlantic Records quickly dropped the band.

JEFF: We always did really well on support slots. It didn't matter who we played with; we always won the audience over. But it was a bit rough for us with Sonic Youth on that tour – and that was strange, because we'd done great shows with them for years. But they were having their first kind of MTV hit at that time with 'Kool Thing', and the audiences were just looking at us like we were Ratt, or some other Poison-type band. We would actually get the 'slow clap' in some places, and it was like, 'Oh, we don't need to deal with this right now.'

STEVEN: I think it was kind of bad timing for us to get the Sonic Youth endorsement. Had we been the Redd Kross lineup of '88– '89, or the band that we would become a couple of years later, that would have been way better than what we were presenting at the dawn of the *Third Eye* release. But we didn't have that same confidence. We tried to do a lot of *Third Eye* live, and it didn't go down very well, which was due to two things: we were missing Victor's playing – Jack Irons was a nice guy, but not a good fit – and we were also missing Victor's backing vocals. We got some backing vocalists to come out with us, and that was cool, but it wasn't like we were brilliant at arranging vocals or giving them direction. It was a pivotal moment for us, but we were wobbly, and we weren't firing on all cylinders.

We were in a weird, awkward, transitional phase with all of this, and it was happening at the exact moment when we were getting a chance, which was a horrible combination. It was our record that had the biggest promotion budget and the best chance to reach the most listeners, but Atlantic realised pretty quickly that it wasn't connecting – they spent all this money on the video for 'Annie's Gone', but I think it only got a couple of spins on *120 Minutes* – and they decided not to put anything else into it. We got this shot, and then we kind of stumbled, and that was something that kept me up a lot of nights in the nineties. And some of it was on us, and a lot of it was on the industry people around us who were cutting their teeth on us.

JEFF: It's a really weird time, too, because it's late 1990; the eighties are over, but it's still a year away from Nirvana and the whole grunge thing. We would've fared much better in that environment, I think, because it was kind of a rebirth of everything that was different. Before that, the edgiest, artiest things that were popular were, like, Guns N' Roses, Jane's Addiction and the Red Hot Chili Peppers, and we didn't fit in with any of that. In the end, it didn't really matter who produced our record or what record it was. It was a question of timing – it was just the wrong time for Redd Kross to be putting out that record.

Third Eye was just a poker chip on red or black. That's what it felt like to me. You make your record, then they give it a few weeks, and if it doesn't start doing anything, they cut their losses. It happened to a lot of people. It wasn't like we had a lengthy partnership with Atlantic, and they'd helped build our career; we hadn't even discussed the idea of doing a second record with them. People always ask us about Atlantic, like there must have been some awful story there with all this drama and fighting, but I have nothing bad to say about them. I mean, we really had no relationship at all with them – it was basically a couple of meetings in New York, and then we were either on the road or in the studio. It was like being on SST, except they paid our bills for a year. And it's not like the album disappeared; it's still out there for people to enjoy. But it was just like, 'Okay, now we have to figure this out again.' We had to finish all our touring for that record, and then reassess.

STEVEN: If *Third Eye* had had the aggressive guitars and wide audio spectrums of our next two albums, or had been a better produced version of *Neurotica*, I think there would have been a very different outcome. Instead, we came limping out with one of these things where people were going, 'Oh, it's good; it just wasn't what I expected.'

Later on, when the book was finally closed on *Third Eye*, Danny Goldberg said something to us like, 'Too bad about that Jellyfish record,' and I really took offense at that. Jellyfish's *Bellybutton* had come out a few months before *Third Eye*. I loved Jellyfish, and I'd even played on that record, but I also felt a friendly competitiveness with them. They'd hit the scene referencing a lot of the same pop culture stuff as us, and wearing similarly groovy clothes, only they were a lot slicker than we were. But Danny Goldberg's comment bothered me, because it seemed to shift blame for our album's lack of success on to this idea that there was only room in the marketplace for one pair of bell bottoms.

So we're dealing with these kinds of reactions at the same time that we're trying to take the next step, trying to get new growth, and our management is booking us into bigger and bigger venues. They booked us into two nights at the Henry Fonda in Hollywood near the end of the tour, and we had like half a room two nights in a row. It was really painful; I felt like such a failure. It's a big ego trip or whatever, but it's hard to not arrive at that place when you have ambition and you put yourself out there, and often the only way the fruits of your ambition are measured is by whether or not the venue is full that night. I was still with Sofia at the time, and Francis Ford Coppola was in the audience for one of those nights, and it was deeply humiliating for me. Granted, he was dealing with his own failure at the time, having just botched his era-defining trilogy…

Sofia and I had a very tight bond for a year or so, and we went through a lot of coming-of-age stuff together. And then she ends up in *The Godfather Part III* and I do *Third Eye*, and both are big flops within a few months of each other. It was a lot for a young couple to weather. For me, *Third Eye* flopping and getting booted off Atlantic was really scary. And her thing was so intense with *The Godfather*. I remember she did an interview and a photo shoot with *Entertainment Weekly* for it, and she came back, like, 'It was amazing! They're going to put me on the cover!' And then the cover came out, and the headline read something like, 'Did she ruin her father's film?'

So she's dealing with that, and I'm dealing with my own sense of failure, but I don't think I had the support system that she had. She had all these friends and family who understood the ups and downs of showbiz, but I didn't have a lot of modelling for it, or know many people who could relate to my experience. And it all took its toll on this young couple living together in an apartment for the first time. I didn't know myself very well, and wound up making some stupid mistakes; and then things finally ended really poorly a year or so later.

We had just finished our first British tour where we were opening for Teenage Fanclub; we played a headlining show the final night at the Islington Powerhaus, this legendary London bar, and the place was packed and we killed it. It was a great night, we were really on our game, and I came off the stage thinking, 'Oh my god, we're gonna get another chance!' And then she called me that night and broke things off.

It's all water under the bridge now, and if I see her by chance at some event, it's all nice and pleasant. But we definitely went through some rough times together.

The events of 1990 may have helped sow the seeds of Steven and Sofia Coppola's eventual split, but the *Third Eye* tour also brought Jeff together with his future bride, Go-Go's guitarist and songwriter Charlotte Caffey. Though a massive fan of Charlotte's for years, Jeff had never actually spoken to her until late 1990, when Redd Kross toured for three weeks with the recently reunited Go-Go's.

JEFF: I was a fan of The Go-Go's since I saw them very early on at the Hong Kong Café. They'd broken up in 1985, but when their greatest hits record came out in 1990, they got back together for a couple of great shows at the Universal Amphitheatre, which I was so stoked for. And then they decided from there to do a tour; they were managed by Gold Mountain, where our manager was working, so we told him, 'We wanna tour with The Go-Go's!'

The tour with them was great. We were playing all these opera houses and incredibly ornate, beautiful theatres all over the country, and their audience liked us; we knew how to adjust things and play up our poppier side. I was talking to Jane Wiedlin the night we were all playing at the First Avenue in Minneapolis, and she said to me, 'Oooh – Charlotte has a crush on you!' And I was like, 'Oh my god!' Once the ice was broken by Jane, I started pursuing Charlotte, we started hanging out, and we've been together ever since.

It all really brought me back to going to see them at the Hong Kong. It would always be like Janet Housden driving, with Joe from The Last and Bill and Frank from the Descendents, and on the way back Bill and Frank would be talking about how they loved Charlotte, and Joe was in love with Jane, and I would just say nothing. But I was a total Charlotte fan.

All the other girls in the band had an early punk image at the time, but Charlotte was always the blonde, California-looking Linda Blair girl. And then when I went to Connie Clarksville to get my first punk haircut, Charlotte was there; Connie had just bleached Charlotte's hair and given her a bob haircut, which was Charlotte's first movement into punk rock. Charlotte was standing only feet in front of me, looking in the mirror going, 'Oh, I like it. It's good.' But I could tell she didn't like it. I was barely 15 at the time.

And then, between the time I saw The Go-Go's do their reunion show at Universal and us touring with them, Steven and I were eating at Kate Mantilini, this diner in Beverly Hills. We're sitting there, and I'm like, 'Oh my god, there's Charlotte Caffey from The Go-Go's!' She walked right past and didn't even look at us. This was about six months before we knew each other, but it was so weird to have all these close encounters before we ended up together. When I tell her these stories, she's like, 'Whatever.' I'll say, 'The Hong Kong was really small and had like a two-foot stage. You *sure* you don't remember this tall, skinny guy with green hair and braces standing there?' And she's like, 'No.' But for me, it was like I was crossing paths with my destiny.

Redd Kross would experience another shakeup in May 1991 when Robert Hecker announced that he was leaving the band. Though it was heartbreaking for longtime fans to see him go, the decision felt like the right one for all concerned. The band had recently acquired two new members – drummer Brian Reitzell and keyboardist Gere Fennelly – and Robert's departure gave Jeff and Steven carte blanche to really revamp the band's sonic and musical approach.

STEVEN: Robert Hecker was losing his mind a little bit. Obviously, Jeff and I were a chaotic environment to be around; we always fought a lot, and we were under a particular amount of stress at that time, so we were probably really hard to cohabitate with. I think we really needed and wanted a lead guitarist who played like Ariel Bender or Mick Ronson, someone who played in a bluesy, seventies arena-rock style. But Jeff had said something critical to Robert about his guitar playing, and Robert had interpreted the criticism to mean that he needed to become *the best guitar player in the world* – which to him unfortunately meant going more and more down a fusion-y, Joe Satriani path, and wearing his guitar up higher and higher. He thought we wanted him to shred more, but we never cared about shredding. And he loved Van Hagar, which we thought was funny, and we were willing to interact with that part of him; but there were creative differences brewing.

JEFF: When we were getting near the end of the *Third Eye* tour, we could kind of tell that Robert had one foot out the door. He was in this crisis over what he was gonna do with his life, which was understandable, because he was practically homeless at the time, and it was definitely a point where we were all reassessing whether or not we wanted to continue to do this. But we had taken a quarter of a million dollars from Atlantic to finance *Third Eye* and these tours, and Robert didn't understand that you don't have to pay the label back if they drop you. He's such an honest person, and he was always agonising about, 'But how am I gonna pay back my part of the debt?' I kept having to explain to him, 'It doesn't work that way, Robert.'

STEVEN: So he was freaking out, and it just kept going down this path where we felt less and less connected. And then the last night of the tour, we were playing this weird show at the Hollywood Palladium where the power went out in the middle of our show – not exactly a victorious homecoming. Backstage after the show, Robert started to cry, and he said to us, 'Dude, I have to leave.' And of course, Jeff and I were ready for him to go; we knew creatively it wasn't working, and that his guitar was getting so high that he had truly lost his mind. But it was also the funniest thing in the world: He's crying, and he's saying to us, 'Dude, I just gotta be new wave. I just *gotta* be new wave!' And we just hugged him and told him, 'It's okay, Robert, it's okay. You should *totally* be new wave.' It was actually a very sweet moment.

JEFF: I still don't really know what he meant by 'I just gotta be new wave,' but I was glad he said it. I knew that it was becoming a problem, trying to work with someone who wasn't into the direction that we were going in. And I would've never, ever fired Robert Hecker, but it was getting impossible. So, I was in complete support of him and his new wave journey. Steven and I knew that we were nowhere near ready to give it up, but we also knew that we needed new blood for the next phase of the group.

We'd gone through the whole drummer audition process again with no luck, but then Andy Sturmer and Roger Manning from Jellyfish said they had a friend from up north who might be good. And that was Brian Reitzell. Brian came down and instantly fit, and we started doing shows with him while Robert was still in the band. But I wanted to do something to expand the sound, and I'd heard about Gere Fennelly. She was this combination of Liberace and Rick Wakeman and Elton John; she'd been a child prodigy pianist and had had jobs playing giant church organs ever since she was 14. She once had an organ gig at this Catholic church where she would play these religious medleys and hymns, and then mix *The Exorcist* theme song in with it; somebody snitched on her, and she got fired. We were definitely on the same wavelength, and she is by far the best musician I've ever known, so we added her and started playing shows as a five-piece. That was when Robert really started to pull away.

STEVEN: I think that lineup with Gere and Brian and Robert lasted for about a three-week period. Robert had always been the one who fulfilled that role of Jeff's jukebox, where Jeff would just turn to him in rehearsal or onstage and go, 'One is the loneliest number…,' and Robert would play it on the spot. But once we got Gere, Jeff would look at her and go, 'Do You Know The Way To San Jose?' And then she would lead us down this Bacharach rabbit hole. So there was a little role overlapping between Robert and Gere, and Robert had lost his energy to adjust. He just needed to be new wave. And we needed to find a new lead guitarist, which was something we hadn't looked for since 1984. Thankfully, we found Eddie Kurdziel.

JEFF: We met Eddie through a mutual friend. Eddie was great because he had been in cover bands in the Midwest in the late seventies playing Foghat and Ted Nugent, but then he'd moved to Florida for a while and had been in a new wave group called The Real Cameras. Eddie was insanely talented, and he was game for anything – he quickly found a way to make that seventies hard rock lead guitar thing work with our more hyper pop stuff. With Eddie, Gere and Brian, we were ready to start the next phase of Redd Kross.

A new chapter: The five-piece Redd Kross lineup with Gere Fennelly, Brian Reitzell and Eddie Kurdziel, 1992. (Photo by Vicki Berndt)

Chapter 20

BRITISH INVASION

Eddie Kurdziel made his official Redd Kross debut on 20 December 1991, when the band's new five-member lineup took the stage as part of the annual Ringling Sisters 'Fun Raiser' at the Roxy, which also included performances by Firehouse, the Steve Wynn Quintet and Permanent Green Light. Redd Kross's eight-song set featured new songs 'Huge Wonder' and 'Super Sunny Christmas' – both of which had just been released on a vinyl-only single from Australian indie label Insipid Vinyl – as well as a stirring rendition of Elvis Presley's 1968 comeback TV special closer 'If I Can Dream.'

Though there would (sadly) be no TV special to mark it, 1992 would be a definite comeback year for Redd Kross. They would only release one little-heard single that year – 'Trance' b/w the Charlotte Caffey co-penned 'Byrds And Fleas', released on the UK indie Seminal Twang – but it kicked off an artistically fruitful period that would see the band produce two of their finest albums and a handful of excellent non-LP singles, as well as spread the Redd Kross gospel to Australia, Europe and the UK, all areas they toured for the first time in '92.

JEFF: Now that we had the new lineup together, the next thing was, 'What do we do?' We'd just toured America for nearly a year, and we hadn't lost anything; if anything, we had moved up a couple of notches. But obviously we didn't have a label, which kind of blew our momentum in terms of making any kind of quick follow-up to *Third Eye*.

At the time, a band in our position – a group that had come out of the punk or alternative scenes and signed with a major label, and then been *dropped* by a major label – would have been considered dead in the dirt. But we hadn't been to Europe yet, and we hadn't been to England yet, and there was a little bit of interest there. And in Australia, as well, which is why we made the 'Huge Wonder'/'Super Sunny Christmas' single.

STEVEN: We did that Australia single right before Eddie joined, then did a few warmup dates in LA and San Francisco with him, and then went to a far-off land – a land where we hadn't 'failed' yet – to start over as an indie band. We were focusing on the international scene, and basically starting over. Rather than just sticking with America and trying to recover from that blow of the disappointment of *Third Eye*, we got a fresh start elsewhere, which was appealing to me.

I always wanted to go overseas, anyway. Jeff and I had randomly gone to Berlin once in 1988 when Jeff had briefly had a German girlfriend, and it left a huge impression on us. We hadn't played Europe yet, no one knew us there, and we were really dying to go. We'd heard so many stories about American musicians like Jimi Hendrix and Suzi Quatro, who had to go to England to find their audience. And we were already so steeped in British Invasion music, so we were really hoping that we'd find 'our people' over there.

JEFF: Teenage Fanclub invited us to come over to the UK at the end of January 1992 and support them on a two-week tour. I was pretty out of it, as far as what was happening in England at the time, but I learned that things had really been happening there as far as guitar pop was concerned. And that was a real thrill to discover, because aside from the Seattle bands and the whole hair metal era, which we still had PTSD from, guitar-oriented music was still pretty scarce in America. It was really refreshing to see the stuff really being mainstreamed there.

We were really lucky to be introduced to the UK via Teenage Fanclub, because we were very like-minded bands. They had just released *Bandwagonesque*, their classic album, and they were playing big university shows that were sold out in advance, and all these kids who were coming to the shows knew all about The Byrds and The Beatles and were into all the same weird shit we're into. So they understood where we were coming from, and it was a really fun time. We instantly had like a very cult-y kind of following; kids would hitchhike from show to show to see us, which was something we'd never seen in America.

STEVEN: It was exciting to be there, but it's funny – I thought the British audiences were kind of baffled by us on that tour. I mean, we weren't hated at all, but there was never a 'Star is Born' kind of moment, where they start out like, 'Who are these mysterious people?' and then by the end, they're eating out of the palms of our hands. It was more like we were sort of strangely circling each other, the band and audience, and by the end of the set we just passively accepted each other.

When we first went to England, people were calling us 'pub rock', and we were insulted. We thought that meant like a lame cover band, a bar band. And we didn't realise that, no, there's this whole rich heritage of pub rock, which I still don't know enough about, which is kind of embarrassing. We also dealt with a lot of lazy journalism in England – like, reviews where all they'd talk about was lava lamps and how monster our elephant flares were. We had given them so much ammunition, of course, but by that point we were wearing drainpipes and Beatle boots.

But in all honesty, I was also very intimidated by going to England. I had no idea who the kids were over there; I hadn't been tuned into the Manchester thing, or any of that stuff. But I knew that grunge was starting to happen over there, and then we're out with this band Teenage Fanclub, these working-class kids from Glasgow who are about our age and owe as much to Big Star as they do to Dinosaur Jr. And they're very welcoming to us, and that was a big coup for us, as well as a moment where I did feel a little bit of community.

Of course, I also felt competitive with them. We were opening for them, and they were packing places like the Brixton Academy, and they knew how to speak that language to those English kids in a way that we didn't. It was mesmerising to see, but it was also mystifying, in that same way that we somehow couldn't connect with a crowd the way J Mascis could. We were really beginning to hit our stride with the new lineup, and I secretly thought we were a better band than all of them. But Teenage Fanclub got to be on DGC. We didn't. And they got to open for Nirvana on tour that year. We didn't.

Nirvana's sudden and massive success would be a significant source of frustration and contention for Redd Kross over the next few years. Not so much because they felt in competition with them (though there was certainly an element of that), but because Redd Kross manager John Silva was now also managing Nirvana – and with the biggest rock band in the world to look after, his attention was elsewhere. Plus, while Kurt Cobain was typically generous about using his band's newfound fame to shine a spotlight on other deserving bands, whether by referencing their music in interviews or bringing them on tour as opening acts, he seemed pointedly unwilling to do the same for Redd Kross. And once again, a series of McDonald brothers crank calls may have been part of the problem.

STEVEN: John, our manager, had cut his teeth on us, and now he was getting his big break. And you think that, okay, some of that good fortune that's happening to him has to do with the fact that he got to cut his teeth on us, and surely this is gonna come back to us somehow. Surely we would be able to reap the benefits of our management that's now able to leverage one of the biggest bands in the world on behalf of their up-and-coming acts. But that never happened, at least not for us.

JEFF: It might have had something to do with this imaginary beef Courtney Love had with us from back before the whole Nirvana thing. Our friend Vicki Berndt knew Courtney from San Francisco; I didn't know her, but she knew a lot of my best friends, so when she moved to LA I was like, 'Wow, who's that girl?' She was kind of a bull in a china shop, just this aggressive, really kind-of-funny person. She worked at an antique clothing store near a coffee house we used to go to, so Steven and I would see that she was in there and be like, 'Let's crank call her!' She would know it was us and then give it right back to us; it was hilarious, but I think she thought it was a feud. She was very suspicious of us; years later, she told me, 'You guys didn't accept me!' And it just wasn't true. I would have loved to be friends with her.

STEVEN: Courtney felt that we'd dissed her back in the day, but she also insisted that, when it came down to not getting the Nirvana tour, it was all about politics and she didn't have anything to do with that. I mean, there's probably some truth to the idea that she told Kurt, 'They were mean to me when I was fat,' which was something we were definitely told at the time. Then again, I had heard, 'Oh, Krist and Dave like *Third Eye*, but Kurt doesn't get it.' So maybe that killed it for us, right there. And Buzz and Dale from the Melvins told us that Kurt was kind of mystified by how happy we seemed, like that was offensive to his sensibilities, so…

237

JEFF: Politics? I don't even know what that means in this case. Maybe because we were a Silva band, it would look like that was the only reason we were getting to tour with them? Maybe that was the political aspect of it because we were connected on some level? I don't know; I've never really spent that much time thinking about it. That's more Steven's thing, because he's so analytical, and I know he's spent many, many moons obsessing over that.

Redd Kross did share one bill with Nirvana in 1992… sort of: both bands played the Reading Festival in the UK that August. On Friday, Redd Kross was the first band to perform on the mainstage, where they were followed by Fatima Mansions, milltown brothers, Mega City Four, PJ Harvey, Public Image Limited, The Charlatans, and headliners The Wonder Stuff. Nirvana, on the other hand, headlined the Sunday show over Nick Cave, Mudhoney, Teenage Fanclub, L7, Pavement, Screaming Trees and the Melvins.

STEVEN: Sunday is the day we should have been on at Reading. I felt like we belonged on the same stage with Teenage Fanclub, who we'd toured with; with L7, who we rehearsed with in the same room in Beverly Hills; with Pavement, who had the same road crew as us; with Screaming Trees, who had opened for us; with the Melvins, who we knew through Bill Bartell; and with Nirvana, who had the same management as us. That would have made more sense. Instead, we were being pushed with these English bands, and we weren't an English band. But that's where we had to go because we had 'failed' in 1990.

This is basically what's happening at the beginning of our band's new chapter. We're getting into the nineties for real, but we're also kind of missing the grunge moment. Bands like Dinosaur Jr. and Mudhoney, bands that weren't as big as us in '88, they've taken off over in England, they're on the cover of

NME, and three decades later they'll be seen as foundational bands for this era. Shonen Knife, a band we wrote a song about in '89 – Kurt mentions them in '92, and then they get signed to Virgin, appear at Reading, and they'll still be a touring enterprise three decades later. So that was all a little weird and frustrating for us. And it still is, at least for me.

Redd Kross were not entirely prophets without honour in this new land, however. Several British labels courted the band while they were over in the UK, and a deal was eventually struck with This Way Up, an Island Records-connected indie helmed by Andrew Lauder. Lauder, a music biz vet whose past signings included such legendary acts as Can, Hawkwind and Motörhead, and who had previously co-founded Radar Records (whose roster included Nick Lowe and Elvis Costello), seemed to have a very keen appreciation for where Redd Kross was coming from.

JEFF: We talked to several labels, including EMI, but we decided to go with This Way Up. They offered a better deal than EMI, and Andrew Lauder just had the history. He was the rock'n'roll historian that had been everywhere, and it was so rare to have higher-ups at record labels that you can actually talk rock'n'roll with. It wasn't just like a bunch of businesspeople.

STEVEN: This Way Up was a cool indie label. They had another band at the time called the Tindersticks, who were just getting ready to put out their first record. It wasn't an obvious fit for us, but Andrew genuinely liked our music. He also had a guy named Dave Bedford working for him, who we genuinely liked and appreciated.

JEFF: At the time, the way they did record release schedules in England was very different than in America. So we just thought we'd do it their way, and concentrate on England, Europe,

Australia and Japan. And, because This Way Up records came out on Mercury in the US, we'd still have a presence there, too. But this was our opportunity to kind of expand our fan base beyond the US borders, and it takes a long time to do that when you've never toured Europe or Australia before. So that's what we spent a lot of our time doing in '92 and '93, both before *Phaseshifter* and after its release.

'Switchblade Sister', the band's first single for the label, dropped in May 1993. A stomping, glam-tastic tune with an instantly infectious chorus, the song – whose title references Jack Hill's 1975 female street gang cult film *Switchblade Sister* – served as a sparkling showcase for the latest incarnation of Redd Kross. Unfortunately, 'Switchblade Sister' wasn't released as a single in the States, where it appeared instead on *2500 Redd Kross Fans Can't Be Wrong*, a limited edition vinyl EP released by Long Beach-based independent label Sympathy for the Record Industry. Still, the song's power and exuberance boded well for the band's next album.

JEFF: We recorded 'Switchblade Sister' at G-Son Studios, the Beastie Boys' old studio in Atwater Village. John Silva managed them, too, and so we were able to use it for free when they were busy doing other stuff; we just had to pay the engineer, Brian Foxworthy, who co-produced the song with us. He was a super-great guy, really fun to work with.

I took the title from one of those trashy films that goes back to our Video Archives days, but I mostly thought about Donita Sparks from L7 while writing it, because she played a Flying V. The song isn't about her, but she was kind of the vision board person in my head.

I meant 'Switchblade Sister' to sound like a hit single from 1973 England, kind of like a Roy Wood or T. Rex song. It had that kind of 1950s chord progression that was really big in England in the early seventies, when there was the whole rock'n'roll revival happening within that whole glitter single thing; that's what we were really going for. And I really wanted to give it an English feel, because I didn't even know if anyone in America would even hear it. At that point, it almost felt like we *were* an English band.

Autographed flyer from a 1994 promotional appearance at Aron's Records in Los Angeles. (Courtesy of Geoffrey Weiss)

Chapter 21

PHASESHIFTER

Released on October 5, 1993, Redd Kross's first new album in three years proved that the muscularity and melodicism of 'Switchblade Sister' weren't any sort of fluke, and that Jeff and Steven's belief in themselves and the latest incarnation of their band had been more than warranted.

Produced by the band and engineered by John Agnello – who'd most recently twiddled the knobs on Dinosaur Jr.'s *Where You Been* and Screaming Trees' *Sweet Oblivion* – *Phaseshifter*'s twelve songs (thirteen in most overseas markets, where 'Any Hour, Every Day' was added as a bonus track) possessed a level of arena-rock power and swagger that had never been fully articulated on a Redd Kross record before, while simultaneously pushing their ridiculously abundant pop hooks to the fore.

At a moment when so much of the alternative rock landscape consisted of Generation X musicians channelling their adolescent trauma, *Phaseshifter* took the opposite tack, joyfully celebrating such life-affirming Gen-X adolescent experiences as watching Led Zeppelin's concert film *The Song Remains the Same* ('Jimmy's Fantasy'), finding vibrators in adults' nightstands ('Ms. Lady Evans') and ditching class to get high ('After School Special').

But the album's lyrics had a foot in contemporary concerns, as well, sarcastically saluting Axl Rose as 'The only God on earth' ('Huge Wonder', re-recorded from the 1991 Australian single), invoking Eva Isaac from TV's *Showtime at the Apollo* ('Lady In The Front Row'), and raising an eyebrow at the media and music industry feeding frenzy that had resulted from Nirvana's success ('Visionary'). The album's one cover song, Frightwig's 'Crazy World', lays the blame for the woeful state of humanity at the door of the war-mongering patriarchy.

Longtime Redd Kross fans might have experienced a moment of déjà vu when they initially dropped the disc into their CD players, as the very first sound on the album was that of 12-year-old Steven McDonald screaming 'Hit it!' from the beginning of 'Standing In Front Of Poseur' on Red Cross's 1980 debut.

STEVEN: Jeff and I were always really into that 'Hit it!', because I'm a squeaky little 12-year-old, but I'm yelling those words like I'm a jazz singer leading a band. Including it on *Phaseshifter* was like us interacting with our past, while also saying to all these other bands, 'We came before you.' We didn't know back when we recorded 'Standing In Front Of Poseur' that the first wave of Southern California hardcore punk rock would one day become so legendary, but we were there, and it mattered to us that people knew it.

JEFF: We'd already lived many lives by the time of *Phaseshifter*. That first EP had been our original debut, but then we'd gone away and come back again with *Born Innocent*, and then we'd kept going away and reinventing ourselves, and each time we'd come back felt like it was another debut. And now that we were making our international debut, it seemed like opening the record with that 'Hit it!' would be a fun way to say, 'This is where we come from.' I mean, who else could've done that?

What other bands from our peer group had actual songs from before their voice changed that they could sample on their latest record?

STEVEN: *Phaseshifter* was the first record after *Third Eye*. And we really felt we had something to prove, because people had thought that we had sold out to a major label, and that we'd made music that wasn't true to us because someone told us to. Which isn't the truth, though we had made music that was a little lost, because we weren't masters of our environment.

Going overseas and starting over had been a very bonding experience, and it really strengthened us as a group. The band sounded great, we really loved the vibe with Gere, Eddie was super-solid, and Brian was a great drummer who was also stepping up as someone who was really competent and could be a big resource as far as helping me with organising and taking care of band affairs. We all wanted to prove that not only were we *not* lame sellouts, but that we knew what we were doing. We immediately got along with John Agnello when we first met with him to talk about engineering the album, but we still had our defensive armour on – we went into the studio with thirteen very well-rehearsed songs, like we had this rigid plan that we would not deviate from under any circumstance.

And then John turned out to be really disarming and easy-going and patient, and absolutely on the same page as us sonically. His favourite album at the time was Alice Cooper's *Billion Dollar Babies*, and he wasn't worried about keeping up with Peter Cetera. Within the first week of working with him at NRG, this new state-of-the-art studio in North Hollywood, we knew we were safe. John could see when we were anxious, and he knew how to relax us. Jeff and I were on good behaviour for that record – we weren't fighting at all – but John knew how to encourage us in the right sort of way. He was also great at sussing out what was needed on any given track, and at helping us make good performance decisions, but with a soft touch. He was about ten years older than us, but he'd started out at the Record Plant in the late seventies and had all kinds of great stories; I think he made coffee during John Lennon and Yoko Ono's *Double Fantasy*, or something like that. I learned so much from him; in retrospect, I think we should have given him a co-production credit on the album, because that would have been a more truthful reflection of how things worked out.

JEFF: John was the first technical person that we were able to really communicate with. He was insanely able technically, but he was also really fun to work with. And because we were so well-rehearsed, it made it possible to just be hyper-focused for those twenty days or so that we spent in the studio, but also be kind of spontaneous when we were putting down each new layer after the basic tracks. And we'd written a bunch of neat songs!

STEVEN: It was very exciting, and also so gratifying – John was such a good fit for us, and the record sounded just like the way I hoped a Redd Kross record could sound, and it did so from our very first sessions. And then when we were mixing the record at Ocean Way, hearing our music coming back at us through the speakers, and sounding so confident and exactly what I would want it to sound like, with the loud guitars and good harmonies, and to be hearing it in a storied room where they only let 'real' musicians in… it felt *great*, you know?

JEFF: 'Jimmy's Fantasy' was one of the bizarro collabs I occasionally did with Bill Bartell. We were chatting on the phone, talking about *The Song Remains The Same* and its silly fantasy sequences, which kind of embarrassed me when I was 12 and watching it at the Old Town Mall in Torrance. I loved the concert stuff, but I hadn't started smoking weed or taking acid yet; but once I did, those parts of the film became just, like, complete comedy.

Bill was like, 'Oh, that'd be a great song – 'Jimmy's Fantasy'!' And then he just started faxing me all these reams of insane Jimmy Page-inspired, fantasy devil worship lyrics. So I pulled out the parts I liked and turned it into my own little thing, with that sort of fun, tongue-in-cheek mysticism that's been a part of every Redd Kross record from at least *Neurotica* on. Musically, it's both pop and heavy; Eddie and I are playing two different guitar riffs, and when we play them together it's like a bomb going off. It's so powerful.

STEVEN: I think 'Jimmy's Fantasy' was also our take on the whole quiet bit/loud bit thing that was happening in alternative rock, where you'd go from a clean sound to a really thick and distorted sound. It seemed kind of revolutionary at the moment, so we were utilising that technique, and this is what we came up with. And for the real nerdballs out there, we were stepping on Sovtek 'Civil War' Big Muff pedals, which now sell for ridiculous amounts on eBay. You could never take them on tour, because not only were their parts totally undependable, but they had this weird latch button that made them look like a small bomb or hand grenade. I think Jeff still has his.

JEFF: 'Lady In The Front Row' is about us being huge fans, and how being on the stage and being in front of the stage go pretty much hand-in-hand for us. I always liked the song 'The People In The Front Row' by the folk singer Melanie, and I liked the way that line sounded so I borrowed it. And then we used to religiously watch *Showtime at the Apollo,* and there was this older woman who was front and centre for every episode, and she would stand up, wave her arms and start swooning if there was a sexy male R&B singer onstage. The song isn't about her, but she was definitely a prompt for it.

STEVEN: Back in the eighties, Jeff would make these bizarre video compilations and then we'd take acid and stay up all night watching them, freaking out over Nicolette Larson into my mom's soap operas into Wally George, or whatever. By now, we were still ingesting our fair share of TV insanity, but just without the acid, and *Showtime at the Apollo* was always part of our Saturday night TV parties. This woman was like the audience barometer – you could tell if they were going to start booing or not based on her reaction.

JEFF: That's one song that we always have in our sets. It's fun to play, and it works really well live.

STEVEN: It's got sort of an 'I Should Have Known Better' vibe to it; Jeff had rented a Rickenbacker 12-string for the recording, and it's in there on the basic tracks. That song was us finding the sweet spot between our reaction to grunge music and our obsession with British invasion, and then throwing our TV/popular culture obsessions into the lyrics. We made a groovy video for it with Rocky Schenck, who had done The Cramps' 'Bikini Girls With Machine Guns' video. We did an all-night shoot at the Hollywood Wax Museum, which was super-fun, and we did it without anything stronger than nicotine or coffee.

JEFF: 'Crazy World' is a song by the band Frightwig; it's from their second album, *Faster, Frightwig, Kill! Kill!*. We've been friends with them from before they even had a record; they were like the sister band of Flipper, but they all had these big, huge voices. It's a feminist song, very political, very anti-war, very anti-patriarchy, and it's always been really satisfying to sing from that point of view. Their version is a lot more arty and psychedelic than ours; ours is just like a wall of mud, and we really rock it out. It's another one of my favourite songs to play live; we improvise a lot of sections for it, and it's kind of mutated through the years.

STEVEN: Covering 'Crazy World' is just us trying to casually put context to our story while also, you know, attempting to show people how superior we are. Because we loved Frightwig and played shows with Frightwig long before Kurt Cobain was ever photographed in a Frightwig T-shirt. With *Teen Babes*, Jeff would say he was giving the hardcore punk kids a rock education; recording 'Crazy World' for this album would have been like giving the grunge kids the same kind of education.

JEFF: The funny thing about our recording of that song is that it became a Mars Bar commercial in Europe. Deanna Chirazi, the writer of the song, received about 50 per cent of the deal we got for the commercial. At the time, she was a single mom with a small kid, and while our share of the money went towards our debt to the label, for her it was enough money to change her life. So that was a really cool and unexpected thing.

STEVEN: On the original single version of 'Huge Wonder', we were just starting to edge towards the beginning of what would be the fully formed *Phaseshifter* sound. It just didn't quite have the thickness that we thought it could have, so we re-recorded it with John Agnello for the album. That's a song that Jeff always felt very comfortable singing, so it kind of became a staple on our set.

JEFF: 'Huge Wonder' is the only song we recorded from the various singles we did between *Third Eye* and *Phaseshifter*. We wanted it to be something like John Lennon's Plastic Ono Band meets Black Sabbath, but the original version wasn't fully baked. By the time we re-recorded it, Eddie had been in the band for over a year, and it was just so much better and heavier when we played it with him. It's kind of a travelogue of Los Angeles at that time – the Sunset Strip and various other points of interests. Just what it was like to visit Los Angeles as a rock'n'roll tourist.

STEVEN: 'Visionary' is our version of seventies arena rock. We're also still trying to square our bitterness and disappointment with what happened with *Third Eye* while watching everybody basking in the glory of the success of Nirvana, all these people on the industry side clamouring to get a piece of them while also taking credit for what they'd done. It's like Ray Davies sings in The Kinks' 'Top Of The Pops' about having friends you'd never think you'd have before. So we're saying, 'Stop saying what this artist did was your idea. Stop trying to take credit for it.'

JEFF: It's kind of poking a bit at the mystique around some people at the time had, as far as 'having the answers for the youth.' I wasn't actually looking for a visionary; I was being sarcastic, and kind of saying, not to follow leaders, but 'watch the parking meters.' That's the attitude I've always had. But it's also looking at that need in all of us; like, I'm always looking for the next thing that's going to turn me on, as far as music is concerned. But there's only a couple of people I can ever put on a certain level where I would just, like, actually join their cult. John Lennon and Bob Dylan are two that affect me pretty deeply, but that's a very high bar.

STEVEN: 'Ms. Lady Evans' is us gassing on the adults in Hawthorne, California when we were growing up. We hated growing up in that place, and we hated the parents we had to deal with, other than ours. One of them, Mrs Evans, was also like a schoolyard supervisor. Someone we knew was babysitting at the Evans's house one time, and we went over there and dug through the parents' night tables looking for their vibrators and stuff. There were all these wife-swapping parties going on at the time; very seventies, like *The Ice Storm*, but the less glamorous, working-class edition. And we're coming to grips with all of that in the song.

JEFF: She was someone who always had it in for me when I was a kid. Sometimes you'll use someone in a song to get revenge in a way that they'll never know about. But there's a danger to doing anything like that, because then they pop in your brain every time you sing it, and sometimes you don't wanna deal with it. But we're always referring to the landscape of our childhood in our songs, so that stuff always pops up. Steven is also using Tom Petersson from Cheap Trick's original Hamer 8-string bass on that song, which Bill Bartell somehow found and bought. It was so hard to play, but Steven sounded great on it.

STEVEN: 'After School Special' is definitely a pop culture reference to the *ABC After School Special*, all those hilarious seventies made-for-TV movies about teens getting pregnant or into drugs or wetting the bed. But it's really about my teenage delinquency, and 'After School Special' is a reference to my various shenanigans.

JEFF: It's also about our friend Sherry; she's the blonde girl on the cover of *Born Innocent*. We only had a couple of friends in our whole high school that really thought the way we did, and she was one of them. She was brilliant; she got out of detention once by telling the teacher that her mother had a brain tumour and that she had to get home before her little brother got home from school, because he liked to play with matches.

STEVEN: Sherry would bring her little brother's Ritalin to school, and we would hang out by the railroad tracks and snort it off our Pee-Chee folders; I would get so high, I wouldn't go to class. A loving thing you could do for your friend in those days was to call in a bomb threat to the school before your friend's PE class, so they didn't have to get dressed for PE. But one time Sherry made a bomb threat to my PE class, and it was after I'd already dressed for PE so it backfired; I wasn't able to go back into the gym and put my regular clothes on because of the bomb threat. So instead of getting me out of class, I was stuck in PE extra long.

Musically, we were riffing on both The Stooges and Mudhoney, kind of like trying to take Mudhoney's song 'Touch Me I'm Sick' and doing our own kind of spin on that concept. It was kind of a playful, 'Oh yeah, you wanna do that? We can do that, too!' It's our equivalent of The Beatles doing 'Helter Skelter' as a reaction to The Who's 'I Can See For Miles.' I remember I sang it through a Twin Reverb with Shure SM57, because that was what Iggy supposedly did on the early Stooges records to get just the right amount of hair on the vocals.

Phaseshifter received rave reviews upon its release, and the band's pop cultural profile seemed to be higher than ever. In the US, Redd Kross performed 'Jimmy's Fantasy' on *The Tonight Show with Jay Leno*, while *Entertainment Weekly* ran a feature on the band (with the awkward title 'The Most Important Band in America?') that featured gushing testaments from Thurston Moore, Sub Pop's Jonathan Poneman and Scott Weiland of Stone Temple Pilots, the latter of whom would soon invite Redd Kross to open for them on a tour of US arenas. In the UK, Redd Kross performed 'Visionary' live on Channel 4's popular late night show The Word, and the band played some 180 dates around the world over 1993 and 1994.

And yet, said world seemed largely oblivious to *Phaseshifter*'s considerable charms. The album charted only in Australia, where it barely crept into the lower reaches of the ARIA Top 100, and the singles 'Jimmy's Fantasy', 'Lady In The Front Row' and 'Visionary' likewise made little dent on the public consciousness; the latter song did significantly better in the UK than the previous two, but still topped out at number 75. A dramatic cover of 'Yesterday Once More', recorded for the all-star Carpenters tribute album *If I Were A Carpenter* was Redd Kross's biggest hit of 1994, climbing to number 45 on the UK Singles Chart.

STEVEN: It was so unfortunate, because *Phaseshifter* was badass. We'd regrouped and were playing better than ever, we'd made an album that was exactly like we wanted it to be, and we had a wonderful experience making it together. The vibe was really good, and we did have some people who were really rooting for us, but we were way more of an underdog at that moment than we'd been a couple of years earlier, before we had a flop on our hands.

In the music industry, you're going up the hill, up the hill, up the hill until you get to the edge of the Grand Canyon, and then you get pushed off and you're supposed to soar. But most people just fall into the canyon and are never heard from again. We fell into the canyon with *Third Eye*, but we didn't quit, and by '93 we were putting out a new record at the same time as Nirvana – *In Utero* came out two weeks before *Phaseshifter*. I thought our record was better than theirs, and still do, and I thought we should have been given the chance to go out with them on that tour. We certainly had the connections to make that happen, right? After all, on John Silva's request, we had encouraged our friends in Sonic Youth to join his management roster. And it's no secret that Nirvana joined the roster a few years later because they wanted to be where Sonic Youth was.

But as far as anybody that really mattered in the industry was concerned, we'd already had our chance, and no one was really gonna get behind us anymore. In the speculatory world of the rock business – and then among artists where it's really just kind of a status game, and you're rubbing up against the people who have higher status than you – we were just not invited to the party anymore. And so we never got to be part of that world that Nirvana broke open, because we were no longer considered the cool kids by then.

Our last show with Robert was at the Palladium in 1991, the show when the power went out. When we were over in the UK in '93, the journalist Everett True was travelling with us for a couple of days to do a story for *Melody Maker*; we were talking about that Palladium show, and he told us that he'd actually been at that Palladium show with Courtney Love, and that she'd told him to trash us in his review of it. And he *did* – he told me that himself. He was like, 'Oh yeah, I reviewed that show. I trashed it. Well, Courtney told me to.' And I was like, 'What the fuck?!? Fuck you!!!' I made a very uncomfortable scene in the van.

JEFF: I mean, it wasn't like we were even aware of that review until Everett True brought it up. We were somewhere in the middle of England, travelling together in this van; Steven had just played the show with the flu, so he was already feeling bad, and he just completely went *off* on Everett: 'Do you know how fucking hard we work doing all this shit? And you're gonna slag us off just because Courtney Love *told* you to?' It was so embarrassing; I was like, 'Oh my god, Steven; just shut up.' He just railed on him, which in retrospect I'm really glad he did. But that's Steven – you don't fuck with his career. Being a prankster, I would find something like that kind of funny. But to him, it was not funny at all.

Eddie Kurdziel in action, 1994. (Photo by Jim Leatherman)

Chapter 22

MISSED BY INCHES

As 1993 rolled into 1994, Redd Kross rolled with it, promoting *Phaseshifter* with raucous shows in Europe, the UK, the US and then Australia. The band were between Australian dates in April when the word of Kurt Cobain's suicide hit the country. Everyone in the music world was shaken by the Nirvana frontman's tragic and untimely death, but the tangle of connections between the two bands made the news hit even harder and weirder for Jeff and Steven.

JEFF: I always associate Kurt's death with something that happened in Australia right before we got the news. I forget which city we were in, but a cab almost ran me over right as I was stepping out of a convenience mart. I was carrying a bag of stuff I'd just bought, and I threw it at the cab, like, 'Fuck you!' And then the cab suddenly stops, and this guy gets out – he's like this giant, barrel-chested, gnarly rugby dude. He's walking towards us, and I'm like, 'Hey man, it's cool. You almost fucking killed me, but it's fine. Get back in your car. It's cool.' But he keeps lumbering towards me. I'm 6 foot 6, so there's no way this dude's gonna sucker punch me, right? The moment he gets close, I kick him in the chest as hard as I can, and he falls down. But then the guy gets up and he finds this eucalyptus tree branch that's twice the size of a baseball bat, and starts running back towards us. We're like, 'Run!'

As we're running, he gets back in his cab and peels around. We're like several blocks from our hotel, and he's following us; right when we get to the hotel, he burns out and does a doughnut right in front of the entrance. We run straight to the elevator, and we're frantically pushing the button. The doors open, we get in, and they close right as he's running down the hall towards us. I never saw him again, but I'm sure he was going to kill us. And then we heard about Kurt right after that, which made it all seem that much more bizarre and surreal.

John Silva managed Nirvana, and he managed us. We were one of his first bands he ever managed, and we'd been with him for years. When the whole Nirvana thing took off, they had so many issues with their fame, and it was just like a constant soap opera. And it was kind of a drag for us; we weren't being tended to the way we should have been because they took up all the bandwidth. And rightfully so, because no one expected them to achieve their level of fame. But then there was Kurt and Courtney, and all the constant dramas with them. They were both going through intense drug addiction issues, and were completely unreliable as a result. But I understand the reason; I mean, I could only imagine what it's like to be someone who's very sensitive, and all of a sudden you're the most famous person in the word, when you weren't even going for that.

When Kurt died, it was a total shock. How do you even process something like that? I mean, the world had a hard time processing it. But for us, it wasn't just the Silva thing. Some of our best friends were extremely close to them. For rock'n'roll people like us and in our world, it was just a big fucking trauma. We were in shock, but we just kind of soldiered on and continued doing our thing, because we didn't know what else to do.

STEVEN: I do seriously love Nirvana, and I do think Kurt was a true visionary, and I would much rather have been hanging out at that party if we'd been invited. But at the same time, he was a fucking burnt-out junkie. And as much as I wanted his acceptance, I also was sober, and I had already learned a lot of lessons about that path. But those were the people that were getting all the shots in that moment – Evan Dando and Butthole Surfers and Kurt Cobain and Perry Farrell – these were the people who were considered the coolest of the cool, and who were getting the breaks and being successful, but who were also fucking strung out on one thing or another, being terribly irresponsible, and taking up all the bandwidth with their behaviour. And not only was it confusing for me, but it was frustrating and embittering, and it was really hard to just go, 'Keep your head up, keep moving forward.'

And it was also really painful, because we were serious veterans compared to our peers at that point. In 1994, Kurt Cobain and I are the same age, and he had been at it for six years, while I had been at it for a decade and a half. I'm the one who had the job that paid for our first demo, and I was 11 at the time. But we couldn't join the party, because Kurt thought *Third Eye* was lame, or Courtney thought we made fun of her because she was fat, or something.

Additionally frustrating for Redd Kross was getting left off the hit soundtrack of Quentin Tarantino's 1994 smash *Pulp Fiction*, after their old Video Archives pal had originally considered using one of their recordings in the film. *Reservoir Dogs*, Tarantino's feature-length debut from 1992, had actually featured some Jeff McDonald-inspired dialogue, and *Pulp Fiction* would have been an even better fit for Redd Kross's sensibilities. But it was not to be.

JEFF: We used to hang out at Video Archives all the time, and I'd always get into movie conversations with Quentin, because he was obviously the biggest buff in the world. But we'd also talk about music, and one time I just started talking about Madonna's 'Like A Virgin' – which was then a big hit – and I was saying that the guy made her feel like a virgin because he made her pussy feel so tight. And he was like, 'Whaaaaat?!?' The size of his dick was so big, it made her feel like a virgin; that's what I was taking from it. I had the dirty interpretation.

We'd have stupid conversations like that all the time because he was so easy to get into the weeds with. So I didn't think anything of it until after *Reservoir Dogs* came out and Roger Avary, a director and screenwriter who later worked with Quentin on *Pulp Fiction*, told me that after we'd had that conversation, Quentin ran out and wrote it all down. I remember seeing *Reservoir Dogs* and thinking that the scene in the diner was really funny. But I had no idea the dialogue was based on a conversation that Quentin and I had had, until Roger Avary told me. It's just classic Tarantino banter, but he takes a lot of his banter from real life – and in this case it was our conversation.

STEVEN: My best friend from high school, Chuck Kelley, also worked at Video Archives, and he eventually got a junior music supervising credit on *Pulp Fiction*; Chuck made a lot of mixtapes for Quentin that influenced that soundtrack heavily.

The Redd Kross cover of 'Blow You A Kiss In The Wind' was actually referenced in the original script of *Pulp Fiction* as, like, offscreen direction – they were going to use it in a scene. But when it came time to actually cut the song into the film, the producers and maybe Quentin as well thought it sounded too lo-fi. But instead of coming to us and seeing if we could remix it or cut a better-sounding version, my friend Chuck suggested that they use his favourite band at the time, Urge Overkill.

I know I'm a little bit of a raw nerve with some stupid resentments, but that one is certainly worthy of being like, 'Ow! Ow!' I guess what I should focus on is, 'Isn't it cool that Tarantino looked to us for dialogue? Isn't it great that he looked to us for what was musically cool?' On many occasions, I have seen interviews with him where he goes on about that great *Bewitched* moment where Elizabeth Montgomery straps on the Vox electric and rocks out as Serena in Samantha's living room, singing 'Blow You A Kiss In The Wind.' I don't know that we turned him on to it, but it was definitely an area where we met minds, as far as that being some kind of monumental moment in our youth. And he wanted to give us credit for it; he wanted to put us in his movie, doing that cover. But Chuck came up with the idea of Urge Overkill doing Neil Diamond; and it did sound beautiful, and it's a great recording. And they won.

I was like, 'Dude, why didn't you come to us first? Why didn't you give us a chance to beat our song?' I even had the 2-inch tape, and I could have remixed it for them. But Chuck is a very authentic dude, and the decision he made in that moment was just him coming from what he thought was a great idea and the best thing for the movie. I don't hold it against him. He wasn't really thinking about the implications to his friend's career, or anything like that; nor should he have. He was just speaking honestly about what he thought was a good idea for the movie. And clearly he was right; it worked. But it would be disingenuous of me not to admit that there was an 'ouch' factor to missing out on that one.

Whatever, it is what it is. We didn't get to open for Nirvana, and we didn't get to be in the soundtrack to *Pulp Fiction*. But we were *inches* from all these things. I mean, it's next to impossible to measure where we would be today if those things had happened, or how much more money would come your way annually as a result of something happening or not happening. It's all so hard to say. But all that stuff really does make it just a little bit easier to continue to make a living from what you do.

Redd Kross was really busy when we were being considered for *Pulp Fiction*, so I wasn't as on top of it as I probably should have been, but had it come up a year or two earlier, John would have pursued that avenue a little harder, instead of being distracted by the whole Nirvana soap opera. Whenever I think about things that did or didn't happen to us, usually I just wanna kind of go like, 'Oh, I blew it. It's my fault.' Like, 'My guitar was stolen, but I was drunk. It's my fault. I'm accountable.' But then there are times when it's just hard not to go, 'Ooh, yeah – that person let me down. They did disappoint me.'

Redd Kross spent much of the summer of 1994 opening for Stone Temple Pilots on a tour of US arenas that also included Meat Puppets and Jawbox; they also opened several dates for STP in the UK that fall. Stone Temple Pilots were a band with considerably less indie cred than most of the big grunge and alternative acts of the moment, and in some ways the tour felt like a consolation prize after missing out on being able to tour with Nirvana. But it nonetheless gave Redd Kross the chance to play arenas for the first time, even if the crowds were often still finding their seats while the band was performing.

STEVEN: In 1994, the worst thing you could do to a grunge band was expose them for having been your average hair metal band five years earlier, and thus prove that they were poseurs. It was kind of an updated version of 1979. I remember some interviews with Mark Arm of Mudhoney, where he was talking about how the guys from Green River who ended up in Pearl Jam were actually hair metal wannabes; just stupid, mudslinging stuff like that. Like, it would somehow hurt your reputation if it got out that you hadn't found out about The Stooges until 1987, and that your real heart lay with Aerosmith's *Rocks*. And of course, Mark Arm's old bandmates in Pearl Jam were now selling millions of records, so take that with a grain of salt.

I didn't know much about the Stone Temple Pilots story, but people at the time were saying that Scott Weiland was singing in an affected way to try and sound like Eddie Vedder, and that their label was marketing them to the alternative grunge world, sending their videos to MTV's *120 Minutes* instead of *Headbangers Ball*. They definitely weren't getting the acceptance of the Mark Arms of the world.

Scott and Dean showed up to our Vancouver show in late '93, when we were on a tour of Canada with the Doughboys. They told us they loved *Phaseshifter* and wanted us to go on tour with 'em. My reaction was, 'They like us and they wanna take us on an arena tour? Awesome.' But I also wasn't really impressed with the music of theirs that I'd heard. It was only once we went out on tour with them and heard them every night that I realised they were a really good classic rock band, one with really solid riffs, and they were firing on all cylinders at the time. I became very impressed by them.

JEFF: We went on every night before Meat Puppets, because they had kind of a hit album at the time. But it was probably very strange for them, too, because the Stone Temple Pilots' record was huge, they had that mainstream audience, and a lot of them didn't know much about bands like us or Meat Puppets; we really had to prove ourselves every night. It was really fun, though; Stone Temple Pilots treated us really well, and we did really well with their audience. But it was definitely an adjustment to go from going on at midnight in clubs to going on at like eight o'clock in arenas.

Stone Temple Pilots had had this instantaneous success, and we were like a legacy group even back then. So there was a lot of apologising from them over their success, because we were cooler – 'You guys should be big stars, not us,' that kind of stuff. And I thought, you know, 'Don't apologise – you're good, and you're successful *because* you're good.' They were great players, and not in that kind of annoying virtuoso way; they were good old-fashioned rock'n'roll players, which were very rare. And Scott was a really great singer.

And they treated us extremely well. Actually, the only time we were ever treated poorly by a headlining act was in 1988, when we were supposed to open for X at the John Anson Ford Theatre in LA – and it wasn't even X's fault, but their roadies were horrible to us. They wouldn't let us move the drums, they wouldn't let us set up our amps where we wanted them, and they were being super rude, and we finally just said, 'Fuck you' and we walked. They thought we were being babies, but we weren't going to be so hampered that we couldn't do our usual performance in front of our own hometown crowd. But we never had any kind of problem with Stone Temple Pilots or their crew. They were incredible.

STEVEN: They had a big show with big stage props, like these two gigantic lava lamps on each side of the stage. And they would act all embarrassed about it with us, like it was inauthentic, or whatever the grunge word du jour would have been for that. And, you know, all we ever wanted was to do those things. We *loved* the big production! Jeff's whole thing was like, 'If I had my way, I would enter the stage riding on a flying BLT sandwich!'

JEFF: That was the bummer about so many big rock bands of the nineties who were in the position to do those kind of arena shows. We grew up going to these ridiculous arena shows with Alice Cooper and KISS, and my brain had stored up a lifetime of production ideas. If you had the budget and the venue to do those kind of things, why be embarrassed to do something with it? Like, I always wanted to play at the Forum because I grew up seeing everyone there. And then to see the Smashing Pumpkins play there, and they're just playing the same show that they'd play at the Roxy or something? It's like, 'What the fuck is this? These lights are not impressive, you need to do more! You need bombs, you need ramps, you need all these bizarre films!' If I was bolder, I would've offered myself up as a stage director for big rock tours. That would have been my side hustle…

It was kind of a wild time. Stone Temple Pilots were dealing with their big onslaught of fame, while having issues with Scott – he was representing the band, but he was also out of it a lot of the time. It was just kind of interesting to watch the soap opera. Various people in the bands were going off the rails on that tour; Scott was one, Cris Kirkwood from Meat Puppets was one, and Eddie from our band was another. Those three were like the problem children of the tour; we'd be like, 'Where's Eddie?' and he'd show up five minutes before we were leaving for the next city, because he'd been out with Scott all night.

STEVEN: It didn't become anything with Eddie like where he didn't show up, or he was hitting bum notes onstage. What he was required to do with us was well within his capabilities; even if he had a terrible flu, he was still gonna be able to pull it off. So a nasty hangover didn't seem to stop him.

JEFF: I mean, how else is a rockstar supposed to behave? Cris, Scott and Eddie were the ones that were behaving normally in that situation; all the rest of us were just being uptight. At the same time, all three of them had big issues that later caught up with them.

When I was growing up, there was always such a mystique to arena shows for me as an audience member. But in reality, we would be hanging out backstage every night, playing Yahtzee with Derrick Bostrom, the drummer of Meat Puppets, right before we went on – like, we'd literally go straight from the Yahtzee game to the stage. If the audience had only known what we were up to backstage, it would have totally destroyed their rock'n'roll fantasy.

Utterly exhausted after spending so much of 1993 and 1994 on the road, Redd Kross were in desperate need of some downtime in the new year. On February 1, 1995, they capped the *Phaseshifter* era with a sold-out homecoming show at the Roxy;

their set featured three new songs ('One Chord Progression', 'Girl God' and 'Secret Life') and a special guest appearance by Robert Hecker, who sang 'Love Is You' and 'What They Say' to the ecstatic crowd. Also on the bill that night were local indie quartet That Dog, whose singer/guitarist Anna Waronker would one day marry Steven.

JEFF: I don't even remember that show – my daughter Astrid was born three weeks later, so I may have been a little preoccupied. But the Roxy has always been one of our favourite clubs. It was the very first club we ever sold out when we were just starting out, and it has the best stage and the best sound. Our shows there are always really magical.

STEVEN: That's the night where Anna and I first met. Jeff was a That Dog fan, and Charlotte and Jeff had gone to see them play a few times. I know there was always talk of Charlotte and Anna writing together, and they did eventually, but I'm not sure if they had started yet. I hadn't seen That Dog, but a neighbour had lent me their 'Old Timer' single, and I remember being really taken by Anna's picture on it. The address on the back of the record was for this independent label in El Segundo, which is the town next to Hawthorne. I just assumed that they put the record out themselves and that they were from El Segundo, and I got really excited; I was like, 'Oh wow, these cool girls with these amazing harmonies, they're from El Segundo! I can talk to 'em about El Segundo Park!' It turned out that they weren't from El Segundo at all. But that's when I met them, and when Anna and I immediately realised that we had some common interest in each other. We started dating pretty soon after that.

And then there were four: Redd Kross, 1997. (Photo by Vicki Berndt)

Chapter 23

SHOW WORLD

In the spring of 1996, Stone Temple Pilots scored a massive US hit with 'Big Bang Baby', the first single from their new album *Tiny Music… Songs From The Vatican Gift Shop*. Between Scott Weiland's uncharacteristically high-register vocals and the song's punchy blend of chugging guitar riffs and psychedelic pop, many listeners mistook 'Big Bang Baby' for a new Redd Kross song. When it turned out to actually be the work of Stone Temple Pilots, some Redd Kross fans accused the band's former tourmates of ripping off their sound and/or somehow stealing their mojo. Others bitterly noted that the success of 'Big Bang Baby' proved there was indeed a wider audience for the kind of music that Redd Kross specialised in making, and that FM radio programmers were clearly more than happy to play said music – just as long as it came from artists who were proven hitmakers, as opposed to, say, Redd Kross. But Redd Kross themselves didn't really see (or hear) it that way.

JEFF: When I write songs, I will often try to go for the feel of a song that I love, and use that as a prompt. 'Big Bang Baby' was a little Rutle-y on the Redd Kross side, sure; it was a very much a sideways version of 'Annette's Got The Hits', and it had a lot of the Redd Kross sass. But when I first listened to it, I didn't even hear that at all. Everyone else said, 'I thought it was you! It sounded exactly like you!' And I'm like, 'Really?' And then when I listened closer, I could hear what they're going for, but I didn't see it at all as some kind of devious plot. It was a tribute, and none of us were anything but flattered.

You know, that kind of stuff would never in a million years get under my skin, because I know what it takes to make rock'n'roll records. You're just everything that you've heard before, and you're just putting it out there again. We already knew that Stone Temple Pilots were huge fans of Redd Kross – they told us that all the time. And the whole time we worked together, whether it was in the studio or on the road, they were always just super-generous to us.

Indeed, by late 1995, Redd Kross had already begun working on the follow-up to *Phaseshifter*, with STP bassist Robert DeLeo producing. The collaboration looked good on paper – a genuine Redd Kross fan leveraging his own talent and success to help the band – and Jeff and Steven had brought some great new songs to the table, including 'Secret Life', a ballad they'd written for (but which had not been included in) Allison Anders' 1996 film *Grace of My Heart*.

Though *Phaseshifter* wasn't a commercial success, the making of that album had been a tremendously fulfilling creative experience for all involved, and Jeff and Steven thought they'd easily be able to pick up where they left off with it. But *Show World*, the new album that eventually emerged in February 1997, had an unexpectedly difficult gestation, one which found Redd Kross changing producers mid-project and losing a member in the process.

JEFF: We thought *Phaseshifter* was successful, in that it was exactly what we wanted; everything about making it was painless, and our fans seemed to like it. So our first choice would have been to just do another album with John Agnello. But at a time when people like Soundgarden were selling millions of records, the fact that we did *not* sell millions of records was a problem, and the label and the businesspeople wanted to try someone new.

STEVEN: Robert DeLeo was going to be our quote-unquote producer. That was my idea; we'd gotten to know him pretty well on tour, and he was really personable and a really great bass player. To me, he seemed like the secret weapon of Stone Temple Pilots – their John Paul Jones. And I think we were a good shoulder for him to cry on when they were going through their frustrations with Scott. And of course, Mercury was all for us working with Robert: 'You're working with someone that's written hit songs? Great!' So we started recording with Robert and his engineer Nick DiDia, who had been working with Brendan O'Brien, at Robert's studio in LA. But we quickly realised that we sorely missed the subtle qualities of working with John Agnello.

John was really good at dealing with the temperament of neurotic, insecure musicians, and he did that by disarming them with his own neuroses and then impressing them with his technical capabilities. It was this nice combination of being able to make it sound better than they'd ever heard yet not threaten them. But Robert and Nick were just like normal dudes; they also had some strong ideas about how to get the tracking done, and they didn't have the same bedside manner as John. They wanted us to record live in the studio with monitors, instead of singing and playing with headphones on; we weren't ready for that, and Jeff didn't like the heavy hand. He was kind of getting into this headspace of, 'I don't know, it just feels like Michael Blum again.' I could feel him retreating, and once Jeff starts to retreat, I become really annoying about trying to get him out of his shell, and things get worse from there. My personality's very dependent, and if I'm supporting him and he's retreating, then I don't know what to do.

JEFF: I have absolutely nothing bad to say about either of those guys. To me, it just really felt like an East Coast/West Coast thing – they're from Jersey, we're from Southern California, and we just have a different way of communicating. And in Robert's defence, he was essentially coming in as a lone man to a very clannish type of situation. We had taken a couple of years off, and I think we were being overly perfectionist. We just expected everything to go smoothly and sound great like it had with *Phaseshifter*; and when it didn't, we kind of lost our confidence.

We parted ways with Robert and Nick, and finished the initial sessions with Brian Kehew, our friend from The Moog Cookbook, as the engineer. Then we took a few months off and came back to finish the record with producer/engineer Chris Shaw, who had worked with Weezer, engineering for Ric Ocasek on their debut album. We brought in some new songs at that point, and some of the songs from the original session made the album, and some original stuff got re-recorded. We had some good times making *Show World*, but at the same time we were not that focused or united; though when I listen to the record now, I don't hear that.

STEVEN: The other big thing that happened before we really got into the record was that Brian Reitzell had become very insistent that Gere had to go. Brian and Gere are friends again these days, but at the time I speculated that it was a marketing concept in Brian's head, where he just thought we'd have more success as a band of four cute dudes – not four cute dudes and their big sister. But it just seemed really out of the blue, and it put me in a horrible position; I had really come to rely on Brian at this point, but I also really loved Gere's energy and vibe, and there was a very specific lane space she occupied, musically and personality-wise, that was such a good fit between me and Jeff. But Brian made it clear that it was him or her, so the options were either extract one person from the group and hope that she'll still play some bits on the record if we need her to… or find a new drummer. It was a terrible vibe to begin a new creative project with. The person I am now would've said, 'Oh, yeah? Okay. I dig what you're saying. Thank you very much for your input. We've got enough going on, we'll find another drummer… today, even.' That's what I should have done. But I was scared, and Brian was someone that was helping me with a lot of logistics stuff. He's a very competent person, and I thought I needed him.

JEFF: Brian was very adamant about downsizing and not having the keyboards anymore; he had a big bee in his bonnet about it, like, 'We have to just scale down and *do* this!' And eventually, we caved, but the only reason I caved was that I knew Gere had her foot out the door already. Although she was very loyal and would've found a way to make it work, being in our band was seriously affecting her ability to earn a living. She could teach piano, she could play in churches, she could go play in private schools and do all this stuff; but those jobs required her to be able to fully commit to it. So in the year or so between the *Phaseshifter* tour and starting the new record, I got a lot of flak from Gere, I guess because I was the perceived leader of the group. She was always like, 'What's going on? What are we doing? What's the plan?'

It was horrible to get the ultimatum from Brian, but we'd all been living really frugally for years, and Gere was at the end of her ability to deal with the struggle of being a touring musician. But it was such a bummer because we were like soulmates. I know Steven still carries some heavy resentments about it, but I'm not sure that he was as aware of Gere's situation as I was, because I was the one she would talk to about it. Still, looking back, it does feel like the first of the straws that eventually broke the camel's back.

Gere Fennelly did play on several of *Show World*'s thirteen songs (the record was expanded to fifteen on its Japanese and Australian CD releases with the bonus tracks 'Sick Love' and 'It's In The Sky'). The finished album was a further refinement of the heavy yet winningly poppy template the band had forged on *Phaseshifter*, and garnered similarly euphoric reviews. But even if sublimely hooky rockers like 'Stoned', 'Mess Around', 'One Chord Progression', 'Follow The Leader' and the album-opening cover of The Quick's 'Pretty Please Me' still radiated an exultant sense of possibility, this phase of Redd Kross was rapidly coming to an end. Then again, Jeff may have been dropping hints of his own burgeoning dissatisfaction in songs like 'Vanity Mirror' and 'Get Out Of Myself.' Meanwhile, the rapidly changing landscape of the major label world was indicating that things were fast approaching 'last call' for the band, at least for a while.

STEVEN: Jeff was the main lyricist on most of *Show World*'s songs, and when I listen back to the record now, I hear a lot of suffering, a lot of struggle. 'Get Out Of Myself', 'Vanity Mirror' and 'Secret Life', too – and maybe even 'You Lied Again.' It's a lot of, 'I can't look at myself, I'm sick of myself' kind of stuff. It's like, okay, you're in a lot of pain here, and this is not working for you; he's getting sicker and sicker of hawking his wares. Jeff McDonald is a commodity now, and it's starting to do psychic damage. When I hear those songs now, it's like, 'Of *course* you were ready to call it quits!'

He'd also become a dad. Jeff and Charlotte had a newborn, and Charlotte was still very much doing The Go-Go's, so they had to figure that out; they eventually landed on the arrangement where Jeff became more of a 'house dad' figure, which was also something that he wanted. Listening to lyrics like 'Vanity Mirror', it doesn't seem anybody's gonna really have to twist this guy's arm and tell him, 'Hey, you could dump all this touring shenanigans and trying to become a pop star, and spend your days at the farmers' market with your terrific little girl instead!'

JEFF: Yeah, there's a lot of dark lyrics on that album, a lot of internal struggles. But the music on *Show World* is still pretty upbeat. Dealing with feelings of like, 'I don't know what the hell's going on with me' and then putting it in a happy-sounding song was always kind of fun for me. But yeah, getting into your thirties, questions come up about the choices you make, and there definitely is a mood in the record that's like, 'Okay, this is a transitional time in my life.'

But I really don't think any one song on there is autobiographical. 'Vanity Mirror' is like my salute to the Flamin' Groovies song 'I Can't Hide', because I'd been listening to their *Shake Some Action* album a lot at the time. 'Secret Life' was a song I pitched to our friend Allison Anders for her movie *Grace of my Heart*, because she needed music of the girl group era for it; I'm a huge Dusty Springfield fan, and it was meant to be kind of a Dusty Springfield melodrama.

'Get Out Of Myself' *is* kind of autobiographical, I guess. People just get sick of themselves, just kind of get sick of being the centre of their own existence at all times, so maybe it's me snitching on my own narcissism. During all the touring and stuff that we had to do for *Phaseshifter*, I did, like, hundreds and hundreds of interviews, and after a while you just get sick of telling your story. Charlotte and I wrote that one together. It was a lot less psychedelic before Chris Shaw got ahold of it; he had some kind of sample on one of his gadgets that gave it this weird, spinning, 'Tomorrow Never Knows' thing and really took it to the next level.

STEVEN: We also really got deep into Beatles – and Byrds – territory on 'Mess Around.' That's Jeff in that old tradition of capo-ing the guitar and playing a D shape and seeing where it leads you. We wrote that one together, but the lyric 'Can't you see/Monogamy/Has always been so hard for me', that's his. That's a great lyric, but I don't know how deep you're gonna get Jeff to go on that conversation.

275

JEFF: Oh my god, every time I sing that song, people think I'm being autobiographical. It was just meant to be a place-holding lyric when we were working on it; I was like, 'I'm *not* singing that,' but that line works perfectly there. It may have been true at one point in my life, but the song is really meant as more of a classic look at the trials and tribulations of love in the form of a rock song. I think people can relate to the sentiment of it at some early point in their relationships, that point where you kind of confess all your weaknesses to the other person, because you're ready to take things to the next level.

But it is embarrassing, because a lot of times people will think our songs are autobiographical, just because I'm singing them in the first person. Sometimes these things just come out, and they're like a soap opera or a TV episode. 'Stoned' is a good example – that's just a little movie about a punk rock squatter girl from Venice who's stoned all the time. It's not about me or anyone I knew at the time; it was just a kind of observation. It's kind of like an Elvis Presley movie track brought up to date.

STEVEN: That's a fun, very Jeff and Steven lyric, with us bouncing things back and forth. It's a simple song, and kind of moralistic, but it's also trying to be kind of humorous. It's like the opposite of the rock'n'roll ethos of 'drugs are good', kind of like Jonathan Richman's song 'I'm Straight', where he talks about 'Hippie Johnny' who is always stoned. For me, 'Stoned' is our most obvious attempt on the record to try and relate to the current radio landscape, using a catchy synth part the way Weezer had done with 'Buddy Holly', which Chris Shaw had also engineered. Mercury released it to radio in the US, but radio didn't pick it up.

JEFF: After all was said and done, we were very happy with the record. We hadn't really been on the road since 1994, so we were really stoked to go out there again, with a new batch of good songs to throw into our set. But though our label was This

Way Up, our record was basically coming out through Island Records in the UK, who also had U2; and all of a sudden we realised, 'Oh my god, U2's putting out their new record the same day we are!'

Our promo team told us not to worry – that U2 records sell themselves. But then *Pop*, the new U2 album, turned out to be one of their weirder ones, and all the radio and promo people at the label had to kind of scramble to save it. I'm not gonna blame U2, but it was just interesting to see how things worked in that world. Like, a band as small as us still has to share bandwidth with the biggest band on our label; and it's still just an office of people who can only be stretched so far dealing with the marketing of our record. Obviously, they're going to put more resources into U2 in that situation, and we knew we were going to suffer for it.

The record industry was already in flux at the time, but then all these labels started either going under or being bought up by, like, the three remaining major conglomerates. This Way Up was consolidated into Seagram Polygram, and all of a sudden we didn't really have a home. It was such an insane time, and so many bands were impacted and had no idea of what to do. It was annoying on a business level, but at the same time we were still able to go out onstage and find the magic. But even that was more challenging than it had been in many years.

STEVEN: We went out on a US tour opening for The Presidents of the United States of America. They were really cool and supportive, but my entitlement and my expectations were getting the best of me. I always thought we were supposed to be opening for Nirvana, and here we are, lucky to get on tour with The Presidents of the United States of America. In reality, what we should have been doing is not opening for anyone; we should have just been doing our own tours. But I think we kept thinking that we were supposed to be expanding our audience and getting to someplace else, and that just being where we were wasn't okay. And that was either coming from us or we were getting that message externally, but I'm sure we were not sufficiently fortified with our own sense of resolve to fend off any external bummers that would've been coming our way. Because we were kind of right there with them, pulverising ourselves.

JEFF: The shows on the *Show World* tour were great for the most part, but there were a couple of times on that tour where I really felt like I was on automatic pilot. That was a bad feeling. Everything seemed fine on the surface, and we managed to make every show kind of mean something. But that 'going through the motions' thing was starting to creep in a little bit, and that was kind of scary. Once that starts to happen, then there's no real reason to be on the road, because everything that's gnarly about travelling so much becomes not worth it.

STEVEN: We did get to go out with the Foo Fighters in the UK; I finally got to open for Dave Grohl, but it was Kurt Cobain I wanted to open for. The story was that each Foo Fighters band member got to choose one band to open for them, and we were Pat Smear's choice. And of course, it was during that time when Pat kept threatening to quit the Foo Fighters, where they would take him to the airport and he'd be like, 'Oh, I forgot my passport!'

I think now he looks at that period as a mistake, and he was just having some kind of meltdown. But he was being super evasive and elusive, and they were having a hard time pinning him down. They finally got him on the plane to England, but he had no luggage, so he arrived with just the clothes on his back. At some point, even the roadies were telling him like, 'Dude, you stink – you've gotta get some new clothes!'

And so he went to some store for full-figure gals in the UK and he got this ladies' matching pants suit. It was very tasteful and cheery; I think it was blue, with yellow sunflowers. And it came with a matching handbag, which he wore onstage with the pants suit, and he kept his picks in the matching handbag. I loved that; that was really funny. But I remember being so grateful when he finally showed up; there was this brief period where some of the Foo Fighters crew were saying to us, 'Your friend is going to ruin this whole tour!'

Of course, we were having difficulties of our own. I don't know if Jeff remembers this, but the band had taken a break for a few weeks after Europe, and then we were supposed to start a short West Coast tour with Sloan opening for us. Brian and Eddie and our crew got in the van and went up to Seattle, and Jeff and I were gonna fly up and meet them. I can't remember what the extenuating circumstances were, but Jeff had gotten strung out in the interim and couldn't go. And so those guys are up in Seattle and ready to tour, and then we had to cancel the whole thing. It was horrible. I can't remember if he ended up in rehab or he detoxed at home, but I think that's when Brian made the resolve to leave. I just felt so sickened by the whole thing, so victimised and abandoned.

JEFF: No, there was only one show that I had to cancel, in Seattle, because I was getting clean and I was not there yet. But that's the only time that ever happened. I've never been on tours when I was wasted. Because you can't maintain; if you have a habit and you can't get drugs every day, you just physically cannot do it. It was during the long stretches of downtime where I would have difficulty; I was having issues with staying sober during those periods. And this was one where the show kind of crept up on me, and I wasn't able to get healthy in time.

I don't mind talking about drugs, although it's really nobody's business. But I don't wanna be labelled a junkie or anything like that, because whenever I had issues with habit-forming drugs, I never broadcasted it. I wasn't wearing it like a badge of honour, like Johnny Thunders or other people in the scene where it was part of their whole identity. I always knew it had to be a temporary situation; it was just sometimes a bigger problem than could be controlled. Sometimes it takes going away for a while until it sticks, which is what fortunately happened.

But I don't think my having to cancel the Seattle show was why Brian left. It was more that we had lost any kind of security as far was what we were going to do next, because everything was falling apart as far as record labels were concerned. *Show World* wasn't a hit, and it was becoming obvious that we were gonna have to slug it out again – which I think Steven and I would have been willing to do, because we have been doing it forever. But it was a bit much for Brian; he had other things he was planning on doing, he needed to make a living, and it was just getting too hairy.

As I remember it, Brian announced he was leaving right after our very last American show that summer. We still had more tour of Japan to do, and after we finished those dates, we were like, 'Okay, enough for now.' The *Show World* tour was over, we didn't have anything in the books for the future, and we just went our separate ways, like we always did when we finished a tour. We just never got back together.

On hiatus in the Hollywood Hills, 2004. (Courtesy of McDonald Family Archives)

Chapter 24

ARE WE GONNA KEEP DOING STUFF?

Redd Kross had taken breaks in the past, but nothing like this. For the next nine years, the band Jeff and Steven had originally formed as The Tourists in 1978 essentially ceased to exist.

Both brothers made the most of the break: Jeff devoted himself to being a stay-at-home dad while making experimental recordings in his spare time, and Steven significantly expanded his musical reach, working as a record producer, A&R person, and touring bassist for hire. Jeff and Steven also continued to make music together in various ways – including collaborating with Charlotte Caffey, Anna Waronker and young Astrid McDonald on the 2002 album *Sound It Out* by Ze Malibu Kids.

Unfortunately, the layoff hit Eddie Kurdziel hard, and the longtime Redd Kross lead guitarist died on June 6, 1999 from a heroin overdose.

JEFF: We never broke up. I remember seeing it printed somewhere that we had officially broken up, but that never happened. It was always just on ice, but unspoken. We had been at it as Redd Kross for twenty years, and we'd been a touring band for a little over a decade. And at that point, Steven and I were like, 'I don't feel like doing anything right now.' I had a family, and I really wanted to be home.

I was really glad to have some time off, where I didn't have to think about making another record. And I was in a position where I was able not to have to worry about it. Charlotte always earned *real* money with The Go-Go's, so that enabled us to not have to really trip out on anything, and it enabled me to be home 100 per cent of the time with our daughter and have an incredible relationship with my family. I wasn't thinking, 'Oh no, my band broke up!' I wasn't missing it. Life was just happening, and I was really enjoying it.

STEVEN: In those twenty years, I had somehow gone from being an early bird to a late bloomer. When Brian first told me he was leaving, I remember being like, 'Well, where are you going? Maybe I want to come too!' Which is kind of sad for me to think about, that I felt I didn't have any agency. I had more options than I felt like I did, but I just didn't see myself as a complete entity.

At the same time, I'm also trying to figure out whether or not my brother wants to keep going, but I'm having a really hard time with the idea of doing all the heavy lifting that would be required for another round of Redd Kross and having to find another record deal. I already knew what it was like to take the major blow of Atlantic dumping us, but now Plan B – redemption via European success – is not working either, and I'm getting the 'We're all out of ideas' kind of vibe from our management.

I kind of felt a little bit like Silva purposely buried us; he wanted us done and out of his life, and rather than just dumping us, he just kind of buried us. But whether that was true or not, the reality is that, if we weren't happy, we were free to leave. He never had a contract with us; that's not how he did business. Which is cool, I think. And we weren't present enough in our own enterprise; if we didn't feel empowered, that's our

284

own fault. Not that John ever was really stoking our ego and encouraging us, but he always had something for us to do, and it kept us motivated. But then once that started going away, then I felt like I was floundering.

My brother had been an undependable partner to me, so I wondered if perhaps there was a greener pasture for me somewhere else. And, as you can hear in his *Show World* lyrics, he was suffering. He'd started messing up again with drugs, and meanwhile he's a new dad and he needs to not be flaking, not be having that struggle. But at the same time, the question hung over our heads: Are we gonna keep doing stuff?

JEFF: Brian had an opportunity to work in film music; he started recording and touring with Air first, but he became really successful as a music supervisor and film composer. Steven really was kind of at a crossroads with what he wanted to do, but he went back to school and studied music for a while. I was happy at home with Charlotte and Astrid. But Eddie was the one who was just kind of lost. He didn't live far from me, and we talked; he would occasionally do an audition for a band – I think he auditioned for The Black Crowes or something – but he didn't really know what he was going to do.

Eddie was an alcoholic, and he never was able to really deal with it. If he got involved with a different drug, whenever he stopped using it he always assumed that he could still drink, and then the drinking would always lead back to the drugs. It was a vicious circle. But he was never the type of person that would ever show up and not be able to play; it's that kind of working-class drug addict or alcoholic thing – first and foremost, you still show up and do your job. That was very much how I was when I was having issues.

He was a brilliant guitar player, and really inspirational to work with. He had this youthful enthusiasm about him, a twinkle. But he'd be doing really well, and then he'd show up and have this kind of dullness, and you could see that the childlike enthusiasm had been dimmed by whatever he was using. He'd had a really troubled upbringing – foster care, parents with alcohol issues – but he always had the most amazing childhood stories. When we'd be sitting in the van after a gig, trading childhood horror stories, his were always the best; he had all these really funny, Huck Finn sort of stories about getting stoned at places like 'Hobo Junction.' But he didn't have the support that we had when we went into hibernation; he had too much free time on his hands, and he just got himself into trouble.

STEVEN: Eddie died less than two years after we stopped playing. I didn't see the moment when he went from, you know, Budweiser and a joint to slamming smack, because we always tried to keep a teetotal vibe on the road: 'You guys can go drink and party after the gig, but keep it away from us.' I suppose there was probably dabbling going on before that, but then it just kind of went into high gear after we got home from Japan. And it's so sad, because he was a really talented, sweet guy, and I think he just was having a hard time imagining what else there could be for him. I feel like, had he stuck around, he would've found many different ways to utilise his skills. Especially with what was about to happen with the music industry and with the internet, and how the whole gatekeeper notion of an artist's 'expiration date' was about to be crushed. But we didn't know that then; and if you were a musician getting into your late thirties, like he was, there was probably the feeling that it had been all a waste.

I wish that I could have been there more for Eddie. But I also didn't have a lot of patience for people who were strung out. Had he come to me with it, I would've been glad to drive him to an AA meeting; I would've been glad to try to hook him up with some people that I thought could help him. But I also would've been quick to acknowledge that I can't do this for him.

JEFF: I had talked to him before he died; I was getting my own shit together, and I was inviting him along for the ride. I told him, 'We *will* play again. I just don't know when – I have absolutely no idea.' I just assumed we would, but I couldn't give him any kind of timeframe; there was just nothing on the horizon. And him passing away was just another reason *not* to get back together, because now Steven and I would have had to put something together again from scratch. And he was busy with his stuff. I was busy with mine.

STEVEN: Jeff and I actually started making music again pretty quickly, though never with any real thought towards 'getting the band back together.' Our publisher had us doing some things, like trying to get songs placed here and there. We made an attempt to get a song into Todd Haynes' 1998 film *Velvet Goldmine* – 'Born To Love You', a very cool 'Bohemian Rhapsody' kind of thing we did with Roger Manning from Jellyfish, which didn't make the film but eventually ended up on our *Hot Issue* compilation.

In 1999, I enrolled in community college. I took some general ed classes, just out of curiosity to see what it would be like, but mostly I took a bunch of music classes. I just wanted to learn theory and try to deepen my understanding of musical language. I even took a popular songwriting class, and I wrote a song where I wrote out all the charts, a Bacharach-style number called 'Waiting For Our Last Time.' The teacher gave me a B or even maybe a B minus; he just thought it was this really corny, lounge-y thing. It later wound up on the Ze Malibu Kids album.

JEFF: Steven, Anna, Charlotte and I had already been making recordings as Ze Malibu Kids on Charlotte's 8-track reel-to-reel tape recorder for a couple of years; during the *Show World* tour, we would sometimes play some of the songs over the PA to see how they sounded. But during our hiatus, we all started getting together to record on Sunday nights, and we had a lot of fun with it, using archaic technology like really old drum machines and cassette tapes. I also did a lot of experimental recordings on my own. I was still very much involved in music, but it was just more for fun.

STEVEN: Ze Malibu Kids were inspired by a trip Jeff and I took to Berlin in 1988, where I ended up sleeping on Blixa Bargeld's couch for ten days, much to his chagrin. Jeff had a West German girlfriend at the time who invited him to Berlin, and just like when we were going to the Whisky a Go Go in 1978, he wanted to bring his little brother with him. She said sure, and I slept in the living room, whereupon it was revealed to me that her roommate was Blixa from Einstürzende Neubauten and Nick Cave and the Bad Seeds – and this was revealed to me when Blixa woke me up by blasting Nick Cave records on his massive stereo system. He was like, 'How long are you with stay?' I said, 'Oh, ten days,' and he just grunted. It didn't get much better from there.

Their apartment complex had a common building that had been turned into a nightclub called the Ecstasy Club, and I spent a lot of time during that trip going there, and being completely baffled by what these people were into – like, everyone was freaking out because Sylvia Juncosa was coming to town. And Blixa was equally baffling, because here was this intense German guy who took himself deadly seriously, but his musical heroes were like Nancy Sinatra and Lee Hazlewood. I mean, we love that stuff also, but we didn't expect these gloomy Germans to dig it in the way they dug it. And so Jeff and I just kind of came up with the idea of this band, Ze Malibu Kids, who would be this kind of holy grail for Blixa and his friends. Like, 'Lee Hazlewood was great, but have you heard Ze Malibu Kids?'

When Jeff and Steven co-produced *Get Skintight*, the 1999 album from Bay Area girl rockers The Donnas, Jeff quickly realised that such gigs were not for him. But Steven, enjoying the challenge as well as the interactions with other artists, went on to produce records by such diverse acts as Be Your Own Pet, Turbonegro, Imperial Teen, Steel Train, The Format and Fun.

STEVEN: Producing The Donnas made me think of the generation gap we'd had with Tommy Erdelyi when we were making *Neurotica*. Only now, Jeff and I were on the other side of that gap.

JEFF: We got it totally thrown back in our face. We thought, 'Oh, we're going to turn them on to so much cool stuff, and take them to the next level.' And then they were playing Cinderella and Poison and Mötley Crüe records for points of reference to what they wanted their record to sound like. The karmic wheel, I guess…

I never really put myself out there as a producer again after that, because I realised that the producer has to kind of manipulate people; you also have to be the shrink, and you also have to be the cheerleader. And that's way beyond my abilities. My nervous system cannot handle that.

STEVEN: Anna and I had both left our bands around the same time, and I remember talking to a guy named Dick Rudolph – the father of actress and comedian Maya Rudolph, who Anna went to school with – about it. Dick had been in showbiz for years, and had produced his late wife Minnie Riperton's albums among other things, and he said to me and Anna, 'Oh, great, now you get to find out all the other things you can do!'

He was the first person I ever talked to that had this attitude, and I remember thinking, 'Wow, that's interesting. Are you tricking me right now?' I had been thinking that I didn't know how to do anything else but be in a band with my brother, and that was scary. But replacing 'have to find out' with 'get to find out' was a little word trick that actually had a very positive effect on my brain. I realised that I didn't have to be a master at any of this; I just had to be willing to sweat it out, show up and do the best I can do, and figure out if there's anything for me there.

I still had a lot of figuring out to do about who I was, which involved trying to open my mind up to branch out beyond the relationship with my brother. At that point in my life, I had very few stories that didn't start off with, 'Well, we did this.' Every story was 'we', and that always meant Jeff and me.

When Redd Kross first went on hiatus, I tried to find my own identity by following Pat Smear's lead and joining a big arena band. So I auditioned for Weezer, and I auditioned for Billy Corgan's band Zwan, which he hadn't yet launched. Both of those seemed like they'd gone really well, but ultimately, I didn't get those gigs. But I wasn't going to give up on music, and I've always been a curious person, so I thought maybe a different approach was in order.

So I worked as a producer, I learned music theory, I learned recording engineering; I upped my game however I could. And after a couple of years, I did nail an audition, which was to go out with Beck as the bass player on his *Sea Change* tour. Greg Kurstin was the band's musical director and keyboard player, and he's really the one who suggested me and hired me. Josh Klinghoffer was playing guitar in the band, and we became friends – and our friendship would lead to him producing the first Redd Kross double album twenty years later.

And I played bass with Sparks for five years, which was a really interesting experience. Aside from the great work and the compensation for my time, I got lot of interesting information about their dedication to their art, and how the Mael brothers navigate the delicate exercise of collaborating and organising creative projects together. Not that they're very revealing – they're very much in the Jeff McDonald camp of close-to-the-vest operations. But at the same time, I could see that they are pretty firm in their roles, and they don't veer from them very much. Ron is the mysterious composer and piano player, and Russell does a lot of the heavy lifting like I do – he was the engineer, and he was the one that was most in touch with their manager. But mostly, those guys, they just really don't let anything deter them.

The first time I saw them play before I started playing with them in 2005, they were playing the Key Club on Sunset Boulevard, which used to be Gazzarri's. It was kind of an awkward phase in their career, where they had just done this dance record called *Balls*. And it just wasn't a career high point. But nearly twenty years later, they'd be playing the Hollywood Bowl.

I also started consulting for labels in the early 2000s, serving as the cool dude that some powerful guy would ask about this or that buzz band du jour. That was the brief, exciting moment where bands like The White Stripes and The Strokes were suddenly getting this chance, though it turned out to be the last time that underground rock was ever a major label concern. I had some A&R gigs with Universal Motown and Atlantic – which was funny, seeing as I had been a failed Atlantic artist – and I liked those jobs, because I didn't have to be in the office, I didn't have to deal with internal office politics, and I didn't have to get everybody excited about my opinion. I wanted to find cool artists I thought were great, and I wanted to help them infiltrate the culture.

Oh yeah – in 2002, I played rhythm guitar with Courtney Love for two shows. Courtney's still kind of a point of contention between Jeff and myself because Charlotte has done some writing with Courtney, and Jeff finds her very entertaining in a rapid-fire Kim Fowley way. But I had done these shows with her, and a few weeks later she invited me to go to a party with her.

Now, by this time I am no longer sober. And on this particular night I was on MDMA, which essentially acted as a truth serum, and I just laid into her for an hour about how angry I was at her. I was definitely bringing my own baggage into the situation, and the whole thing was not entirely heroic on my part. But for the people who don't love her, who feel so resentful of her in certain ways and for certain reasons, I felt like I was saying things directly to her face that many would have applauded.

But Jeff's never been on that page with me, and I'm not even sure if I ever told him the full story of that night. I *definitely* didn't tell him that I was on MDMA. But I guess now he'll find out.

291

Redd Kross rock Barcelona's 2012 Primavera Club Festival with Jason Shapiro on lead guitar. (Photo by Jordi Vidal/Redferns via Getty Images)

Chapter 25

RESEARCHING THE BLUES

The 1990s and early 2000s films of LA director Allison Anders often contained a small treat or two for Redd Kross fans, in the form of cameo appearances by Jeff, Steven or both. Their combined turn in *Grace of My Heart* as members of The Riptides – a Beach Boys-like group who can't get their heads around the complex new music of their visionary songwriter – was perhaps the most memorable and amusing, but they also appeared as members of The Sherry McGrale Band in 2001's *Things Behind the Sun*, while Jeff briefly popped up in 1992's *Gas Food Lodging*, and delivered a small but affecting performance in 1999's *Sugar Town* as a desperate, drug-addicted songwriter.

But in 2006, Anders would give Redd Kross fans the sweetest treat of all by luring the band out of their lengthy hiatus to perform at the annual Don't Knock the Rock Film and Music Festival. Though only about three hundred people were in attendance for their July 1 reunion concert – which featured the *Neurotica* lineup of Jeff, Steven, Robert Hecker and Roy McDonald – at Disney Hall's Roy and Edna Disney CalArts Theater (aka REDCAT), the evening's success gave new life to the band and their career.

JEFF: I guess I was part of Allison Anders' 'ensemble cast' – I always had small parts in her movies, going back to *Gas Food Lodging*. Allison's a huge rock'n'roll fan and a film fan, and so am I; we met when we were both hanging out on the LA punk scene, and we just became buds. We had one writing session, where we decided we were going to write a film together. I wanted to write a movie musical about an all-girl lowrider gang, but nothing ever came of it. Her next film was *Mi Vida Loca*, which *was* about a girl gang, but it was much more serious than what I wanted to do – all my ideas were pretty ridiculous and campy. Though now that I think of it, I should call her up, because that film could probably be rebooted as a Broadway musical.

It was always really fun to be in Allison's films, but my favourite was *Grace of My Heart*, because it was about that whole Wrecking Crew–Brian Wilson–Carole King period of music that I'm really passionate about. Matt Dillon played a character in that film that was loosely based on Brian Wilson, and Steven and I and Brian Reitzell were his band. We got to film a really fun *Where the Action Is* type of scene, where we're playing music on the beach in Malibu, and then we did another scene with Matt Dillon where he's playing us his opus in the studio, and we're freaking out on him because his music's getting too weird. Steven says something like, 'How are we supposed to perform this live?'

Back before airplanes had screens on the back of every seat and you could just choose what you wanted to watch, they would announce at the beginning of the flight, 'Our film tonight is blah blah blah,' and everyone had to watch the same movie. We were on a flight to England to meet with our label there about *Show World*, and *Grace of My Heart* was playing on the plane, and I suddenly realised that I was wearing the same shirt that I'm wearing in that film. I got up to go to the bathroom, walking really slow down the aisle to see if anyone made the connection. No one noticed.

Allison was curating this music and film festival at the REDCAT, and she asked us if we wanted to play it. I always had the best time working with her, so I was just immediately like, 'Okay, we'll do it!' But until that moment, I had no plans for putting Redd Kross back together or anything like that. It was only because Allison asked.

STEVEN: Well, two things really happened around the same time: Allison was doing her film festival, but there was also a promoter in Spain, a guy named David Jimenez that had been writing me forever, who had a company called Love To Art. We had always thought of *Show World* as just a flop around the world, but apparently 'Mess Around' got a lot of traction over there in Spain, and our 1997 show at a festival in Madrid was considered legendary, and we had somehow become this legendary band in Spain during our hiatus. And now David was offering us not only a spot at that year's Azkena Rock Festival, but a prime spot on the main stage. It was like, 'Can we actually get it together to play a big European festival?' The whole thing was really scary and intimidating. At that same time, that's when Allison was reaching out to Jeff playing the Don't Knock the Rock thing. So those two things are what really kind of put the fire under us to give Robert and Roy a call, and see if they wanted to get together and play.

JEFF: Roy and Robert were into it. I had just recently got back in touch with Roy, and though Robert and I hadn't worked together since he left Redd Kross to be new wave, we had always stayed in touch. We just put together a set, and that's when I realised what was looming ahead for me. I just remember thinking, 'Man, I haven't done this in a decade!' It was the longest I'd gone without performing in front of an audience since I was a child. Would I even remember how to behave on stage?

So that was strange, but the show was very, very fun. We had Be Your Own Pet open for us – Steven had just produced their album – and it was all these music and cinema people in the audience, so it felt very natural, like we were playing in front of our peers in this small theatre. And we've been doing this ever since.

STEVEN: It was a pretty magical night. And then we played the Azkena Festival, which was amazing, and suddenly we were in demand. Promoters started offering to fly us places, and we could kind of pick and choose which shows we wanted to do. We played about ten shows in 2007, and then in 2008 we started working on a new record... only, it would take us until 2012 to actually get it out.

JEFF: I had written a bunch of songs during our hiatus, recording them on Charlotte's old reel-to-reel in our basement, along with various bits and pieces and just random ideas I'd come up with. I would keep those unfinished pieces in my iTunes library, and sometimes they'd pop up on shuffle and I'd go, 'Oh, that's great,' and then I'd finish them.

STEVEN: Jeff had this backlog of songs from nine years of just going down to the basement with nothing better to do, but they were some of the best things he'd ever written. I went through it all and came up with about thirty-five minutes of great Jeff McDonald material, and that became *Researching The Blues*. He'd written all the songs, so the way we worked it out ego-wise was that I'd produce the record. We recorded the meat of the record in eight or nine days at a place in LA called Kingsize Studios, just as a three-piece. Roy lived like an hour away from us, and he had a job and a family, so we tried to be as efficient as possible about getting him in to the studio.

JEFF: We were self-financing it, and we just powered through the basic tracks. We weren't telling people that we were making a new album; we were just kind of doing it for ourselves. We figured once we found somebody who wanted to put it out, then we'd do the normal touring stuff and be in public again. But I think between not really having any deadlines for it and our own undiagnosed ADHD, it kind of turned into our own little *Chinese Democracy*.

STEVEN: We just kind of worked with Robert when he could do it; I think he came by for one or two sessions. Not to diminish his contribution to the record, because I love what Robert did on it, but in reality he didn't play on every song. We got Knut Schreiner, aka 'Euroboy' from Turbonegro, to play lead guitar on 'Uglier'; I'd produced Turbonegro's *Party Animals* record, so when the band was in town to do a show, I managed to grab him and bring him to the studio. Working with Knut and talking to him about music was always a mind-blowing experience for me; he plays like James Williamson viewed through the lens of a Nordic scientist. I think he's now a civic planner in Oslo.

What slowed things down was that we didn't really have the wherewithal or the know-how to finish the record and mix it ourselves. Also, I'd started playing and touring with Off!, a new punk band with Keith Morris, so that took up a lot of my time. I eventually taught myself Pro Tools well enough to put the kind of fun, splashy, trashy mix on the record that it has, which I'm proud of – it's definitely a garage-y affair. So then I started sending out the record and trying to get people interested in it. I sent it to Sub Pop, Matador and Merge, but Merge were the only ones who bit.

Released in August 2012, *Researching The Blues* was a garage-y affair indeed, its ten songs ditching the expansive sound and arrangements of *Phaseshifter* and *Show World* in favour of a raw and viscerally exciting attack. But as songs like 'Uglier' (co-written by Jeff and Steven with Charlotte and Anna), 'Choose To Play', the ringing 'Stay Away From Downtown' and the hard-riffing title track attested, Jeff's flair for alluring melodies and indelible hooks hadn't atrophied at all during the band's long absence.

JEFF: It's a really fun record, but I especially love 'Stay Away From Downtown.' I'd originally written it as a submission for the soundtrack to *Permanent Midnight*, the Ben Stiller film based on the Jerry Stahl novel. We'd demoed it with Steven on bass and Joey Waronker on drums, and I did all the vocals. That demo was more in the style of Fleetwood Mac; they didn't use it in the film, and that version eventually ended up on our *Hot Issue* compilation. But when we were rehearsing for the Don't Knock the Rock show, we just kind of turned it up and jammed it out, and it was like, 'Yeah!' And that's the version we recorded for *Researching The Blues*.

STEVEN: We did a really cool video for 'Stay Away From Downtown', although it wasn't exactly as I'd envisioned it. I'd wanted it to look like a Beat Club thing, that seventies German TV show where you'd have, like, Black Sabbath or T. Rex playing in front of this weird imagery. It kind of became a more indie rock version of that; you weren't supposed to see the boundaries. But it's one of those examples of where you go for something and you fail at it, but that ends up making something new and cool instead.

Filling in on lead guitar (and donning matching KISS-inspired makeup and a gold-and-silver leather jacket) for the 'Stay Away From Downtown' video was Jason Shapiro, former guitarist for late eighties/early nineties LA glam weirdos Celebrity Skin. Jason also went out with the band on their two dozen live dates in 2012, becoming Redd Kross's go-to lead guitarist from then on.

STEVEN: Although we never did a lot of touring for the album, we did a couple of short tours, sporadic dates and festival one-offs around that time. But Robert couldn't really do that stuff with the flexibility that I was looking for; Jason could, and we had known him since the Celebrity Skin days. Mentality-wise, we get along with him really well, and we share a lot of people and experiences in common; he gets enthusiastic about the same music that Jeff and I love, and we can speak in shorthand with Jason. He's kind of like our Ariel Bender.

JEFF: Robert decided years ago that he couldn't continue to do the sporadic kind of touring and stuff that we wanted to do, because he was concentrating on his education and his job. Jason was in Celebrity Skin, one of the best LA bands of all time, and he's a brilliant guitar player. It's just really fun to have someone who's kind of ready-made for us in the band – someone who thinks like us and comes from the same demented school of rock'n'roll.

STEVEN: I guess there's a part of me that gets a little miffed when people are like, 'Oh, the *Neurotica* lineup – that's all I really care about!' I mean, as a KISS fan, I totally get it. But not to compare Roy and Robert to Peter Criss and Ace Frehley, who were drug addicts and undependable and probably very frustrating for Gene and Paul to work with, but we've had a lot of great Redd Kross lineups over the years, and life's realities and practical matters can make it difficult to get everyone on the same page at the same time.

The creative core of Redd Kross has always been Jeff and me. Will we ever play with Robert and Roy? I'm not gonna rule that out. But at the same time, I'm not gonna give in to people that are only interested in us if certain conditions are made. If you're not gonna tune in if those guys aren't with us, or you only like the Janet and Tracy era, then you miss out. Calvin Johnson from K Records once told me that we'd basically peaked on our first EP. I was like, 'Okay, you fucking snob.' It's not like I needed him to, like, fawn over me, but I've worked my ass off over the last forty-five years. I don't need some snot face telling me that it's all been downhill since I was 12.

Roy stopped playing with us around 2015. He's always had the struggle between his work life and doing music, and then by the time he rejoined Redd Kross he was already in The Muffs. He finally decided that he could only really be in one other band besides his day job, and of course there was no competing with the formidable power of the late, great Kim Shattuck, so I understood, but it was hard for me. But I'm glad he spent that time in The Muffs.

After Roy left, we started bringing in Dale Crover, who I'd already been playing with in the Melvins around 2015. The Melvins' ethos is very much the opposite from the Redd Kross ethos. Jeff always wants to maintain the mystique of our band, like, you don't want to do anything to spoil your entrance.

JEFF: Oh yeah, seeing The Cramps at Devonshire Downs on their *Psychedelic Jungle* tour left a huge impression on me. I remember seeing this door briefly open next to the stage, and there was Poison Ivy, just sitting there in a tiny broom closet. I realised, 'She's not hanging out – she's just sitting there until they go on.' And then when they hit the stage that night, it gave me the same feeling I got when I would see the major bands at the big arenas. So The Cramps really re-introduced me to that whole concept of 'mystique.' And from that point on, it would always be like, 'No hanging around before the performance!'

STEVEN: The Melvins, on the other hand, are working musicians who, whenever they're on tour, are always also in the opening band, or the opening band has members in their band, or the opening band is also doing merch, because that's a cheaper, more practical way to tour. So Dale and I decided that we would play in both bands; I'll play bass in the Melvins and he'll play drums in Redd Kross, and when we toured together across Europe in 2017 – and then in the States after we recorded

Beyond The Door – we did double-duty. That's been one way I've been able to tie in my very, very lucky 'day job' with the Melvins with my passion project, Redd Kross.

But for various reasons, Redd Kross wasn't able to really do more than three weeks of touring on *Researching The Blues*. Which was a shame, because it got a lot of traction; people were excited about having a new Redd Kross record for the first time in fifteen years, and 'Stay Away From Downtown' was a little bit of an indie punk hit. I never felt like we got the chance to really capitalise on that moment.

Part of it was that the other guys in Off! seemed really threatened by what was going on with Redd Kross; their agent would never give me any help with trying to figure out a schedule where I could do stuff with Redd Kross at the same time, much less do a tour supporting Off! We did open for an Off! record release party in LA, where we only played our first EP, but that was it. Bands are weird, you know?

JEFF: All the tour dates we did for *Researching The Blues* were just great. It was the first record we'd made for a while that was completely indie, and it was kind of fun just to be on our own. We played off that record for a couple of years, and it seemed like it started getting more of an audience several years after it was released, which is almost always the case with our records. The new record will come out, and people will say they like it, but then about five years later they'll start saying, 'It's one of your best records!' That's why, whatever head space we're in when we're making a record, we just do our thing; our only expectations are that the record will *exist*. Some records are very popular out of the gate and then just disappear. Ours find their audiences, but they just do it at a snail's pace.

The *Beyond the Door* lineup with Dale Crover and Jason Shapiro, 2019.
(Photo by Tony Molina Filmworks)

Chapter 26

BEYOND THE DOOR

The buzz around *Researching The Blues* and Redd Kross's brief tour to support it was enough to trigger renewed interest in the band and their back catalogue, and by now there was sufficient room in the marketplace for vinyl reissues of their records. Frontier Records – a label that had passed on their demos over two decades earlier – struck first, reissuing *Born Innocent* in 2013, while Australia's Blank Recording Co. served up a new vinyl pressing of *Third Eye* in 2015. Jeff and Steven got into the game themselves, reissuing an expanded version of *Teen Babes From Monsanto* in 2015 on their own Not On Label imprint, and following it up in 2016 with *Hot Issue*, a new odds'n'sods collection released on their own Redd Kross Fashion Records, which also released a self-titled collection of Jeff McDonald home demos the following year. By 2023, thanks in part to new arrangements with Merge Records and Third Man Records, the entire Redd Kross album catalogue would be available to the public via vinyl reissues and digital streaming services.

JEFF: There was a really fun period after *Researching The Blues* where I started going through the songs and albums that we still owned the rights to, as well as old demos, and getting things like the expanded *Teen Babes* and *Hot Issue* together. And I also put out a solo album of home recordings I did in the late nineties, and an album of experimental music called *The Outrageous Incantations Of Beatrice Winters*. I got them all mastered or remastered, did the artwork with Jon Krop, and literally mailed them out myself. A live record from the *Show World* tour, *Oh Canada* – that was another one I did. They would sell out immediately, and then I would have like literally thousands of records to pack and address, because at this point Steven was doing Off! and the Melvins, and we were in between Redd Kross projects.

And then when we started touring again, we started finding other people to put out our other records. *Third Eye* has been reissued several times on other labels, but I don't deal with that one because we don't own it. But Third Man put out *Phaseshifter* and *Show World*, and then Merge put out an even more expanded *Teen Babes* and reissued *Hot Issue*; and then we found the *Neurotica* demos and Merge put out a special edition of that album, with the demos on one LP and *Neurotica* on the other. And Steven got back the rights to our first EP, and we found the demos for that, so we curated a special version of that. Now we're at a point where all of our records are out there for the real collectors and the people who buy vinyl, and they're also all streamable through services like Spotify and Apple Music. Everyone who wants to hear those records can do so, which is great. But once we start playing live again, we don't know what the fuck we're going to do. There are so many songs to pick from – which ones do we learn to play again? If we do just one song off every album, that's a set right there.

When we toured with the Melvins on the only tour we did for *Beyond The Door*, we played under an hour each night; and because we were on such a tight schedule, we did the same set every night. Steven likes to do that, because he's been in the Melvins machine for too long, but I do *not* like to do that. The last tour we did, we learned a load of songs, and we wrote different setlists like every night; we would change 'em, change opening songs, drop songs, bring in songs. So if you were following us and saw us three nights in a row, you would never see the same show.

It can be really scary, too – when we did a festival show with Superchunk, Laura Ballance from Merge was like, 'You guys write a new setlist every night? That would give me diarrhoea!' But it's something I'm always fighting for, both because I know 99 per cent of the bands out there are doing the same set every night, and because changing things up is a good defence against going on automatic pilot.

Beyond The Door, Redd Kross's first new album since *Researching The Blues*, only added to the glut of possible setlist variations. Despite being more or less thrown together on deadline from spare parts and half-written songs, the album contained a really strong batch of Jeff tunes, like the Stones-meets-early Bee Gees power pop of 'What's A Boy To Do', a loopy return to *The Song Remains The Same* with 'Fantástico Roberto', and the Kim Shattuck co-penned kiss-off 'Jone Hoople.' *Beyond The Door* also included some excellent Steven contributions, like the garage-pop celebration of 'The Party Underground', his co-write with Jeff on the swaggering title track, and 'There's No One Like You', a sweet and funny song penned by Steven and Anna about their young son Alfie.

Throw in a raucous opening rendition of Henry Mancini's theme from the 1968 film *The Party*, a ripping closing cover of Sparks' 'When Do I Get To Sing 'My Way'' (re-recorded from a version Steven had cut for his self-titled 2017 Melvins EP), and guest appearances from Gere Fennelly, Buzz Osborne and Josh Klinghoffer, and *Beyond The Door* was yet another Redd Kross album brimming with hooks, sass and unrepentant joy.

Released in August 2019 by Merge Records, *Beyond The Door* got the band out the door and on to the road for two months opening for the Melvins, with headlining jaunts scheduled for the US and Europe in 2020. Unfortunately, like just about everyone else on the planet, Redd Kross's 2020 plans were thwarted by Covid-19.

JEFF: *Beyond The Door* was done in more of a home studio situation than *Researching The Blues*. We just kind of collected the basic tracks and then worked on them periodically at Steven's home studio. But since we actually had a record label this time, we were given a deadline, so we finished it in a reasonable amount of time.

STEVEN: I probably took on too many roles on that record. I was not only the singer, bass player and arranger, I was also the engineer and a co-producer. So by the end of the project, I was pretty zombified.

I was also in three bands at the time; I was in Off! and the Melvins, and Redd Kross worked the least of the three. It's hard to be in someone else's band in a supporting role, especially at this point in the game – and especially when you have your own rock band, too, but it can't function well enough to get it together and make a record without you lighting a fire under people's asses. But I knew from looking at the Melvins' plans that if Redd Kross could get a new record out in 2019, we could do a US tour with the Melvins. So that glimmer of opportunity made me want to see if I could make that happen for the band. All things considered, I think it came out okay.

JEFF: Steven and I hadn't collaborated in the same room writing songs for ages. We've never had any rules of how things are done, but usually someone has a bunch of songs and then we go through them and go, 'This one's good, this one's not, this one's great,' etc. But this time, we were sitting down and writing lyrics and making each other laugh. It was fun.

STEVEN: The title track is just Jeff and I facing each other in my little music room with acoustic guitars in a classic 'John and Paul' collaboration. It came together quickly, whereas many of the songs on the record were sort of cobbled together from other pieces that had already existed.

The title itself comes from a 1974 horror movie which Jeff and I are obsessed with. We saw it as kids, and it was like a cheap rip-off of *The Exorcist* crossed with *Rosemary's Baby*. When *The Exorcist* first came out, Jeff used to always grind on me to go to the mall and see it with him; we were kids and it was rated R, but the plan was that we'd 'pimp tickets' – we'd get some adult to buy us tickets so we could get in. Which is what Jeff eventually did, but I refused to go; I put my foot down, and somehow I got out of it. But I was ready for the movie *Beyond the Door*, which came out like a year later. We tricked our mom into taking us; it starred Juliet Mills from *Nanny and the Professor*, so we were like, 'Oh, come on, Mom – Nanny's in it!' Little did she know it was going to be a pregnant Nanny levitating, swivelling her head around and spitting up Campbell's Soup.

JEFF: 'Fantástico Roberto' is the sequel to 'Jimmy's Fantasy' – I was looking through my computer and found all these lyric ideas that Bill Bartell had sent me at the same time he was bombarding me with the ideas for 'Jimmy's Fantasy', but these ones were about Robert Plant. I picked through Bill's ideas and went from there. I think the song is actually my demo, and then we kind of played on top of it.

STEVEN: Yeah, 'Fantástico Roberto' came from a basement tape of Jeff's, just like 'When Do I Get To Sing 'My Way'' required some archaeology on my part – I'd covered that myself on an EP I did for the Melvins, and I think we used the same vocal here for practical reasons, though it's a slightly different version. That was a song that was always on the set during the five years I played with Sparks. I never loved their mid-nineties electronic house arrangement of it, but it's still a really great song about frustration in the world of music that's obviously easy for me to relate to. And I thought, to take it to an extra level, what if we do it *my* way, and turn it into a guitar rock song?

JEFF: I wanted to do 'The Party' because I thought it would be a great way to open the album, as well as a great way to open the show. My idea was that we'd go onstage with the recording blasting while we're plugging in and fiddling around, and then halfway through, the band would drop into the song and finish it. We haven't actually got the chance to do that, but I love *The Party* soundtrack, and I love Mancini. Henry Mancini was of course an early influence on Redd Kross because Steven learned the *Peter Gunn* theme in school orchestra and worked it into 'Annette's Got The Hits', so this was kind of bringing it full circle.

STEVEN: I didn't write much on this album; mostly it was me trying to be supportive to Jeff's songwriting and then slipping a few things of my own onto the record, like 'There's No One Like You.' That one's a love song to my son; I wasn't skilled enough to know how to put some words together in a way that it wouldn't come out like a Hallmark card, but Anna helped me do it. She was like the midwife; she helped me birth the lyrics. And the truth is, I meant every word – so much so that I was crying the entire time while recording the vocals.

It's hard to put something like that out there when you know your audience is made up of grizzled old rockers, many of whom will never be breeders themselves. But the song is just what it is; it's not particularly Redd Kross, but it's a very honest account of feeling grateful for this little human being in my life.

The funniest line to me is the one about, 'You said you didn't like me 'cause I'm not a Jew.' I mean, I hate to hit controversial topics right now, but it's a true story. Alfie is 56 per cent Ashkenazi Jew, thanks to his mom's 100 per cent. And actually, we since have learned I'm 12 and a half per cent Jewish because, thanks to 23 and Me, we found out that my grandma was adopted, and we didn't know she was actually 50 per cent Jewish.

Anyway, Alfie came home at 9 years old from his first Shabbat, which our neighbour had invited him to. He's always giving me a hard time; I'm the parent that gets viewed as the more disciplinary of the two because I say 'No' every once in a while. And he was just nailing me at that moment about something or other, and he goes, 'You know why I don't like you? You're not Jewish!' And I'm like, 'What?!?' And maybe it speaks more about tribalism or whatever other hot topic we can map onto that right now, but I just thought it was really funny that my 9-year-old said that to me. And that's really what the song came out of.

JEFF: The lyrics to 'Jone Hoople' were co-written with Kim Shattuck, just a few months before she passed away. She didn't have the ability to talk or move at that point because of ALS, but she could write with her eyes using this special computer device she had. We had been friends going back to when she was in The Pandoras, so I asked her if she wanted to write lyrics to this song, and she was like, 'Oh yeah, let's collaborate!' It's a classic Kim diss track, as anyone who knows The Pandoras and The Muffs will recognise; even when she was horribly ill, she was still Kim, 100 per cent. The majority of the lyrics are hers; I just had to make a few edits here and there to squish 'em into our music. It's like Kim's 'You're So Vain' – it's about someone specific, but I can't say who it is.

STEVEN: We were calling the song 'Jone Hoople' before we even had Kim's lyrics, because I had been listening to Mott The Hoople a lot, and 'All The Way From Memphis' has always been a reference point for us. We'd tried to put some of that same feel in the song '1976' on *Third Eye*, though actually I think we were also referencing 'Turn To You' by The Go-Go's, with its great piano solo. But that modulated kind of seventies take on Jerry Lee Lewis-style piano is a favourite genre we try to visit every once in a while. And we love Gere – she's the queen of all sorts of different styles of piano – so this song was a good opportunity to get her on to the album.

Overall, I would say *Beyond The Door* is a solid album, but the record just ended up taking so much out of me. I was also recording with Off! at the time, and I was touring with the Melvins constantly. At some point when we were making *Beyond The Door*, it took two weeks longer for Jeff to get his lyrics written than we'd planned, which put the record into time that I had promised for Off! They got deeply offended, and then (or so it seemed to me) eventually kicked me out of the band over it – and in a really brutal way, or at least in a way that didn't need to be so petty and calculating and hurtful, especially for middle-aged men.

I had put a lot of time and effort into that band. I had also been engineering their latest record, and at one point I said I needed to take a break, and I was begged not to. And then, after I spent ten years of keeping all these balls in the air, playing a million different roles to different people and trying to keep everybody happy, and there was a new Off! album that I'd engineered for them basically in the can… I was out on tour for *Beyond The Door*, and I got this phone call from them where they unceremoniously fired me. Ultimately, whatever their stated reasons were, they didn't like me making a Redd Kross record.

But, hey, it was an opportunity for me to work on Redd Kross. The record came out, and we did like a nine-week support tour that fall with the Melvins, and then we were planning this big European headlining tour in 2020, which was something we hadn't done since the nineties, and we were hoping to do a big

American headlining tour as well. Buzz was gonna do a solo year in 2020, so I had this window where I could, for lack of a better term, take a break from my day job with the Melvins. And not to denigrate them at all with that term; it's my livelihood, and it's also creatively satisfying to be in that band. But everything was coming together in a way that was going to allow Redd Kross to actually enjoy a 'routine record cycle' for the first time since the late nineties, and I was really stoked about it.

Well, we all know how that turned out. We were just about to leave for Europe when the pandemic hit, so that got squashed. All the opportunities to sell *Beyond The Door* the hard way, night after night, got squashed with it – and not just the physical sales, but the songs and the legacy of the record, too. I really thought we'd be able to go out there and just kill it night after night, and then that would become another part of the story of that record. And instead, it was kind of still-birthed by the pandemic, something that of course happened to so many other artists at the time, as well. Looking back now, it's made the legacy of *Beyond The Door* a little harder for me; it was our first new record in seven years, but it never really got a chance to have a life.

Redd Kross, 2024. (Photo by Steve Appleford)

Chapter 27

REDD KROSS

Given the lingering effects of the pandemic, Redd Kross's generally less than brisk rate of production, and the dispiriting fate of *Beyond The Door*, the odds of a follow-up surfacing any time soon seemed woefully slim. And yet, right as this book was going to print, a new Redd Kross album emerged from the mist.

And this was not just another Redd Kross album, but rather the first-ever Redd Kross double LP in the band's four decades-plus history. Simply titled *Redd Kross*, and housed in an all-red sleeve paying lovingly humorous tribute to the same self-titled Beatles album that young Jeff and Steven bought back in 1970 with their combined take from Coke bottle returns, the album featured eighteen masterfully crafted punk, power pop and psychedelia-tinged bangers that were written and recorded in an unexpectedly prolific burst between the summer of 2023 and early 2024.

Produced by Josh Klinghoffer, who also played drums and a variety of other instruments on the record, *Redd Kross* the album was an uncharacteristically lavish offering from a band that has always specialised in short, sharp LPs. But as usual, Jeff and Steven had the songs and spirit to back it up, as tracks like 'Candy Coloured Catastrophe', 'Terrible Band', 'Way Too Happy' and 'Born Innocent' – the latter a track written for the closing credits of Andrew Reich's Redd Kross documentary of the same name – happily affirmed.

JEFF: I've always been a fan of records that barely clock in at thirty minutes; even during, like, the eighties and nineties, when everyone put bonus tracks and all that crap on CDs simply because they could, most of the albums we were making were like twenty-nine to thirty-three minutes. And this one's... not that. But after we got about halfway through recording it, we thought, 'Let's just go for a double record!' We had so much good material, and expanding it to eighteen songs gave Steven a chance to sing more lead vocals, because he would always just have a couple of songs in the past. I'm really excited about it.

Also, the double album thing is kind of fun, because it's like, what other band has been together for forty years and *then* their 10th album is the double record? Bands that have been together as long as we have, usually they're scraping and scouring for material, or re-recording their old songs. We'll see what people think, but I hope everyone loves it.

STEVEN: I feel really happy with it, too. As far as the album title goes, I really think this is the best example of a record we've done that *could* be self-titled. Not only is it a perfect example of what it is that we love to do, but it's also a total team effort – Jeff and I co-wrote the majority of the songs on the record, and we were able to make the whole thing in a really harmonious, unified and satisfying fashion, as opposed to the combative, 'grabbing for the steering wheel' thing that we did so often in the past. I'm really proud of the work, and really proud that we didn't fight while doing it.

I credit much of that to the loving help of our producer, Josh Klinghoffer, who's been like a younger sibling to us. Josh has been very helpful and brilliant and all the things a producer needs to be. But he's also really sensitive to internal band dynamics, especially those of our particular generation; he kept the Red Hot Chili Peppers afloat for a decade, and then he walked into Pearl Jam as a kind of 'jack of all trades' auxiliary member, so he's definitely a guy who knows how to read the room and act accordingly. He's very aware of family dynamics, as well, and he knows how to roll with it when he sees me and my brother having our unique, complicated relationship.

Dale couldn't play drums for us this time out because he was still recovering from his emergency back surgery when we went into the studio. But it was also kind of serendipitous in a way – because, among Josh's many other talents, he actually started out as a drummer. He has a fun, energetic style that's really good for Redd Kross, and having him play drums was a great way to get him really involved in the songs. He also played a lot of guitar on the album, which kind of allowed Jeff to take more of a lead singer role in the process.

I've known Josh since the Beck tour we did together in 2004, and we've stayed connected since then even though we've both been really busy in that time. It was so great to have someone else in there with us that I've known for twenty years – not that he was necessarily biased towards me, because I think he's very naturally egalitarian, but because I just felt supported in a way that I've never felt in the studio. And then Jeff was on such great behaviour, and we just really got along. Nobody got kicked in the balls this time.

JEFF: Working with Josh was incredible. We're all very like-minded, but he's also so talented; any idea that we would have, or he would have, he would go pick up an instrument and just lay it down. Jason came down on a couple of weekends to do some lead guitar parts, but mostly it was just me, Steven, Josh and his engineer Michael Craver working together in Josh's studio. There were no outside guests this time, and Josh was essentially a member of the band during the recording process.

It went so easily. It was so much fun. And it was such a different way of recording for us, because normally we've had our songs together and then rehearsed them, and then went in the studio and did things quickly. This time, we would have the song, but then we'd all learn it at the same time while we were recording it, so the songs all have a real freshness to them. I mean, it's kind of scary working that way, because you have to make a lot of decisions on the fly; you can't just sit on them for a while. But it really prevents you from working things into the ground, and it gives things a loose kind of vibe. That loose vibe is something that I think is almost like a special effect these days because everything in digital recording is about being perfect on the grid. You know, just being yourself is a special effect these days.

STEVEN: The dynamic with Josh was also interesting, because throughout our career I've usually been the youngest person in the studio. But Josh was born literally, like, around the time we recorded our first EP in '79. You might expect someone twelve years younger than me and sixteen years younger than Jeff to automatically fall into a supportive role just by nature of the difference in age, but at the same time, he's the only person in the room who has travelled around the world playing stadiums every night. Josh has done so much more than us, in so many ways, and he knows how to gently take the authority that comes with that experience and do something constructive with it.

I honestly don't know if the chemistry we had on this record will ever happen again. One thing I've kind of come to slowly understand is that chemistry is not only hard to define and put into words, but it's also extremely fragile. So I am just very grateful that we kind of stumbled on to the chemistry that worked for this record.

A couple of months before we started work on this record, I bought box seats to see Sparks play at the Hollywood Bowl. I

316

took Jeff and Anna, and I invited Josh, who I'd actually played with in Sparks, to go with us. I wanted to see where the Mael brothers had taken things from the first time I saw them at the Key Club during what, in retrospect, was the beginning of their third act. And to see them at the Hollywood Bowl was deeply inspiring, because for five years I'd had a front-row seat to see exactly what kind of effort and energy they put into what they do. And at times, I thought they were a little batshit crazy, to be honest; but seeing them at the Hollywood Bowl reminded me that you kind of *have* to be a little batshit crazy to achieve what they have achieved.

I got to watch them that night with people that I feel relate to that, and I was hoping that maybe we would all be inspired by them together. And then three months later, Jeff, Josh and I were in the studio making an album that I love. And a lot of that came from the inspiration of the Mael brothers and their unwavering, Don Quixote-like obsession with showing people what they can do.

After seeing an early cut of Andrew's documentary, I also had a burning desire to make good on all the nice things people were saying about us. I know everyone at times deals with imposter syndrome, but try watching ninety minutes of people you really respect saying how great you are — and that the only reason you're not a household name is because the households are just wrong. More than anything, the *Born Innocent* movie just really pushed me to see if I could try and bridge the gap between what people were saying about us and my own belief of how much we had either succeeded or failed to show people what we were actually capable of. I'm so relieved and grateful to be able to say that we've wildly exceeded my hopes.

JEFF: Why has Redd Kross lasted this long? I think the number one reason that we've been able to do this through all these years is because we're intense fans. We love music. I am a huge fan of live music, I'm a huge fan of records – old records, new pop, anything – and I never get tired of digging around to find something great. As long as we're coming from that place, we'll always do something that's interesting and fun, because we're doing what we believe in. And we've always done that, even before we had the ability to really play our instruments, or before we really knew how to write songs. We always just kind of did what we wanted to do.

I always had a vision of some kid finding *Born Innocent* in a thrift store bin and starting a band because of it. I remember finding the first Love album in a thrift store; I'd never heard of it, never heard of them, but I bought it for a quarter and became a lifelong fan. I've always felt that if we made records that we believed in, they'd always find an audience. Maybe not a big audience, but they will always find people – and then those people will want to freak out their friends with it and turn other people on to it, which is exactly how Steven and I still experience music to this day. I mean, it's a lifelong, nonstop project. It's like archaeology; you're just always on the lookout for something interesting.

STEVEN: Ultimately, I think our whole trip is sort of viewed as that we're these people who unapologetically embrace popular culture or, you know, disposable junk culture. And I guess I want to feel like I'm in on that, like I've got some kind of highfalutin academic take on us and what Jeff and I do. I would love to think that I'm the *architect* of it, you know? But in some ways, I have to admit, I think I am also just a product of my environment, and I am susceptible to its influences.

So much just comes down to good fortune, too. I always think of the fact that, by some bizarre chance, Black Flag were starting around the same as us, just 4 miles down the road from where we were growing up. I mean, we had to be insanely dedicated and weird to track that down and figure out how to engage with it at such ridiculously young ages. But at the same time, if we'd been born 40 or 400 miles from Hermosa Beach instead of 4, that weirdness and insane dedication we had back then might not have taken us anywhere nearly as interesting. I mean, it's totally okay to have an ordinary experience, but the fact that mine has been so bizarre, even with all of its ups and downs, is something I never lose gratitude for.

JEFF: What is the legacy of Redd Kross? I don't even know; I never think about it. I think we're fortunate enough that there are still people who care about us, forty-five years after we first went into a recording studio. But as far as in the grand scheme, I don't know. I just know that we're a band that a lot of people have heard of – and just to get to that point is nearly impossible. Forget billion-selling records; just to be a band that a lot of people have even *heard* of is pretty amazing. That's one thing I know.

I would never record an AI song, because I just think it's immoral. But when I was just sitting around Josh's studio during our recording sessions for the new album, I started messing around with AI a bit and seeing what kinds of lyrics it would come up with, because the prompts were just so much fun; that's where the creativity in it really lies, I think. And at one point, I had it write a song called 'In the Style of Redd Kross' – that's what the prompt was. And the song it wrote was totally like, 'Bell bottoms and hair flying in the wind.' Like, it had enough information to write a really clichéd song about us.

STEVEN: I would hope that our music would be our legacy; that's the part of our story that I hope would be the most important to people – and that the work is something I can be proud of, and something I can be remembered for. But the reality with my life is that Jeff and I are very different people, and there's been a lot of challenges because of it. And I think there are some definite reasons why, in forty-five years of working with my sibling, our body of work is not as massive as

I would like it to have been. There's the brother dynamic, the band dynamic, and the various external forces that have been brought to bear on both of those things, and it's been quite an interesting ride to find myself in the middle of all of it.

But at the same time, I would hope that people can find something relatable and maybe even inspiring in the human parts of our story, especially the parts that are about perseverance. Like, how does someone recover from disappointment? How do they deal with failure, or just the perception of failure? How do they recalibrate? How do they keep moving forward? People who are not musicians might not be able to relate to certain specifics of our story, but I think most people can relate on some level to what we've gone through, because life is messy, and everybody has their similar trials, regardless of their medium or occupation. What I'm really pushing for nowadays is that I think I have a killer third act in me, and that this is the moment where the perseverance finally pays off. I was such an early starter, and yet now I'm pushing to be a late bloomer.

JEFF: I think about myself at 60, and then I remember my grandfather at 60. And it's like, he wouldn't have been touring the world in a rock'n'roll band, being a total weirdo. We're really fortunate to be of an era where you could do something like this at any age. And I think of the people that came before us; like, I always think of Sonic Youth, because they were ten years older than us, and I remember seeing them playing to teenagers when they were in their thirties and forties. It was like, 'We could do that!' And we do. And then, seeing The Rolling Stones being fantastic at, like, age 80 or whatever they are, and realising that we're part of that first generation that can do this, is still inspiring. And as long as it's authentic, we can keep on doing it, too.

ACKNOWLEDGEMENTS

Jeff and Steven would like to thank Janet and Terry McDonald, Charlotte Caffey, Astrid McDonald, Kevin Devine, Anna Waronker, Alfie McDonald, Dale Crover, Buzz Osborne, Andrew Reich, Steve Appleford, Rob Reynolds, Mary Wigmore, Dan Epstein, Jon Krop, Larry Hardy, Craig Wedren, Lee Sobel, and everyone who's ever played in Redd Kross.

Dan would like to thank Lee Sobel, Andrew Reich, David Barraclough, Claire Browne, Randy Bookasta, Lyn DelliQuadri, Irwin Epstein, Rebecca Epstein, Carole Roth, Shannon McGrane, Bob MacKay, Chris Jackson, Eric Sugg and Robin Rhode, Jason Walker, Doug Edmunds, Eric Colin Reidelberger, Matt Devine, Jessica Ricci, and especially Jeff and Steven McDonald. And, of course, Paul Stanley.